JAMESTOWN EDUCATION

Annotated Teacher's Edition

SIGNATURE READING

LEVEL
F

Mc Graw Hill **Glencoe**

New York, New York   Columbus, Ohio   Chicago, Illinois   Peoria, Illinois   Woodland Hills, California

Signature Reading Levels

Level	Reading Level
D	2—4
E	3—5
F	4—6
G	5—7
H	6—8
I	7—9
J	8—10
K	9—10
L	10—12

Contents

To the Teacher

Signature Reading is a sequential, nine-level program for remedial, on-level, and advanced students in grades 2 and above. It is designed to teach students not only which skills and strategies to use while reading but also when to use them. Developmental in approach, the program provides a wealth of practice to reinforce and improve existing skills while developing new skills and strategies.

The philosophy of *Signature Reading* is based on four main principles, which are reflected in the pedagogical structure of the lessons.

Effective readers apply appropriate skills and strategies in the reading process. *Signature Reading* uses high-interest, student-centered selections to develop the variety of skills and strategies that students need. To become effective readers, students must master a variety of strategies as well as a set of skills. Different strategies may be used for different types of reading, but they are always used by good readers. By using skills and strategies together, students learn the difference between them and the roles each of them play in the reading process. This enables them to isolate and focus on those they need help with as they move toward the goal of becoming better readers.

Effective readers participate in—and evaluate—their own learning process. *Signature Reading* teaches students to become active participants in their own education. Each selection provides activities for self-assessment, including a comparison of the students' personal evaluation with an objectively measured score. This becomes a "reality check" for students and a third level of development beyond skills and strategies. Students record and graph their scores, providing ongoing visual testimony to their improvement. This participation in the learning process will be both motivational and lifelong. Students will continue to apply these self-evaluation principles as they gain confidence and become independent readers.

Effective readers adapt their knowledge of skills and strategies to a wide variety of genres. *Signature Reading* provides a wide variety of authentic stories and articles to give students the exposure they need to different kinds of reading. Students learn which skills and strategies are most effective for reading mysteries, humorous stories, biographical sketches, how-to articles, and many other genres of literature.

Effective readers know how and when to vary their reading rate to accommodate the demands of the text. *Signature Reading* takes into account the fact that good readers are efficient readers and that rate does matter. Slowing down a student's reading rate can undermine rather than improve comprehension. However, the teacher must use discretion when employing timed reading. For some students, the primary goals of understanding what is read and how they should read it will be challenging enough.

Each book contains these main comprehension, literary, and word-study strategies:

- Recognizing Main Ideas
- Making Inferences
- Identifying Causes and Effects
- Identifying Problems and Solutions

- Comparing and Contrasting/Classifying
- Following Sequence/Steps in a Process
- Reading Content-area Materials

- Using Graphic Aids/Organizers
- Recognizing Literary Forms
- Recognizing Literary Elements
- Word Study/Vocabulary

Signature Reading works because . . .

- it places students at their instructional level.
- it teaches the strategies students need to become independent readers.
- it shows students how and when to apply those strategies.
- it helps students understand what they read and how they should read it.

Signature Reading is . . .

- **interactive**

   Clear models guide students' responses.

   Personal checklists help students reflect upon their learning.

   Extensions and resources provide ways to "learn more about it."

- **sequential**

   Nine volumes cover reading levels 2–12.

   Each book features graduated readabilities.

   Students increase their reading levels as they strengthen their skills.

- **student-centered**

   Selections are high-interest but low readability.

   Everything students need is contained in the student book.

   Students can work alone or with others, with or without the teacher.

- **all-inclusive**

   A variety of approaches accommodates a variety of learning styles.

   Graphic organizers help students visualize the strategies.

   Suggested multimedia activities and resources engage aural, kinesthetic, and spacial learners.

Instruction before, during, and after reading ensures success for students.

Before Reading

- **Building Background** prepares students for reading by accessing prior knowledge or providing background.
- **Vocabulary Builder** gets students thinking about relevant vocabulary and concepts.
- **Strategy Builder** introduces and defines strategies necessary for reading the selection.

During Reading

- **Strategy Break** models how to apply the strategies presented in Strategy Builder.

After Reading

- **Strategy Follow-up** enables students to apply the strategies presented and modeled.
- **Personal Checklist** helps students reflect on their learning.
- **Vocabulary Check, Strategy Check,** and **Comprehension Check** assess students' performance.
- **Extending** provides ways to learn more about some aspect of the selection.
- **Resources** suggests books, magazines, brochures, Web sites, recordings, and other materials that students can use to complete the Extending activities.

Blackline Masters

- Jamestown Placement Test (T15–T18)
- Student Scoring Charts (T19)
- Reading Rate Chart (T23)
- Skills and Strategies Tests (T25–T28)

Additional Teaching Resources

- Timed Readings
- Test Answers

For a sample of how it works, turn the page. ➡

Sample Lesson

Building Background

Prepares students for reading by helping them access their own prior knowledge or by giving them background information.

Vocabulary Builder

Gets students thinking about relevant vocabulary and/or concepts before they read. Vocabulary is chosen to enhance students' understanding of the selection's "big ideas."

Strategy Builder

Introduces and defines strategies necessary for reading the selection.

LESSON 14 Greg LeMond

appendicitis

cyclist

defeat

gunshot wounds

internationally famous

rescue helicopter

top form

willpower

CLIPBOARD
Difficult Time

CLIPBOARD
Exciting Time

Building Background

In this selection, you will read about a famous American bicycle racer named Greg LeMond. The selection describes his experiences in the Tour de France, the most famous bicycle race in the world. The map below shows the route of the 1989 Tour de France.

The 1989 Tour de France

BELGIUM

START
LUXEMBOURG

FINISH
Paris
FRANCE

SWITZERLAND

Vocabulary Builder

1. Before you read this selection, think about how each word or phrase in the margin might describe an exciting time or a difficult time in Greg LeMond's life. Then list each word or phrase on the appropriate clipboard.

2. As you read the selection, look for other words related to difficult and exciting times in LeMond's life. Add them to the clipboards.

3. Save your work. You will use it again in the Vocabulary Check.

Strategy Builder

How to Read a Biographical Sketch

- A **biography** is the story of a person's life, written by someone else. A **biographical sketch** is the story of a part of a person's life.

- Biographical sketches describe events in the order in which they happened. Therefore they are written in time order, or **sequence**.

- To make the sequence as clear as possible, writers often use **signal words**. Examples include *first, then,* and *a few days later.*

- The following paragraphs explain how Greg LeMond began cycling. Pay attention to the sequence of events as you read. Use the underlined signal words and phrases to help you.

> Greg had always loved sports that he could do on his own—hunting, backpacking, and freestyle skiing. <u>When he was 14</u>, he went to a camp for skiers. One of the best ways to stay in shape, he was told, was bicycle riding. And that's how it started. Greg and his dad, who was trying to lose a little weight, rode 20 miles every day.
>
> <u>Soon</u> Greg entered races for 14- and 15-year-olds and won almost every one. He became almost unbeatable in the United States. But being number one in the U.S. didn't count for much. All the top cyclists raced in Europe. Could Greg beat *them*? <u>When he was 16</u>, Greg decided to find out. He entered the World Championship for Juniors—and finished ninth.

Strategy Builder

Provides an authentic example of the strategies that were just introduced.

- If you wanted to show the sequence of events in the paragraphs above, you might use a **sequence chain** like this one:

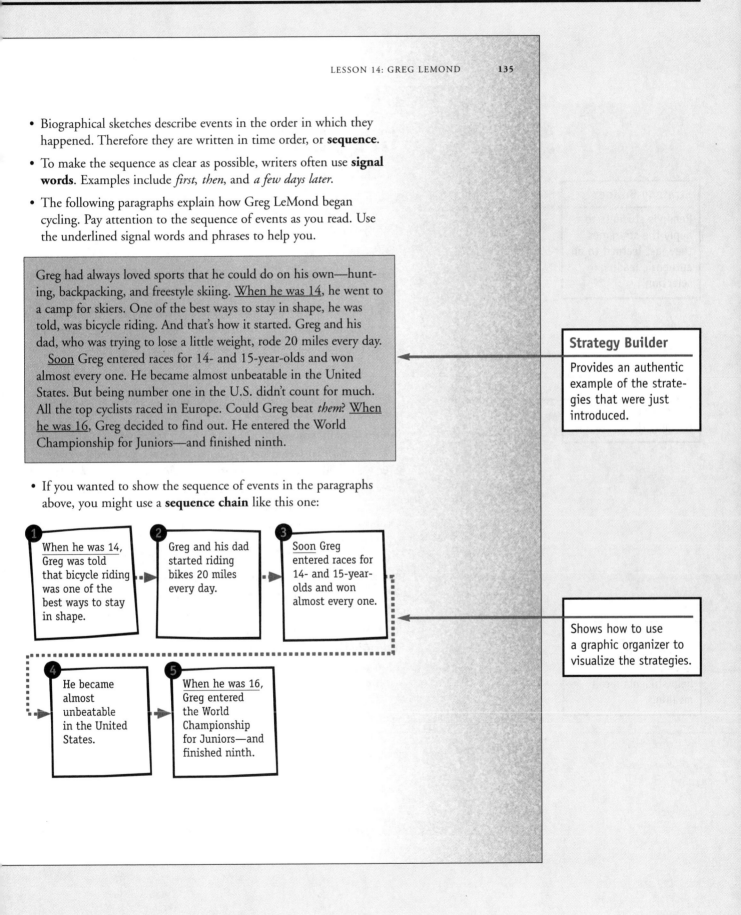

Shows how to use a graphic organizer to visualize the strategies.

Sample Lesson

Greg LeMond

by Jim O'Connor

As your read the first part of this biographical sketch, apply the strategies that you just learned. Underline the signal words as you read. They will give you a more exact picture of when things happened.

The Tour de France is the most important bicycle race in the world. It travels about 2,500 miles around Europe over quiet country roads, twisting mountain passes, and busy city streets.

In Europe, bicycle racing is bigger than the Super Bowl is here. Bigger even than the World Series. And for three weeks each summer the race swings through France like a traveling circus and rock concert rolled into one. When the Tour ends in Paris, the winner is the world's number one **cyclist**.

In 1986, for the first time ever, an American won the Tour. He was a 24-year-old from Utah named Greg LeMond. Overnight Greg became **internationally famous**. And his future as a top racer seemed guaranteed.

The next winter Greg went to California to visit his family. On April 20, Greg went wild-turkey hunting with his uncle and his brother-in-law. The three men separated and moved through a field of berry bushes. Greg lost sight of the others. He stopped and then began to move again. Suddenly he was hit in the back with a full blast of buckshot. His brother-in-law had accidentally shot him.

Greg's uncle ran home and called 911. Then Greg had a stroke of luck. A **rescue helicopter** was flying nearby. It heard the police radio calls and flew Greg to a hospital with a center for **gunshot wounds**.

This quick trip probably saved Greg's life. He had 60 holes in his back from the one blast of buckshot and was bleeding from every one of them. If the trip had been any longer, he would have bled to death.

Greg spent the next six days in the hospital in terrible pain. Doctors removed most of the pellets. But two were in the lining of his heart. The doctors had to leave them there. Greg didn't know if he would ever race again.

"For three or four weeks," Greg recalled, "I'd sit at home in a chair, shaking with pain. I'd just cry and cry."

But little by little, Greg forced himself to take short walks. It was two weeks before he could go two blocks without tiring. Finally one day he

---

Strategy Builder

Reminds students to apply the strategies they just learned to an authentic reading selection.

Gives examples of how to apply the strategies.

Presents target vocabulary in dark type to help students recall meaning.

climbed on his wife's bike and pedaled up and down the driveway. It wasn't the Tour de France—but Greg was riding again.

Soon Greg tried to bike a couple of miles each day. Then he took longer rides in the hills. But just as he was getting back to normal, Greg had more bad luck. He was rushed to the hospital with **appendicitis**. The doctors operated on him again.

That wiped out the 1987 season for Greg. He was sure he could come back to **top form** in 1988. But for the first time, Greg's **willpower** was not enough. By the '89 season, his ranking had dropped from #2 to #345!

⬣ **Stop here for the Strategy Break.**

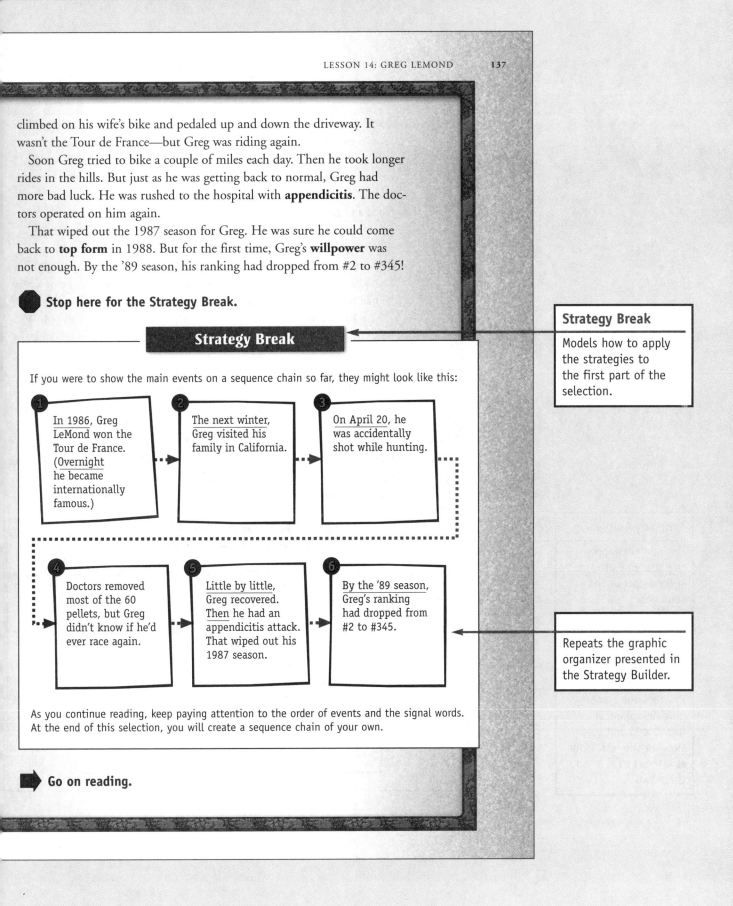

Strategy Break

If you were to show the main events on a sequence chain so far, they might look like this:

1 In 1986, Greg LeMond won the Tour de France. (Overnight he became internationally famous.)

2 The next winter, Greg visited his family in California.

3 On April 20, he was accidentally shot while hunting.

4 Doctors removed most of the 60 pellets, but Greg didn't know if he'd ever race again.

5 Little by little, Greg recovered. Then he had an appendicitis attack. That wiped out his 1987 season.

6 By the '89 season, Greg's ranking had dropped from #2 to #345.

As you continue reading, keep paying attention to the order of events and the signal words. At the end of this selection, you will create a sequence chain of your own.

➡ **Go on reading.**

Strategy Break

Models how to apply the strategies to the first part of the selection.

Repeats the graphic organizer presented in the Strategy Builder.

Sample Lesson

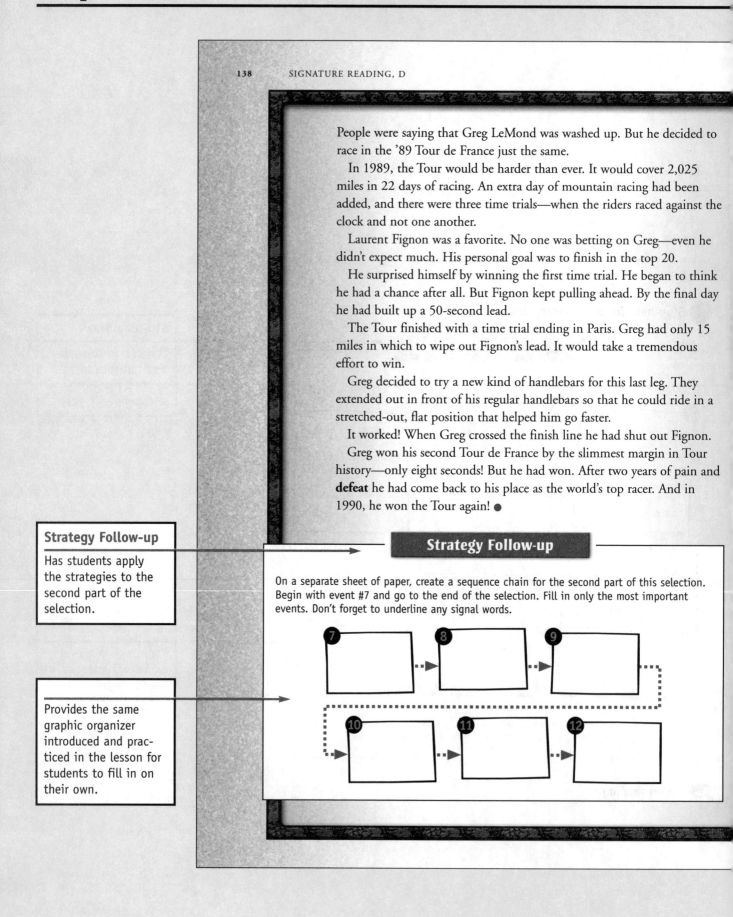

People were saying that Greg LeMond was washed up. But he decided to race in the '89 Tour de France just the same.

In 1989, the Tour would be harder than ever. It would cover 2,025 miles in 22 days of racing. An extra day of mountain racing had been added, and there were three time trials—when the riders raced against the clock and not one another.

Laurent Fignon was a favorite. No one was betting on Greg—even he didn't expect much. His personal goal was to finish in the top 20.

He surprised himself by winning the first time trial. He began to think he had a chance after all. But Fignon kept pulling ahead. By the final day he had built up a 50-second lead.

The Tour finished with a time trial ending in Paris. Greg had only 15 miles in which to wipe out Fignon's lead. It would take a tremendous effort to win.

Greg decided to try a new kind of handlebars for this last leg. They extended out in front of his regular handlebars so that he could ride in a stretched-out, flat position that helped him go faster.

It worked! When Greg crossed the finish line he had shut out Fignon.

Greg won his second Tour de France by the slimmest margin in Tour history—only eight seconds! But he had won. After two years of pain and **defeat** he had come back to his place as the world's top racer. And in 1990, he won the Tour again! ●

Strategy Follow-up

On a separate sheet of paper, create a sequence chain for the second part of this selection. Begin with event #7 and go to the end of the selection. Fill in only the most important events. Don't forget to underline any signal words.

Strategy Follow-up

Has students apply the strategies to the second part of the selection.

Provides the same graphic organizer introduced and practiced in the lesson for students to fill in on their own.

✓ Personal Checklist

Read each question and put a check (✓) in the correct box.

1. How well were you able to use the map on page 134 to follow the Tour de France?
   - ☐ 3 (extremely well)
   - ☐ 2 (fairly well)
   - ☐ 1 (not well)

2. Before you read this selection, how many vocabulary words were you able to put on the appropriate clipboards?
   - ☐ 3 (6–8 words)
   - ☐ 2 (3–5 words)
   - ☐ 1 (0–2 words)

3. How well were you able to create a sequence chain for the second part of this selection?
   - ☐ 3 (extremely well)
   - ☐ 2 (fairly well)
   - ☐ 1 (not well)

4. How well do you understand how important the Tour de France is to bicycle racers?
   - ☐ 3 (extremely well)
   - ☐ 2 (fairly well)
   - ☐ 1 (not well)

5. How well were you able to understand why Greg's win in 1989 was such a great accomplishment?
   - ☐ 3 (extremely well)
   - ☐ 2 (fairly well)
   - ☐ 1 (not well)

Vocabulary Check

Look back at the work you did in the Vocabulary Builder. Then answer each question by circling the correct letter.

1. In 1986, what event made Greg LeMond internationally famous overnight?
   - a. He was the first American to win the Tour de France.
   - b. He was shot in the back while hunting for turkeys.
   - c. His ranking as a cyclist dropped from #2 to #345.

2. Which word describes an exciting time in Greg's life?
   - a. appendicitis
   - b. defeat
   - c. willpower

3. Which phrase describes a difficult time in Greg's life?
   - a. gunshot wounds
   - b. internationally famous
   - c. top form

4. Which situation is an example of willpower?
   - a. a rescue helicopter flying nearby
   - b. racing again after a serious injury
   - c. sitting in a chair and crying

5. Which situation describes Greg in top form?
   - a. having appendicitis
   - b. being shot in the back
   - c. racing to a first-place finish

Vocabulary Check

Follows up on the words presented in the Vocabulary Builder and used in the selection.

Personal Checklist

Helps students reflect upon their performance through the lesson.

Add the numbers that you just checked to get your Personal Checklist score. Fill in your score here. Then turn to page 203 and transfer your score onto Graph 1.

Check your answers with your teacher. Give yourself 1 point for each correct answer, and fill in your Vocabulary score here. Then turn to page 203 and transfer your score onto Graph 1.

Scoring Box

Helps students tally their scores and graph their progress.

Sample Lesson

Strategy Check

Follows up on the strategies presented and practiced in the lesson.

Comprehension Check

Checks overall comprehension of the selection.

Strategy Check

Look back at the sequence chain that you created in the Strategy Follow-up. Then answer these questions:

1. In the 1989 race, when was Laurent Fignon ahead by 50 seconds?
   a. after the first time trial
   b. after the second time trial
   c. by the final day of the race

2. When did Greg decide to try a new kind of handlebars?
   a. during the first time trial in 1989
   b. during the last leg of the 1989 race
   c. during the 1990 race

3. Which phrase is *not* an example of signal words?
   a. only eight seconds
   b. by the final day
   c. when Greg crossed the finish line

4. Which phrase tells when Greg regained his place as the world's top racer?
   a. by the final day of trials
   b. for the last leg of the race
   c. after two years of pain and defeat

5. Which sentence shows the correct order of events in this selection?
   a. Greg wins the first time trial, wins the '89 race, then wins the '90 race.
   b. Greg is ahead the last day, wins the first time trial, then wins the '90 race.
   c. Greg switches handlebars, wins the first time trial, then falls behind.

Comprehension Check

Review the selection if necessary. Then answer these questions:

1. How many miles does the Tour de France cover?
   a. about 25
   b. about 250
   c. about 2,500

2. What made the 1989 Tour de France harder than ever?
   a. An extra day of mountain racing had been added.
   b. There were three time trials.
   c. Both of the above answers are correct.

3. Who or what wiped out the 1987 season for Greg?
   a. a hunting accident
   b. appendicitis
   c. Laurent Fignon

4. Which of the following was a difficulty for Greg LeMond?
   a. gunshot wounds
   b. extended handlebars
   c. being an American

5. How many times does the selection say Greg LeMond has won the Tour de France?
   a. one time
   b. two times
   c. three times

Check your answers with your teacher. Give yourself 1 point for each correct answer, and fill in your Strategy score here. Then turn to page 203 and transfer your score onto Graph 1.

Personal
Vocabulary
Strategy
Comprehension
TOTAL SCORE
✓ T

Check your answers with your teacher. Give yourself 1 point for each correct answer, and fill in your Comprehension score here. Then turn to page 203 and transfer your score onto Graph 1.

Personal
Vocabulary
Strategy
Comprehension
TOTAL SCORE
✓ T

Extending

Choose one or more of these activities:

RESEARCH THE TOUR DE FRANCE

Using the resources on this page or others, find out more about the Tour de France. Try to find such information as when it started, who started it, what route the first race covered, how many people usually compete, which countries have won, which country and/or person has won the most times, and how the race has changed over the years. Present your findings to the class in an oral or written report.

MAP THE ROUTE OF THE 1989 TOUR DE FRANCE

Follow these steps to map a three-dimensional route of the 1989 tour de France:

1. Find a good clear map of Luxembourg, Belgium, and France. Make sure the map includes physical features such as mountain ranges.
2. Trace the borders of the three countries onto a sturdy piece of cardboard.
3. Cover the borders with a layer of clay.
4. Look at the physical map to find the mountain ranges. Use more clay to make the mountains stand out.
5. Use the map on page 134 and brightly colored yarn or string to map the route of the 1989 Tour de France. Glue the yarn or string into place.

CONDUCT TIME TRIALS

Choose an activity that can be timed, such as outdoor running or walking races, completing a multiplication fact sheet, or building a tower of blocks. Using a stopwatch, set up time trials and have individual classmates race against the clock to complete their chosen activity. Record everyone's times, and post a ranking from shortest to longest times. (You can leave students' names off if you'd like.)

Resources

Books

Hautzig, David. *1,000 Miles in 12 Days: Pro Cyclists on Tour.* Orchard Books, 1995.

Lovett, Richard A. *The Essential Touring Cyclist: A Complete Guide for the Bicycle Traveler,* 2nd ed. International Marine/Ragged Mountain Press, 2000.

Porter, A. P. *Greg LeMond: Premier Cyclist.* Lerner Publications, 1990.

Web Sites

http://www.cnnsi.com/cycling/1998/tourdefrance/map
This 1998 Tour de France site features maps, race results, and information on the cities that the race passes through.

http://www.lvvelo.org
This is the Lehigh Valley Velodrome bicycle race site.

Video/ DVD

L. L. Bean Guide to Bicycle Touring. L. L. Bean, 1986.

Resources

Lists resources that students can use to complete the Extending activities.

Extending

Provides ideas and activities for learning more about some aspect of the selection.

Scope and Sequence

	COMPREHENSION	STUDY/CONTENT AREA	LITERARY	VOCABULARY/ WORD STUDY
LESSON 1	Identifying Problems and Solutions	Using Graphic Organizers (Problem-Solution Frame)	Author's Purpose Recognizing Story Elements Recognizing Irony	Synonyms Antonyms
LESSON 2	Making Predictions	Using Text Elements	Recognizing Humor Reading Contemporary Fiction	Multiple-Meaning Words
LESSON 3	Summarizing Nonfiction	Using Graphic Organizers (List)	Reading an Informational Article	Multiple-Meaning Words
LESSON 4	Following Time Sequence Signal Words	Using Graphic Organizers (Sequence Chain)	Reading an Autobiographical Sketch Point of View	Specialized Vocabulary
LESSON 5	Identifying Problems and Solutions	Using Graphic Organizers (Problem-Solution Frame)	Reading Science Fiction Recognizing Story Elements	Suffixes
LESSON 6	Comparing and Contrasting	Using Graphic Organizers (Features Chart)	Reading Contemporary Fiction Using Context	Definitions
LESSON 7	Following Time Sequence Signal Words Classifying	Using Graphic Organizers (Sequence Chain)	Reading a Biographical Sketch Point of View	Suffixes
LESSON 8	Following Time Sequence	Using Graphic Organizers (Time Line)	Reading a Biography	Suffixes
LESSON 9	Outlining Main Ideas and Supporting Details	Using Graphic Organizers (Outlines) Using Text Elements	Reading an Informational Article	Compound Words
LESSON 10	Making Predictions	Using Text Elements	Reading Contemporary Fiction Using Context	Specialized Vocabulary
LESSON 11	Identifying Causes and Effects	Using Graphic Organizers (Cause-and-Effect Chain)	Reading Contemporary Fiction Recognizing Story Elements	Prefixes Compound Words
LESSON 12	Outlining Main Ideas and Supporting Details	Using Graphic Organizers (Outlines) Using Text Elements	Reading an Informational Article	Compound Words
LESSON 13	Following the Steps in a Process	Using Graphic Organizers (Sequence Chain)	Reading a How-to Article Author's Purpose	Synonyms Compound Words Multiple-Meaning Words
LESSON 14	Identifying Details	Using Text Elements	Reading a Play Identifying Mood	Prefixes Multiple-Meaning Words
LESSON 15	Using Mood and Foreshadowing to Predict	Using Text Elements	Reading a Mystery Recognizing Foreshadowing Recognizing Suspense	Synonyms
LESSON 16	Using Foreshadowing to Predict	Using Text Elements	Reading Contemporary Fiction Recognizing Foreshadowing Using Context	Prefixes
LESSON 17	Comparing and Contrasting	Using Graphic Organizers (Features Chart)	Reading an Informational Article	Compound Words
LESSON 18	Summarizing Nonfiction	Using Graphic Organizers (Word Map) Using Text Elements	Reading an Informational Article	Specialized Vocabulary Compound Words
LESSON 19	Identifying Causes and Effects	Using Graphic Organizers (Cause-and-Effect Chain and Features Chart)	Reading a Folktale Recognizing Story Elements	Suffixes
LESSON 20	Using Folktale Elements to Make Predictions	Using Text Elements Using Graphic Organizers (Features Chart)	Reading a Folktale Recognizing Story Elements	Suffixes

Jamestown Placement Test

The Jamestown Placement Test (pages T16–T18) will help you determine at which level—introductory, middle, or advanced—your students should be placed to receive maximum benefit from *Signature Reading*.

Administering the Test

This silent reading comprehension test will take approximately 20 minutes. It is not timed, so allow time for most students to finish. Collect your students' test-answer sheets as they finish. Tell students that they may skip any question that is too difficult for them to answer. The Jamestown Placement Test may be duplicated for student use.

Answer Key for Student Placement Test

1. b	5. b	9. b	13. c
2. b	6. b	10. c	14. c
3. a	7. c	11. a	15. a
4. b	8. a	12. d	

Student Placement Level Based on Score

	Student Score (number correct)	Placement Level
Level D	8–10	Introductory
Level E	8–10	Introductory
Level F	8–10	Introductory
Level G	10–13	Middle
Level H	10–13	Middle
Level I	13–15	Advanced
Level J	13–15	Advanced
Level K	13–15	Advanced
Level L	13–15	Advanced

Jamestown Placement Test

Name _____	**Date** _____
Class _____	**Score (Number Correct)** _____

Directions

Read the passage. Then read each question and fill in the circle before the correct answer. You may look back at the passage. You may skip a question if the question is too difficult. Raise your hand when you are finished, and your teacher will collect the test.

On a calm, clear December afternoon in 1945, Flight 19 took off from the south coast of Florida on a routine Navy training mission. The five Avenger planes that made up Flight 19 would never return. Incredibly, a Martin Mariner plane sent to rescue Flight 19 was also lost without a trace.

Whenever planes or ships disappear in the infamous Bermuda Triangle, the wildest stories are heard. Many people think that the waters off the coast of Florida are the deadliest in the world. Legends tell of hundreds of ships and airplanes simply disappearing in the Bermuda Triangle.

1. Navy Flight 19 took off from
   ○ a. Bermuda.
   ○ b. Florida.
   ○ c. a Navy aircraft carrier.

2. How many planes made up Flight 19?
   ○ a. three
   ○ b. five
   ○ c. seven

3. Flight 19 was on a
   ○ a. training mission.
   ○ b. secret mission.
   ○ c. rescue mission.

4. The Bermuda Triangle is interesting because
   ○ a. it has been proven very dangerous.
   ○ b. many people think it is dangerous.
   ○ c. the Navy expected trouble there.

5. One thing we know about Flight 19 is that
   ○ a. it was rescued by Martin Mariner.
   ○ b. it was lost forever.
   ○ c. it would not become part of the legend.

Go on

Jamestown Placement Test

Name _____   **Date** _____

Day had broken exceedingly cold and gray when the man turned aside from the main Yukon trail and climbed the high earthbank, where a dim and little-traveled trail led eastward through the fat spruce timberland. It was a steep bank, and he paused for breath at the top, excusing the act to himself by looking at his watch. It was nine o'clock. There was no sun nor hint of sun, though there was not a cloud in the sky. It was a clear day, and yet there seemed an intangible pall over the face of things, a subtle gloom that made the day dark, and that was due to the absence of sun. This fact did not worry the man. He was used to the lack of sun in this first season of the year. It had been days since he had seen the sun, and he knew that a few more days must pass before that cheerful orb, due south, would just peep above the skyline and dip immediately from view.

6. This story takes place
- ○ a. in Siberia.
- ○ b. in the Yukon Territory.
- ○ c. during an Arctic expedition.

7. In what season is the story set?
- ○ a. winter
- ○ b. fall
- ○ c. spring

8. The sky above the man was
- ○ a. clear and cloudless.
- ○ b. bright with sunlight.
- ○ c. dim and cloudy.

9. What did the man see around him?
- ○ a. wild animals
- ○ b. trees
- ○ c. barren land

10. The man may be described as
- ○ a. scared.
- ○ b. depressed.
- ○ c. unafraid.

Go on

Jamestown Placement Test

Name _____   **Date** _____

The Yellow Emperor was an important god in ancient times. He was a very powerful figure and had many children, some of whom were gods and some humans. He took great interest in the human race. Because he protected them and helped them to lead a peaceful, settled life, he was often considered to be an earthly emperor, the first to rule over China.

One of his greatest deeds was his defeat of a monster named Chiyou.

Chiyou started life as quite a lowly god. His task was to be a runner for the Yellow Emperor, one who cleared the way for him when he went on a journey. Chiyou was, however, very ambitious, and he planned to overthrow the Yellow Emperor and take his throne. Chiyou gathered as his followers some 80 minor gods who were discontented with the Yellow Emperor's reign.

11. Who was Chiyou?
    ○ a. a lowly god who served as a runner for the Yellow Emperor
    ○ b. one of the Yellow Emperor's ministers
    ○ c. the Yellow Emperor's rainmaker
    ○ d. the thunder god

12. What did Chiyou want?
    ○ a. to be a more important god
    ○ b. to lead the Yellow Emperor's army
    ○ c. to be the Yellow Emperor's assistant
    ○ d. to overthrow the Yellow Emperor and take his throne

13. Chiyou gathered together some 80 minor gods who
    ○ a. refused to join Chiyou.
    ○ b. wanted their own kingdoms.
    ○ c. were discontented with the Yellow Emperor's reign.
    ○ d. were content to be minor gods.

14. What do you think of the Yellow Emperor?
    ○ a. He did not care about his people.
    ○ b. He wasn't a good warrior.
    ○ c. He was a good ruler.

15. Chiyou may be described as
    ○ a. ambitious.
    ○ b. lazy.
    ○ c. loyal.

STOP

Name _____   Date _____

Graph 1

For each lesson, enter the scores from your Personal Checklist and your Vocabulary, Strategy, and Comprehension Checks. Total your scores and then compare them. Does your Personal Checklist score match or come close to your total scores for that lesson? Why or why not?

Go down to Graph 2 and shade your scores for the lesson you just completed.

Graph 2

Now record your overall progress. In the first column for the lesson you just completed, shade the number of squares that match your Personal Checklist score. In the second column for that lesson, shade the number of squares that match your total score. As you fill in this graph, you will be able to check your progress across the book.

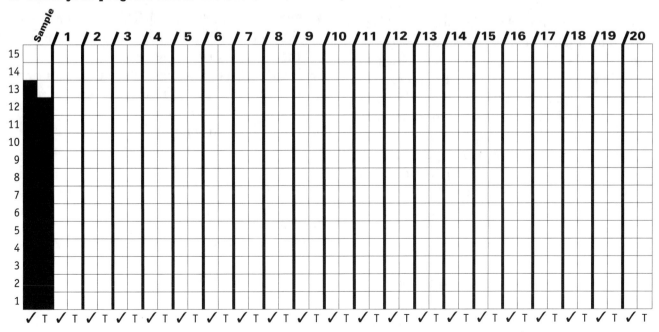

Timed Readings

Timed readings are designed to challenge your students to increase their reading rate while maintaining a high level of comprehension. When combined with the Personal Checklist at the end of each lesson, a timed reading will provide students with yet another way to reflect upon and evaluate their own reading performance.

Some Things to Consider

Timed readings may not be appropriate for every student. The primary goals of *Signature Reading* are to help students understand both *what* they read and *how* they should read it. For some students, these goals will be challenging enough. If you feel that timed readings are more than some students can handle, skip this section.

There is no ideal reading rate. Because so many different variables affect the way students read a selection, no one reading rate is ideal. Help students evaluate their reading rates on a selection-by-selection basis, keeping in mind the following:
- The readability levels in this book span two grade levels. In general, students will have an easier time reading the selections at the beginning of the book than they will have at the end.
- The number of words is not consistent from selection to selection. This obviously will affect how long it takes students to read each selection. (For the exact number of words in each selection, see the charts on page T21.)
- In general, fiction takes less time to read because students have had more exposure to stories and are familiar with how to read them.
- In general, nonfiction takes longer to read because its content is often unfamiliar and consequently more difficult. Readers must slow down to make sure they understand the concepts, graphics, and specialized vocabulary being presented in nonfiction.

When measuring rate, consistency is key. In order to get the most accurate rates possible, it is important to conduct timed readings often, at regular intervals, and in a consistent manner. Not having to refamiliarize themselves with the procedure every time will allow students to keep their rates as consistent and accurate as possible.

For additional timed readings, see *Timed Readings* (fifty 400-word nonfictional passages with questions), *Timed Readings in Literature* (fifty 400-word fictional passages with questions), and the three *Timed Readings Plus* series (25 two-part lessons with questions).

Selection Lengths

The following charts list the length of each selection in Level F. In case you would like to conduct timed readings using fiction or nonfiction only, the selections are divided for your convenience.

Directions for Conducting Timed Readings

1. Before students begin, instruct them to read the selection straight through, without stopping for the Strategy Break(s). Also tell them to read at a slightly faster-than-normal speed, but well enough to understand what they are reading.
2. Write the intended start-time on the board. When the clock reaches that time, tell students to begin reading.
3. At thirty-second intervals, write the new time on the board.
4. When each student finishes the selection, he or she should look at the board and write down the last time that you recorded.
5. Then the student should subtract the start time from his or her finish time to get a total reading time.
6. Using the charts on page T21, find the number of words in the selection that the student just read. Round that number up or down to the nearest increment of 25, beginning with 600 words.
7. Then use the student's total reading time, the approximate number of words in the selection, and the table on page T22 to figure the student's approximate reading rate, or number of words per minute.
8. Provide each student with a copy of the graph on page T23. If necessary, help students graph their approximate reading rate by shading the appropriate number of squares.

Fiction

Selection Title	Number of Words
L. 1: Shoeshine Whittaker	834 words
L. 2: The Big Toe Contest	906 words
L. 5: Two Fat Boys from Venus	976 words
L. 6: Put the Brolly in the Boot and Let's Go	901 words
L. 10: Too Tall Twyla	1328 words
L. 11: Dava's Talent	680 words
L. 14: Dracula (Part 1)	1011 words
L. 15: Dracula (Part 2)	1897 words
L. 16: When Disaster Strikes...	1023 words
L. 19: The Magic Bowl	1236 words
L. 20: Talk	824 words

Nonfiction

Selection Title	Number of Words
L. 3: The Trail of Tears	703 words
L. 4: At Last I Kill a Buffalo	1805 words
L. 7: The Contest	1197 words
L. 8: The Fabulous Miss Bly	935 words
L. 9: Bungee Jumping: A Leap of Faith	754 words
L. 12: Feeling Sleepy?	848 words
L. 13: How to Be a Super Sorter: Five Steps for Managing the Mess	819 words
L. 17: Seed Travel	696 words
L. 18: Vegetables	783 words

Words per Minute

Number of Words

Minutes	600	625	650	675	700	725	750	775	800	825	850	875	900	925	950	975	1000	1025	1050	1075	1100	1125	1150	1175	1200	1225	1250	1275	1300	1325	1350	1375	1400
25.0	24	25	26	27	28	29	30	31	32	33	34	35	36	37	38	39	40	41	42	43	44	45	46	47	48	49	50	51	52	53	54	55	56
24.5	24	26	27	28	29	30	31	32	33	34	35	36	37	38	39	40	41	42	43	44	45	46	47	48	49	50	51	52	53	54	55	56	57
24.0	25	26	27	28	29	30	31	32	33	34	35	36	38	39	40	41	42	43	44	45	46	47	48	49	50	51	52	53	54	55	56	57	58
23.5	26	27	28	29	30	31	32	33	34	35	36	37	38	39	40	41	43	44	45	46	47	48	49	50	51	52	53	54	55	56	57	59	60
23.0	26	27	28	29	30	32	33	34	35	36	37	38	39	40	41	42	43	45	46	47	48	49	50	51	52	53	54	55	57	58	59	60	61
22.5	27	28	29	30	31	32	33	34	36	37	38	39	40	41	42	43	44	46	47	48	49	50	51	52	53	54	56	57	58	59	60	61	62
22.0	27	28	30	31	32	33	34	35	36	38	39	40	41	42	43	44	45	47	48	49	50	51	52	53	55	56	57	58	59	60	61	63	64
21.5	28	29	30	31	33	34	35	36	37	38	40	41	42	43	44	45	47	48	49	50	51	52	53	55	56	57	58	59	60	62	63	64	65
21.0	29	30	31	32	33	35	36	37	38	39	40	42	43	44	45	46	48	49	50	51	52	54	55	56	57	58	60	61	62	63	64	65	67
20.5	29	30	32	33	34	35	37	38	39	40	41	43	44	45	46	48	49	50	51	52	54	55	56	57	59	60	61	62	63	65	66	67	68
20.0	30	31	33	34	35	36	38	39	40	41	43	44	45	46	48	49	50	51	53	54	55	56	58	59	60	61	63	64	65	66	68	69	70
19.5	31	32	33	35	36	37	38	40	41	42	44	45	46	47	49	50	51	53	54	55	56	58	59	60	62	63	64	65	67	68	69	71	72
19.0	32	33	34	36	37	38	39	41	42	43	45	46	47	49	50	51	53	54	55	57	58	59	61	62	63	64	66	67	68	70	71	72	74
18.5	32	34	35	36	38	39	41	42	43	45	46	47	49	50	51	53	54	55	57	58	59	61	62	64	65	66	68	69	70	72	73	74	76
18.0	33	35	36	38	39	40	42	43	44	46	47	49	50	51	53	54	56	57	58	60	61	63	64	65	67	68	69	71	72	74	75	76	78
17.5	34	36	37	39	40	41	43	44	46	47	49	50	51	53	54	56	57	59	60	61	63	64	66	67	69	70	71	73	74	76	77	79	80
17.0	35	37	38	40	41	43	44	46	47	49	50	51	53	54	56	57	59	60	62	63	65	66	68	69	71	72	74	75	76	78	79	81	82
16.5	36	38	39	41	42	44	45	47	48	50	52	53	55	56	58	59	61	62	64	65	67	68	70	71	73	74	76	77	79	80	82	83	85
16.0	38	39	41	42	44	45	47	48	50	52	53	55	56	58	59	61	63	64	66	67	69	70	72	73	75	77	78	80	81	83	84	86	88
15.5	39	40	42	44	45	47	48	50	52	53	55	56	58	60	61	63	65	66	68	69	71	73	74	76	77	79	81	82	84	85	87	89	90
15.0	40	42	43	45	47	48	50	52	53	55	57	58	60	62	63	65	67	68	70	72	73	75	77	78	80	82	83	85	87	88	90	92	93
14.5	41	43	45	47	48	50	52	53	55	57	59	60	62	64	66	67	69	71	72	74	75	78	79	81	83	84	86	88	90	91	93	95	97
14.0	43	45	46	48	50	52	54	55	57	59	61	63	64	66	68	70	71	73	75	77	79	80	82	84	86	88	89	91	93	95	96	98	100
13.5	44	46	48	50	52	54	56	57	59	61	63	65	67	69	70	72	74	76	78	80	81	83	85	87	89	91	93	94	96	98	100	102	104
13.0	46	48	50	52	54	56	58	60	62	63	65	67	69	71	73	75	77	79	81	83	85	87	88	90	92	94	96	98	100	102	104	106	108
12.5	48	50	52	54	56	58	60	62	64	66	68	70	72	74	76	78	80	82	84	86	88	90	92	94	96	98	100	102	104	106	108	110	112
12.0	50	52	54	56	58	60	63	65	67	69	71	73	75	77	79	81	83	85	88	90	92	94	96	98	100	102	104	106	108	110	113	115	117
11.5	52	54	57	59	61	63	65	67	70	72	74	76	78	80	83	85	87	89	91	93	96	98	100	102	104	107	109	111	113	115	117	120	122
11.0	55	57	59	61	64	66	68	70	73	75	77	80	82	84	86	89	91	93	95	98	100	102	105	107	109	111	114	116	118	120	123	125	127
10.5	57	60	62	64	67	69	71	74	76	79	81	83	86	88	90	93	95	98	100	102	105	107	110	112	114	117	119	121	124	126	129	131	133
10.0	60	63	65	68	70	73	75	78	80	83	85	88	90	93	95	98	100	103	105	108	110	113	115	118	120	123	125	128	130	133	135	138	140
9.5	63	66	68	71	74	76	79	82	84	87	89	92	95	97	100	103	105	108	111	113	116	118	121	124	126	129	132	134	137	139	142	145	147
9.0	67	69	72	75	78	81	83	86	89	92	94	97	100	103	106	108	111	114	117	119	122	125	128	131	133	136	139	142	144	147	150	153	156
8.5	71	74	76	79	82	85	88	91	94	97	100	103	106	109	112	115	118	121	124	126	129	132	135	138	141	144	147	150	153	156	159	162	165
8.0	75	78	81	84	88	91	94	97	100	103	106	109	113	116	119	122	125	128	131	134	138	141	144	147	150	153	156	159	163	166	169	172	175
7.5	80	83	87	90	93	97	100	103	107	110	113	117	120	123	127	130	133	137	140	143	147	150	153	157	160	163	167	170	173	177	180	183	187
7.0	86	89	93	96	100	104	107	111	114	118	121	125	129	132	136	139	143	146	150	154	157	161	164	168	171	175	179	182	186	189	193	196	200
6.5	92	96	100	104	108	112	115	119	123	127	131	135	138	142	146	150	154	158	162	165	169	173	177	181	185	188	192	196	200	204	208	212	215
6.0	100	104	108	113	117	121	125	129	133	138	142	146	150	154	158	163	167	171	175	179	183	188	192	196	200	204	208	213	217	221	225	229	233
5.5	109	114	118	123	127	132	136	141	145	150	155	159	164	168	173	177	182	186	191	195	200	205	209	214	218	223	227	232	236	241	245	250	255
5.0	120	125	130	135	140	145	150	155	160	165	170	175	180	185	190	195	200	205	210	215	220	225	230	235	240	245	250	255	260	265	270	275	280

Name _____   **Date** _____

Timed Readings
Signature Reading, F

Shade the correct number of squares to show your approximate reading rate (number of words per minute).

Words per Minute

290 280 270 260 250 240 230 220 210 200 190 180 170 160 150 140 130 120 110 100 90 80 70 60 50 40 30 20

Lesson

1 2 3 4 5 6 7 8 9 10 11 12 13 14 15 16 17 18 19 20

Tests

Each test covers the skills and strategies presented in five lessons plus a Learning New Words section. The questions check how well students understand and can apply the skills and strategies they have learned. They do not require students to remember specific details of selections. These tests may be reproduced for classroom use.

ANSWER KEY

Test 1 (page T25)
for Lessons 1–5 and Learning New Words

1. a	6. a
2. a	7. b
3. c	8. b
4. b	9. c
5. a	10. a

Test 3 (page T27)
for Lessons 11–15 and Learning New Words

1. b	6. b
2. a	7. c
3. a	8. b
4. c	9. c
5. b	10. c

Test 2 (page T26)
for Lessons 6–10 and Learning New Words

1. c	6. b
2. b	7. c
3. a	8. c
4. a	9. c
5. a	10. a

Test 4 (page T28)
for Lessons 16–20 and Learning New Words

1. b	6. c
2. a	7. c
3. c	8. b
4. b	9. c
5. a	10. b

Name _____   **Date** _____

| **Test 1** | **for Lessons 1–5 and Learning New Words** |

Answer each question by circling the correct letter.

1. The words *speck* and *spot* are
   a. synonyms.
   b. antonyms.
   c. multiple-meaning words.

2. Which graphic organizer would be most helpful in following an autobiographical sketch?
   a. sequence chain
   b. problem-solution frame
   c. comparison chart

3. When you summarize a text, you
   a. track how a character changes from beginning to end.
   b. try solutions until you get to the end result.
   c. list or retell in your own words the most important ideas

4. In the sentence *The judge was fair, he did the right thing* what does *fair* mean?
   a. average, nothing special
   b. treated everyone equally
   c. a traveling carnival

5. Which type of writing usually contains a problem and a solution?
   a. fiction
   b. nonfiction
   c. biographies

6. Find the antonym of *clean.*
   a. muddy
   b. cloudy
   c. black

7 Which type of graphic organizer would contain an end result?
   a. sequence chain
   b. problem-solution frame
   c. comparison chart

8. Which of the following is not an example of nonfiction?
   a. an autobiographical sketch
   b. science fiction
   c. a how-to article

9. What do you look for in a story to help you predict what will happen?
   a. specialized vocabulary
   b. signal words
   c. context clues

10. An autobiographical sketch is written in
   a. first-person point of view.
   b. second-person point of view.
   c. third-person point of view.

Name _____   **Date** _____

Test 2   for Lessons 6–10 and Learning New Words

Answer each question by circling the correct letter.

1. If you needed to remember how things in a story were alike and different, you would use a
   a. sequence chain.
   b. problem-solution frame.
   c. comparison chart.

2. Which of the following is true about a biographical sketch?
   a. the story is about the author's whole life
   b. the story is about part of someone else's life
   c. the story has some real and some fictional elements.

3. Choose the sentence with the signal words underlined.
   a. <u>After that</u> she went home.
   b. After that <u>she went</u> home.
   c. After that she <u>went home</u>.

4. Which set of words is an example of specialized vocabulary?
   a. fungicide, irrigation, greenhouse
   b. hesitate, accurate, forfeit
   c. muddiest, dirtiest, filthiest

5. A time line will best help you keep track of events in
   a. a biography.
   b. a fictional story.
   c. an informational article.

6. The suffix –er turns a verb into a noun that means
   a. full of ____.
   b. a person who ____.
   c. the process of _____.

7. Outlining main ideas and details will be helpful in
   a. a biography.
   b. a fictional story.
   c. an informational article.

8. An expert in chemistry is called a
   a. chemical.
   b. chemicor.
   c. chemist.

9. You are reading a story about the Big Dipper. Which of these is a main idea?
   a. Some people see a cart when they look at the Big Dipper.
   b. Slaves used its North Star to find their way to Canada.
   c. The Big Dipper is part of Ursa Major (the Great Bear).

10. You are writing a paragraph about soccer. To think of as many related words as possible, you could use
   a. a concept map.
   b. a comparison chart.
   c. a time line.

Name _____   **Date** _____

Test 3 for Lessons 11–15 and Learning New Words

Answer each question by circling the correct letter.

1. The prefix *trans-* means
   a. again.
   b. across.
   c. ability.

2. You are sleeping one morning, then your alarm goes off and you wake up. This is an example of
   a. a cause-and-effect relationship.
   b. a biographical sketch.
   c. a first-person point of view.

3. Sequence chains are most helpful in
   a. following the steps in a process.
   b. finding the main idea and supporting details.
   c. understanding specialized vocabulary.

4. Which type of writing does not usually contain mood?
   a. a play
   b. a fictional story
   c. a biography

5. When an author provides clues about something before it happens, it is called
   a. predicting.
   b. foreshadowing.
   c. context.

6. Find the compound word.
   a. translator
   b. catnap
   c. rediscover

7. What type of graphic organizer often contains Roman numerals (I, II, III, etc.)?
   a. cause and effect chain
   b. time line
   c. outline

8. An informational article contains
   a. suspense and foreshadowing.
   b. a topic, main idea, and supporting details.
   c. signal words.

9. You are reading a how-to article. What is the author's purpose for writing?
   a. to entertain
   b. to persuade
   c. to inform

10. Find a synonym for *stake.*
    a. meat
    b. mail
    c. stick

Name _____   Date _____

Test 4   for Lessons 16–20 and Learning New Words

Answer each question by circling the correct letter.

1. Which prefix means *with* or *together*?
   a. un-
   b. co-
   c. pre-

2. Which group of words is about seeds?
   a. pod, parachute, glide
   b. hover, navigate, controls
   c. produce, fertilizers, irrigation

3. Which graphic organizer would be most helpful in making predictions?
   a. time line
   b. comparison chart
   c. neither

4. The type of writing that gives facts and information about a particular topic is
   a. fiction.
   b. nonfiction.
   c. biography.

5. One element of folktales is
   a. one-sided, flat characters.
   b. a complicated plot.
   c. both of these.

6. You will often find repetitive patterns in
   a. informational articles.
   b. fiction.
   c. folktales.

7. The prefix *sub-* means
   a. over.
   b. between.
   c. below.

8. You should use a comparison chart when you want to
   a. make predictions.
   b. compare and contrast.
   c. identify the problems and solutions in a story.

9. Which type of writing contains animals that sometimes act like people?
   a. informational articles
   b. fiction
   c. folktales

10. The best strategy for understanding nonfiction is
    a. identifying problems and solutions.
    b. summarizing.
    c. making predictions.

Shoeshine Whittaker
LESSON 1 (pages 6–15)

Summary

Shoeshine Whittaker arrives in Mudville, the muddiest, cruddiest town in the West. When he begins to give guaranteed shoeshines, he finds he must clean up the whole town to make sure the shoeshines last. But there is a problem: the townspeople are not accustomed to such clean surroundings.

Selection Notes

Irony
Explain to students that irony occurs when the results of an action are exactly the opposite of the expected results. For example, in Shoeshine Whittaker, you would expect the townspeople to thank him when he makes the town spotless. What do they do instead? Why is this ironic?

Vocabulary: Words About Dirt and Cleaning

- clean
- down
- dusty
- muddiest
- sparkled
- spot
- dirtiest
- dulling
- gleamed
- shining
- speck
- up

Strategy Focus: Identifying Problems and Solutions

Taught elsewhere: Lesson 5
In this story, students will learn to identify the problem in a fictional story, name the solutions, and define the end result. They will use a problem-solution frame to accomplish this.

In Lesson 5, students will identify problems and solutions in a science fiction setting.

Fiction • 834 words

The Big Toe Contest
LESSON 2 (pages 16–25)

Summary

When we meet Hayden Tucker, he is lifting weights with his big toe in preparation for The Big Toe Contest at the River County Fair. However, when he arrives at the fair, he discovers that the contest is not exactly what he imagined.

Selection Notes

Humor
Humor often comes from taking things out of context. The whole story of "The Big Toe Contest" occurs because Hayden misunderstands the meaning of "big toe". Ask students if they can think of any times when they misunderstood something. Were the consequences as funny as Hayden's?

Vocabulary: Words for Predicting the Plot

- fair
- toe

Strategy Focus: Making Predictions While Reading the Story

Taught elsewhere: Lesson 10, Lesson 20
In this story, students will learn to make predictions about what will happen next. They should base their predictions on information or clues that the author provides.

In Lesson 10, students will practice making predictions based on context clues in the story. In Lesson 20, students will use elements in a folktale to make their predictions.

Fiction • 906 words

The Trail of Tears
LESSON 3 (pages 26–33)

Summary

This selection tells the heartbreaking story of the relocation of the Cherokee nation from the Smoky Mountains to Oklahoma. Government troops rounded up the Cherokees, split their families, and forced them to walk 1000 miles to Oklahoma. More than 1/4 of those who set out died of cold, hunger, or exhaustion on this terrible march.

Selection Notes

More History

Encourage students to research government treatment of Native Americans in the 19th century, particularly the Cherokee and the Trail of Tears. If you think students are not ready to find their own materials on the subject, bring some books and encyclopedias into the classroom.

Vocabulary: Words About the March

- exhaustion
- forced
- heartless
- relocate
- stockades
- exiles
- frightened
- orders
- round up

Strategy Focus: Summarizing Nonfiction

Taught elsewhere: Lesson 18

In this selection, students will learn how to summarize nonfiction. They will retell sections of the story in their own words, sorting through the text to include only the most important ideas. They will practice this strategy again in Lesson 18.

At Last I Kill a Buffalo
LESSON 4 (pages 34–43)

Summary

In this story a young Native American boy tells of his first buffalo hunt at the age of eight. He tells about the anticipation before the hunt, watching his father prepare, how he felt during the excitement of the chase and what he learned from the experience.

Selection Notes

Turning Points

In many Native American cultures buffalo hunting was a turning point from childhood to adulthood. Ask students if they have any traditions to mark the end of childhood and the beginning of growing up. If they could make up a tradition or a ceremony to celebrate this important time, what would it be?

Vocabulary: Words About Buffalo Hunting

- buffalo hunt
- quivers
- justified
- herd
- praised
- tipi
- rawhide
- honesty
- fatal wound

Strategy Focus: Reading an Autobiographical Sketch

Taught elsewhere: Lesson 7, Lesson 8

In this selection, students will read part of an autobiography. They will learn to find signal words to help them put the events of the story in the correct order. Students will be able to organize the events on a sequence chain in the order they happened.

In Lesson 7, they will practice making sequence chains for a biographical sketch.

Nonfiction • 703 words

Fiction • 1805 words

Two Fat Boys from Venus
LESSON 5 (pages 44–53)

Summary
Since there are no good haircutters on Venus, two Venusian boys come to Earth to get a haircut. Most of the people they meet scream and faint when they see them, but finally they run across a young boy who agrees to cut their hair. He also inspires them to become haircutters themselves.

Selection Notes
Science Fiction
Discuss with students the elements in this story that make it different from standard fiction. Ask students if they prefer this type of story over other types of fiction. Why or why not?

Vocabulary: Words for Predicting the Plot

- abundant
- customer
- Earth
- gorgeous
- inhabitants
- Venus
- courteously
- decent
- fainted
- haircutters
- screamed
- Venusian

Strategy Focus: Identifying Problems and Solutions
Taught elsewhere: Lesson 1
In this story, students will learn to identify problems and solutions in a science fiction setting.

   In Lesson 1, students learned to identify the problem in a fictional story, name the solutions, and define the end result. They used a problem-solution frame to accomplish this.

Fiction • 976 words

Learning New Words
(pages 54–55)

Synonyms
From Lesson 1
- dirtiest
- gleamed
- speck
- muddiest
- sparkled
- spot

Ask students if they can think of even more synonyms of these words.

Antonyms
From Lesson 1
- clean
- down
- dulling
- dusty
- up
- shining

Have students think of five additional antonym pairs and share them with the class. Combine the words into a master list and distribute it to the class.

Multiple-Meaning Words
From Lesson 2
- fair
- toe

From Lesson 3
- orders

Ask students to point out the context clues that helped them pick the correct definitions on page 55.

Put the Brolly in the Boot and Let's Go
LESSON 6 (pages 56–65)

Summary

In this story Jenny, an American girl, goes to England to visit her cousins. At first, she is confused by many of the words her cousins use. But after a while both Jenny and her cousins begin to enjoy learning about the differences between American and British English.

Selection Notes

Coping Strategies

Jenny's mother had told her that her relatives spoke English, but when Jenny arrived she had a lot of trouble understanding them. Help students understand her feelings by having them share times when they thought they knew how to handle a situation, but suddenly things changed. How did they deal with the new situation? Was it successful?

Vocabulary: Words for Predicting the Plot

- bangers
- bonnet
- chemist
- loo
- surgery
- valise
- biscuits
- boot
- crisps
- lorry
- tea

Strategy Focus: Comparing and Contrasting

Taught Elsewhere: Lesson 17

In this story students will use a comparison chart to find similarities and differences between life in America and life in Great Britain. In Lesson 17 students will use an expanded version of the chart to compare and contrast information in a nonfiction selection.

Fiction • 901 words

The Contest
LESSON 7 (pages 66–75)

Summary

In this selection, we meet famous singer Marian Anderson as a young girl about to enter a voice contest. The young Marian is nervous and unsure of her abilities, but her teacher's unwavering confidence and her own natural abilities lead to a splendid performance. Finally, the judges announce the winners.

Selection Notes

Point of View

This story is told from an omniscient point of view—that of someone outside the story who knows the thoughts and feelings of all the characters. Ask students to think about how the story would be different if it were told from the point of view of Marian's coach.

Vocabulary: Words for Predicting the Plot

- abscess
- ambitious
- flourish
- precious
- trill
- accompanist
- aria
- lanced
- recitative
- unanimous

Strategy Focus: Reading a Biographical Sketch

Taught Elsewhere: Lesson 4, Lesson 8

In this selection, students will read part of a biography. They will learn to find signal words to help them put the events of the story in the correct order. Students will be able to organize the events on a sequence chain in the order they happened.

In Lesson 4, students practiced using signal words to make sequence chains for an autobiographical sketch.

In Lesson 8, students will apply what they learn about sequence to the story of someone's entire life.

Nonfiction • 1197 words

The Fabulous Miss Bly
LESSON 8 (pages 76–85)

Summary
In 1885, Elizabeth Cochrane responded to an article in the paper saying that women could not do a good job outside the home. She felt that they could, and she asked the editor of that paper for a job. He gave it to her, and it was the start of a fabulous career of reporting, traveling, and adventure.

Selection Notes
Editorials
In this story Elizabeth Cochrane responded to a newspaper editorial. Remind students that editorials are stories written by people to express their opinions in a newspaper. They are different from regular news stories, which are supposed to be only fact, not opinion. Ask students to name something in their town or school they would like to express an opinion about. If they wrote an editorial, what would it say?

Vocabulary: Words About Newspaper Publishing
- article
- editorial
- reporter
- topic
- editor
- published
- reports

Strategy Focus: Reading a Biography
Taught Elsewhere: Lesson 4, Lesson 7
In this lesson, students will apply what they have learned about sequence to the entire story of a person's life. They will learn to use a time line to show events in the order that they happened over an extended period of time.

In Lesson 7, students read part of a biography. They learned to find signal words to help them put the events of the story in the correct order. Students will be able to organize the events on a sequence chain in the order they happened.

In Lesson 4, students practiced using signal words to make sequence chains for an autobiographical sketch.

Nonfiction • 935 words

Bungee Jumping: A Leap of Faith
LESSON 9 (pages 86–93)

Summary
This article gives the history of the daredevil sport of bungee jumping. It begins in the sport's earliest stages in England and the South Pacific, and explains how it became popular in the United States and spread around the world. It also tells about the dangers of the sport.

Selection Notes
Motivation
This selection touches on what would motivate people to try bungee jumping. Ask the class if they would like to try bungee jumping. Why or why not? Write their reasons for and against on the board. As students read, have them compare the class motivations to those listed in the article.

Vocabulary: Words for Predicting the Plot
- cords
- daredevil
- plunge
- vines
- courage
- gorge
- thrill
- yo-yo

Strategy Focus: Outlining Main Ideas and Supporting Details
Taught Elsewhere: Lesson 12
In this lesson, students will use a basic outline format (Roman numerals and capital letters) to organize the main ideas and supporting details in an informational article. They should include only the most important ideas and details.

Students continue to practice outlining in Lesson 12.

Nonfiction • 754 words

Too-Tall Twyla
LESSON 10 • (pages 94–103)

Summary
The Midcity boys basketball team has a problem. They are one player short for their championship game, and this year they really have a shot at winning. Reluctantly, they ask Too-Tall Twyla, a good player on the Midcity girls team, to be their sixth player on the bench. But during the game, their star player gets injured, and Twyla must take his place.

Selection Notes
Debate
In recent years there has been growing debate about whether or not girls should be allowed to compete on the same playing field with boys in school sports. Ask students what they think about this. Does the type of sport being played make a difference? Remind students to support their arguments as well as they can, not just voice opinions.

Vocabulary: Words for Predicting the Plot
- coed
- routines
- MVP
- accurate
- forfeit
- nickname
- hesitate
- stunned

Strategy Focus: Making Predictions While Reading a Story
Taught Elsewhere: Lesson 2, Lesson 20
In this lesson, students will practice making predictions based on context clues in the story.

In Lesson 20, students will use elements in a folktale to make their predictions.

In Lesson 2, students learned to make predictions about what will happen next. They based their predictions on information or clues that the author provided.

Fiction • 680 words

Learning New Words
(pages 104–105)

Compound Words
From Lesson 9
- daredevil

Ask pairs of students to create sentences using each compound word on page 104.

Suffixes
-er and -or
From Lesson 8
- reporter

From Lesson 9
- editor

Give students 60 seconds to generate a list of as many words as possible using the -er and -or suffix. Remind students that these words should all be nouns, not verbs or adjectives.

-ist
From Lesson 7
- accompanist

Repeat the exercise above for the -ist suffix.

Dava's Talent
LESSON 11 (pages 106–113)

Summary

Dava is the son of a shepherd in Morocco. All the men in his family have been shepherds. Dava would like to be one, too, but there is one problem: the sheep won't listen to him. One day his father gets hurt and Dava has to lead the sheep home himself. At first, they will not listen to him, and he is afraid he will lose them all. But then he discovers a special talent.

Selection Notes

Exploring Cultures

Assign students to find out more about Morocco: its culture, history and government. Give each student a specific piece of information to look for. When everyone has found the information, discuss it as a class. Point out similarities and differences between Morocco and the United States.

Vocabulary: Words About Sheep

- bleat
- herd
- sheared
- shepherd
- flock
- lambs
- sheepcote

Strategy Focus: Identifying Causes and Effects

Taught elsewhere: Lesson 19

In this story, students will learn how to identify and track cause-and-effect relationships; what happened and why. Students can organize them on a cause and effect chain. In Lesson 19, students will examine a series of cause-and-effect relationships in which one event causes another.

Fiction • 680 words

Feeling Sleepy?
LESSON 12 (pages 114–121)

Summary

This selection discusses kids and sleep: how much they need, how much they are getting, and what happens if they don't get enough. The article states that kids who don't get enough sleep don't do as well in school and have more difficulty controlling their emotions than those who are well-rested.

Selection Notes

Survey

In small groups have students collect the answers to the first three questions in Building Background, and report the information to the class for their group. Do students get enough sleep according to the chart? What could they do (or stop doing) that would let them sleep more each night?

Vocabulary: Words About Sleep

- catnaps
- internal "clock"
- readjusting
- functions
- reaction time

Strategy Focus: Outlining Main Ideas and Supporting Details

Taught elsewhere: Lesson 9

In this lesson, students will use a basic outline format (Roman numerals and capital letters) to organize the main ideas and supporting details in an informational article. They should include only the most important ideas and details.

Students previously practiced outlining in Lesson 9.

Nonfiction • 848 words

How to Be a Super Sorter: Five Steps for Managing the Mess
LESSON 13 (pages 122–131)

Summary

This selection tells how to take a messy room and make it clean for good. Broken into chunks, a big job doesn't seem so monumental. The five steps to a clean room include the big sort, planning where things should live, deciding what to keep or toss, making cleaning a habit, and taking the project one step at a time.

Selection Notes
How-to Articles

Be sure students understand that how-to articles are meant to inform and teach the reader. Sometimes they are also entertaining, but not always. How-to articles can be found in books, magazines, and newspapers about a variety of subjects. Have students name something they would like to read a how-to article about.

Vocabulary: Words About Cleaning and Sorting

- keepsakes
- tackle
- train
- monumental
- tidy
- whirlwind

Strategy Focus: Following the Steps in a Process

In this article, students will learn to pay attention to the sequence in which an author presents things. Using a sequence chain, students will be able to show the steps in a process in their proper order.

Nonfiction • 819 words

Dracula (Part 1)
LESSON 14 (pages 132–141)

Summary

In Part 1 of this play based on Bram Stoker's famous novel, the scene is set as young Jonathan Harker arrives at Count Dracula's castle, to help Dracula buy a castle in England. After a few odd occurrences, Harker begins to suspect something is very wrong. One night he is visited by a beautiful woman in a flowing gown with razor-sharp teeth. Dracula arrives and stops her from harming Harker, but by then Harker has realized that Dracula is a vampire.

Selection Notes
The Settings of a Play

Remind students that plays were meant to be performed on a stage. Ask students why the play is broken into scenes (each scene is a new location; sets must be changed). Is this a logical way to break things up? Why or why not?

Vocabulary: Words for Predicting the Plot

- horror
- foreboding
- fury
- vanishes
- transforms
- property
- Count Dracula
- rosary
- vision
- vampire

Strategy Focus: Identifying Mood

In this lesson, students will learn to identify the mood of a story and the descriptive details that set the mood. For this particular play, students will be able use the characters' diaries to access their thoughts and emotions as well as their words and actions. Students will combine all the mood-setting details into a chart.

Fiction • 1011 words

Dracula (Part 2)
LESSON 15 (pages 142–153)

Summary

In the second half of the play, we go to England to meet Harker's fiancée, Mina. She has come to spend the summer visiting her friend, Dr. Seward. He runs a mental hospital next to the Carfax estate, the one that Dracula has bought. Over the next month, Mina becomes very ill. Dr. Seward sends for his mentor Dr. Van Helsing, who tells him that Mina has been bitten by a vampire. The only way to save her is to find the vampire during the day and drive a wooden stake through his heart.

Selection Notes

Folklore

Transylvanian legends say that vampires are afraid of rosaries and crucifixes. Ask students to find other elements of vampire folklore used in the story. (afraid of garlic, can't be seen in mirrors, can turn himself into a dog or wolf, etc.)

Vocabulary: Words for Predicting the Plot

- crucifix
- fiancée
- hypnotize
- witnesses
- eternity
- haunted
- intrusion
- stake

Strategy Focus: Using Mood and Foreshadowing to Predict

Taught Elsewhere: Lesson 14 (Mood), Lesson 16 (Foreshadowing)

In this lesson students begin with making predictions based on specified clues provided by the author. By the end of the play, they will be finding their own clues within the selection, as well as making predictions. Students will practice making predictions again in Lesson 16.

Learning New Words
(pages 154–155)

Prefixes

re-
From Lesson 11
- readjusting

trans-
From Lesson 14
- transforms

Have students generate a list of words using the *re-* and *trans-* prefixes, then use the words to play charades.

Compound Words

From Lesson 11
- sheepcote

From Lesson 12
- catnaps

From Lesson 13
- keepsakes
- whirlwind

For each compound word on page 154, ask students to create an antonym word or phrase.

Multiple-Meaning Words

From Lesson 13
- tackle
- train

From Lesson 14
- vision

After you have reviewed students' answers to the questions on page 155, ask them to create one sentence for each of the definitions that were not used.

Fiction • 1897 words

When Disaster Strikes . . .
LESSON 16 (pages 156–165)

Summary
Stacey and her father were helping to sandbag during a flood. Needing a rest, Stacey talks her father into taking her up in his helicopter to look for people and animals that could be trapped in the rising water. Just before the helicopter takes off, Stacey grabs a rope ladder and life jackets in case they find someone. Now Stacey must fly the helicopter while her father attempts to rescue three people from the flood.

Selection Notes
Natural Disasters
With the class discuss the types of natural disasters that occur in your area. Do students think that one type of natural disaster is worse than another? Which one, and why? What should people do when they hear about the possibility of a natural disaster?

Vocabulary: Words About Rescues
- copilot
- rope ladder
- submerged
- hovered
- life jackets
- navigated
- controls

Strategy Focus: Using Foreshadowing to Predict
Taught elsewhere: Lesson 15
In this lesson students continue to make predictions about what will happen based on clues they find in the selection. They first practiced this strategy in a play in Lesson 15.

Fiction • 1023 words

Seed Travel
LESSON 17 (pages 166–173)

Summary
This article covers why seeds need to travel, and the various methods for doing so. It's a seed's job to claim new living space for its species, and to make sure that it will have enough water and sunlight to survive. Seeds travel in many ways, depending on the type of plant they come from. Some seeds use rockets, pods, or parachutes to get away from their parent plants. Some seeds have wings, and others float or hitchhike through the air.

Selection Notes
Environmental Science
As students read through the article, have them list the different types of seed travel and the climate in which each occurs. Using this information, have students answer the following question: Is the type of seed travel chosen by each plant affected by its climate?

Vocabulary: Words About Seeds
- glide
- launch
- parachute
- species
- hitchhike
- nourishes
- pods
- whirls

Strategy Focus: Comparing and Contrasting
Taught Elsewhere: Lesson 6
In this selection students will use an expanded version of the comparison chart (called a features chart) to compare and contrast the various methods of seed travel listed in the article.

Students practiced using a comparison chart to find similarities and differences between life in America and life in Great Britain in Lesson 6.

Nonfiction • 696 words

Vegetables
LESSON 18 (pages 174–181)

Summary
This selection explains what vegetables are and how they are grown. Because of modern farming methods, the vegetables we find in the stores come from all over the world. Different types of vegetables come from different parts of the plants. Root vegetables are things like carrots and radishes. Cabbage and lettuce are examples of leafy vegetables. Seed vegetables include peas and some types of beans.

Selection Notes
Specialized Vocabulary
Have students continue adding words they know to the vegetables word map they began in the Vocabulary Builder. Tell them to share their word maps with a partner, and explain to their partner any words their partner doesn't understand.

Vocabulary: Words About Farming
- fertilizers
- greenhouses
- pesticides
- truck farms
- fungicides
- irrigation
- produce

Strategy Focus: Summarizing Nonfiction
Taught Elsewhere: Lesson 3
In this selection students will again practice summarizing nonfiction. They will retell sections of the story in their own words, sorting through the text to include only the most important ideas. They were first exposed to this strategy in Lesson 3.

Nonfiction • 783 words

The Magic Bowl
LESSON 19 (pages 182–191)

Summary
Little Wong and his mother worked for a rich farmer. Little Wong was required to travel farther and farther every day to find grass for the rich man's horses. One day he finds a field in which the grass grows back as soon as he cuts it. He and his mother discover the source of the magic that makes the grass grow— a small earthenware bowl. The farmer takes their bowl away and destroys it in his greed.

Selection Notes
Moral of the Story
A story with a moral is one that tries to teach something about the values of a particular culture, what is considered bad or good. Traditional tales such as "The Magic Bowl" often have morals embedded in them. What do students think is the moral of this story? Why?

Vocabulary: Words for Predicting the Plot
- greedy
- jealous
- wisely

Strategy Focus: Identifying Causes and Effects
Taught Elsewhere: Lesson 11
In this lesson students will examine a series of cause-and-effect relationships in which one event causes another. They will track the relationships on a cause and effect chain.

Students used a simpler cause-and-effect chain in Lesson 11.

Fiction • 1236 words

Talk
LESSON 20 (pages 192–201)

Summary

This folktale tells of a man who dug up a yam to take it to market. The yam did not like this attention and asked the man to leave him alone. The man was shocked that the yam spoke to him, and became even more shocked when his dog agreed with the yam. The man started hearing voices from the trees, branches, and rocks. He ran into a fisherman, weaver, and bather who began to run with him when inanimate objects began talking to them.

Selection Notes

Personification

Personification, animals or objects acting like people, is a common element in folktales. As students read the story, have them think about what reasons an author would have for wanting animals and objects to act like people. Use the information they gave in Building Background to start the discussion.

Vocabulary: Words for Predicting the Plot

- complaints
- gazelle
- peace
- tone
- ford
- patiently
- punish
- yam

Strategy Focus: Using Folktale Elements to Make Predictions

Taught Elsewhere: Lesson 2, Lesson 10 (Predictions) In this story, students will use the repetitive elements in a folktale to make their predictions. These repetitive elements include flat characters, repetitive patterns, and irony.

In Lesson 2, they learned to make predictions about what will happen next. They learned to base their predictions on information or clues that the author provides.

In Lesson 10, students practiced making predictions based on context clues in the story.

Learning New Words
(pages 202–203)

Prefixes

co-

From Lesson 16

- copilot

Give students 60 seconds to list as many words as they can using the prefix co-. Review the lists with the class, and make sure that students understand the definition of each word.

sub-

From Lesson 16

- submerged

In small groups ask for student volunteers to use each *sub-* word on page 202 in a sentence. The other group members must check to see that the word was used correctly according to the definition given.

Suffixes

-ly

From Lesson 19

- wisely

From Lesson 20

- patiently

Have students name the *–ly* adjectives that are the opposites of those listed on page 203.

Compound Words

From Lesson 17

- hitchhike

From Lesson 18

- greenhouses

Ask students to think of more compound words using one or more of the words on page 203. Examples: *toothbrush, bedroom, seashell.*

Fiction • 824 words

JAMESTOWN EDUCATION

SIGNATURE READING

LEVEL F

McGraw Hill **Glencoe**

New York, New York   Columbus, Ohio   Chicago, Illinois   Peoria, Illinois   Woodland Hills, California

JAMESTOWN EDUCATION

Reviewers

Marsha Miller, Ed.D
Reading Specialist
Elgin High School
1200 Maroon Drive
Elgin, IL 60120

Kati Pearson
Orange County Public Schools
Literacy Coordinator
Carver Middle School
4500 West Columbia Street
Orlando, FL 32811

Lynda Pearson
Assistant Principal
Reading Specialist
Lied Middle School
5350 Tropical Parkway
Las Vegas, NV 89130

Suzanne Zweig
Reading Specialist/Consultant
Sullivan High School
6631 N. Bosworth
Chicago, IL 60626

The McGraw·Hill Companies

ISBN: 0-07-861720-0 (Pupil's Edition)
ISBN: 0-07-861721-9 (Annotated Teacher's Edition)

Send all queries to:
Glencoe/McGraw-Hill
8787 Orion Place
Columbus, OH 43240-4027

1 2 3 4 5 6 7 8 9   113   09 08 07 06 05 04

Contents

How to Use This Book

Working Through the Lessons

The following descriptions will help you work your way through the lessons in this book.

Building Background will help you get ready to read. In this section you might begin a chart, discuss a question, or learn more about the topic of the selection.

Vocabulary Builder will help you start thinking about—and using—the selection vocabulary. You might draw a diagram and label it with vocabulary words, make a word map, match vocabulary words to their synonyms or antonyms, or use the words to predict what might happen in the selection.

Strategy Builder will introduce you to the strategy that you will use to read the selection. First you will read a definition of the strategy. Then you will see an example of how to use it. Often, you will be given ways to better organize or visualize what you will be reading.

Strategy Break will appear within the reading selection. It will show you how to apply the strategy you just learned to the first part of the selection.

Strategy Follow-up will ask you to apply the same strategy to the second part of the selection. Most of the time, you will work on your own to complete this section. Sometimes, however, you might work with a partner or a group of classmates.

Personal Checklist questions will ask you to rate how well you did in the lesson. When you finish totaling your score, you will enter it on the graphs on page 205.

Vocabulary Check will follow up on the work you did in the Vocabulary Builder. After you total your score, you will enter it on page 205.

Strategy Check will follow up on the strategy work that you did in the lesson. After you total your score, you will enter it on page 205.

Comprehension Check will check your understanding of the selection. After you total your score, you will enter it on page 205.

Extending will give ideas for activities that are related to the selection. Some activities will help you learn more about the topic of the selection. Others might ask you to respond to the selection by dramatizing, writing, or drawing something.

Resources such as books, recordings, videos, and Web sites will help you complete the Extending activities.

Graphing Your Progress

The information and graphs on pages 204–205 will help you track your progress as you work through this book. **Graph 1** will help you record your scores for the Personal Checklist and the Vocabulary, Strategy, and Comprehension Checks. **Graph 2** will help you track your overall progress across the book. You'll be able to see your areas of strength, as well as any areas that could use improvement. You and your teacher can discuss ways to work on those areas.

clean

dirtiest

down

dulling

dusty

gleamed

muddiest

shining

sparkled

speck

spot

up

Shoeshine Whittaker

Building Background

What did the dust say during a rainstorm?
"If this keeps up, my name will be mud!"

What do you call a jackrabbit that's stuck in mud?
"Unhoppy."

Did you smile or laugh (or groan) as you read any of these jokes? The creators of the jokes had a purpose for writing them: to entertain you. What other things have your read or seen lately that were meant to be entertaining?

Authors write for one or more of these purposes: to **entertain** (make you laugh or smile), to **inform** (explain or describe something), to **persuade** (try to get you to agree with their opinion), to **express** (share their feelings or ideas about something). Skim the story you are about to read. For what purpose or purposes do you predict Helen Ketteman wrote "Shoeshine Whittaker"?

CLIPBOARD 1

Antonym Pairs

1. clean
   dusty

2. down
   up

3. dulling
   shining

Vocabulary Builder

1. Study the vocabulary words in the margin. Each word is half of a pair of **antonyms** (words with opposite meanings) or **synonyms** (words with similar meanings).

2. Write the antonym pairs on the first clipboard. Write the synonym pairs on the second clipboard. (Hint: Look at the word endings for a little help.)

3. As you read "Shoeshine Whittaker," underline any other antonym or synonym pairs that you find.

4. Save your work. You will use it again in the Vocabulary Check.

CLIPBOARD 2

Synonym Pairs

1. dirtiest
   muddiest

2. gleamed
   sparkled

3. speck
   spot

Strategy Builder

Identifying Problems and Solutions

- In some stories, the main character or characters have a **problem**. Throughout the story, they try to solve it. Sometimes they try more than one **solution**. By the end of the story, they usually come up with the solution that works—the **end result**.

- As you read the following paragraph, notice Billy's problem and what he does to solve it.

> Billy the Kidd thought he was in goat heaven. He lived next to Burger Doodle's favorite dumping ground. He loved nosing around in the bags of trash, looking for things to eat. Life was good—until the day the Burger Doodle became the Dino Dry Cleaners!
>
> Now where would he find good things to eat? First he tried the bookstore, but all they had were books and cardboard boxes. They were filling but not very tasty. Next he tried the pizza place, but the owners chased him away. Finally, he decided to wait outside the ice cream shop. Bingo! Before he knew it, there was an ice cream cone standing upside down on the ground like the tower of a candy castle.

- If you wanted to show Billy's problem and solutions, you could put them on a **problem-solution frame**. It would look like this:

What is the problem?
The Burger Doodle has become the Dino Dry Cleaners.

Why is it a problem?
Now Billy the Kidd doesn't know where to find good things to eat.

Solutions	Results
1. He tries the bookstore.	1. All they have are books and cardboard boxes— filling but not very tasty.
2. He tries the pizza place.	2. The owners chase him away.
3. He waits outside the ice cream shop.	3. END RESULT: He finds an upside down ice cream cone to eat.

Shoeshine Whittaker

by Helen Ketteman

As you read the first part of this story, apply the strategies you just learned. Look for the problem that Shoeshine Whittaker faces—and why.

Mudville, which sat on the bank of the Mud River, was the **muddiest**, cruddiest town in the West. There wasn't a nook or a cranny in Mudville that wasn't covered with dirt.

One **dusty** summer morning, a stranger drove his wagon into town. The long tails of his black coat flapped as he bounced over the rutted road. He wore a bright red vest with shiny buttons that **sparkled** in the sun, and a tall top hat tilted over one eye.

"Whoa there, Miss Clara," he said, pulling to a stop at Fanny Ambrose's Saloon and Fine Eating Establishment. As he climbed **down** from his wagon, Sheriff Blackstone strode **up**. "Who might you be, stranger, and what's your business in Mudville?"

The stranger swept off his top hat and bowed. "Shoeshine's the name, and shoeshine's the game, and I figure I've found the best whang-dang town anywhere. For **shining** shoes, that is."

Sheriff Blackstone narrowed his eyes. "What in thunderation are you talking about?"

Shoeshine laughed and took a stool off his wagon. "I'll give you a free demonstration. Have a seat."

A crowd gathered as the sheriff put up his feet. Shoeshine whistled. The sheriff had the **dirtiest** boots he'd ever seen.

Shoeshine opened a wooden box filled with tins, brushes, and rags. "This is going to be one whing-ding of a challenge," he said, rolling up his sleeves. He brushed clumps of mud off the sheriff's boots. Then he opened a tin of polish and rubbed and scrubbed. Finally, he stood back. "Now that, Sheriff, is a shoeshine!"

The crowd gasped. Sheriff Blackstone blinked. "Why, my boots are as shiny as a mirror. If that don't beat all!"

Shoeshine set out a sign that read:
FINEST SHOESHINE IN THE WEST
GUARANTEED
ONLY 5 CENTS

Soon the whole town was lined up for shoeshines. By the end of the day, everyone in Mudville had beautiful, shiny shoes.

Shoeshine Whittaker counted his money. "Four whole dollars and fifty cents, Miss Clara. We have struck it rich. Tomorrow we'll head for the next town." He thanked the people and rode out of town to set up camp for the night.

Early the next morning, the sheriff shook Shoeshine awake.

"What is it?" asked Shoeshine, rubbing his eyes.

"You're under arrest for cheating the folks of Mudville, that's what! There ain't a shiny boot left in town, and your sign said 'guaranteed.'"

"But, Sheriff, I can't guarantee—"

"Shoeshine Whittaker, your sign said 'guaranteed.' Unless you can back that guarantee, you'll have to stand trial."

 Stop here for the Strategy Break.

Strategy Break

If you were to create a problem-solution frame for this story so far, your frame might look like this:

What is the problem?
Shoeshine Whittaker's sign said "guaranteed."

Why is it a problem?
There's not a shiny boot left in Mudville. Unless Shoeshine can back his guarantee, Sheriff Blackstone will arrest him.

Solutions   **Results**

As you read the rest of this story, pay attention to how Shoeshine solves his problem. Keep track of his solutions, the results, and the end result. When you finish the story, you will complete the problem-solution frame.

Go on reading to see what happens.

Shoeshine gulped. "I'm the best in the West, so there's only one thing to do. Take me back to town, Sheriff. And get me rags—a mountain of rags."

Soon the townspeople had brought Shoeshine a huge pile of rags. He rolled up his sleeves. "Stand back," he shouted as he started working.

He rubbed and scrubbed and shined and polished. By noon, Mudville City Jail and Stable sparkled in the sun, and Hayden Clopstop's General Dry Goods Store and Dentist's Office shone a bright cornflower blue. Even Hayden Clopstop was surprised.

"I plumb forgot I had painted it blue," he said.

Shoeshine polished and rubbed all afternoon. By sunset, half the houses and the wooden sidewalks **gleamed**. Shoeshine worked all night long, too.

By morning, even the surface of Main Street was glistening. There wasn't a **speck** of dust or a **spot** of loose dirt in the whole town. The townspeople couldn't believe their eyes. Mudville had never looked like this.

Once again, Shoeshine set up his stool. "Now your shoes will stay **clean**. Shoeshine Whittaker guarantees it."

People lined up to have their shoes shined. By noon, the sun was high in the sky and reflecting off the shiny surfaces of the street, sidewalks, buildings, and shoes. The glare half blinded the people of Mudville. Their eyes hurt, and their heads ached.

"Now things are too shiny," complained Sheriff Blackstone.

Shoeshine pulled his hat over his ears and muttered under his breath. "These folks of Mudville are whing-dang-dingy! There's only one thing to do."

"Give me an hour, Sheriff," said Shoeshine. "I know just what you need."

Shoeshine hurried down to the Mud River. He dug mud out of the riverbank, tying it into small bags. When he returned, he set up a new sign that read:

SHINE DULLER

ONLY 25 CENTS A BAG

The townspeople lined up with their quarters. "You just take a rag and rub a bit of duller on any surface that's too shiny," announced Shoeshine. "Works great!"

The people bought every last bag Shoeshine had, and they spent the rest of the day **dulling** things up. By sunset, Mudville was back to normal.

Everyone waved to Shoeshine as he rode out of town. "You come back and visit us again, Shoeshine Whittaker," yelled Sheriff Blackstone.

Shoeshine listened to the clink of coins as Miss Clara pulled the wagon down the road. "I probably will, Sheriff," said Shoeshine, waving his top hat. "I probably will." ●

Strategy Follow-up

Now complete the following problem-solution frame with information from the second part of the story.

What is the problem?
Shoeshine Whittaker's sign said "guaranteed."

Why is it a problem?
There's not a shiny boot left in Mudville. Unless Shoeshine can back his guarantee, Sheriff Blackstone will arrest him.

Solutions | Results

1. Shoeshine rubs and scrubs until everything in Mudville is glistening. ➡ 1. The people complain that everything is too shiny.

2. Shoeshine digs mud out of the riverbank and sells it as "shine duller" for 25 cents a bag. ➡ 2. **END RESULT:** The people dull things up, and Mudville gets back to normal—and Shoeshine doesn't get arrested.

✓Personal Checklist

Read each question and put a check (✓) in the correct box.

1. How well do you understand why the sheriff makes Shoeshine Whittaker return to Mudville?
    ☐ 3 (extremely well)
    ☐ 2 (fairly well)
    ☐ 1 (not well)

2. How well were you able to list synonym and antonym pairs in the Vocabulary Builder?
    ☐ 3 (extremely well)
    ☐ 2 (fairly well)
    ☐ 1 (not well)

3. How well were you able to use the information in Building Background to predict the author's purpose for writing this story?
    ☐ 3 (extremely well)
    ☐ 2 (fairly well)
    ☐ 1 (not well)

4. How well were you able to complete the problem-solution frame in the Strategy Follow-up?
    ☐ 3 (extremely well)
    ☐ 2 (fairly well)
    ☐ 1 (not well)

5. How well do you understand why the people of Mudville are happy at the end of this story?
    ☐ 3 (extremely well)
    ☐ 2 (fairly well)
    ☐ 1 (not well)

Vocabulary Check

Look back at the work you did in the Vocabulary Builder. Then answer each question by circling the correct letter.

1. Which vocabulary word is a synonym for the word *speck*?
    a. dusty
    (b.) spot
    c. clean

2. Which synonym pair describes Mudville when Shoeshine Whittaker arrives?
    (a.) dirtiest/muddiest
    b. speck/spot
    c. gleamed/sparkled

3. Which antonym pair can be used to describe directions?
    a. clean/dusty
    (b.) down/up
    c. dulling/shining

4. Which word from the story is a synonym of *gleamed* and *sparkled*?
    a. brushed
    b. covered
    (c.) shone

5. After Shoeshine sells all of his mud, the townspeople spend the rest of the day dulling things up. Which vocabulary word is an antonym of *dulling*?
    a. dusty
    b. dirtiest
    (c.) shining

Add the numbers that you just checked to get your total score. (For example, if you checked 3, 2, 3, 2, and 1, your total score would be 11.) Fill in your score here. Then turn to page 205 and transfer your score onto Graph 1.

► Personal
Vocabulary
Strategy
Comprehension
►TOTAL SCORE

Check your answers with your teacher. Give yourself 1 point for each correct answer, and fill in your Vocabulary score here. Then turn to page 205 and transfer your score onto Graph 1.

Personal
► Vocabulary
Strategy
Comprehension
TOTAL SCORE

Strategy Check

Review the problem-solution frame that you completed in the Strategy Follow-up. Then answer these questions:

1. Shoeshine rubs and scrubs everything until Mudville is glistening. What is the result?
   a. Shoeshine digs mud out of the riverbank.
   b. The sheriff threatens to arrest Shoeshine.
   c. The people complain that everything is too shiny.

2. Why does Shoeshine rub and scrub until everything in Mudville is glistening?
   a. because the sheriff has threatened to arrest him
   b. because everyone wants a muddy, cruddy town
   c. because everyone wants a town to match their shoes

3. What is the end result of Shoeshine's problem?
   a. Shoeshine rubs and scrubs everything until Mudville is glistening.
   b. The people dull things up, and Mudville gets back to normal.
   c. Shoeshine gets arrested for not backing his guarantee.

4. Why is the end result humorous?
   a. because Mudville ends up muddy and cruddy, just the way it started
   b. because Mudville ends up gleaming and glistening, just the way it started
   c. because Mudville starts out gleaming but ends up muddy and cruddy

5. Aside from the fact that Shoeshine doesn't go to jail, what else makes him happy with the end result?
   a. He gets to make Mudville a clean place again.
   b. He gets to shine the shoes of everyone in Mudville.
   c. He gets to sell mud that people could have gotten for free.

Comprehension Check

Review the story if necessary. Then answer these questions:

1. Why is Shoeshine Whittaker happy when he first rides into Mudville?
   a. He knows that lots of people will need their shoes shined.
   b. He knows that no one there will need their shoes shined.
   c. He knows that he can sell the people lots of mud.

2. What does Shoeshine probably mean by "guaranteed"?
   a. He guarantees that everyone's shoes will stay shiny forever.
   b. He guarantees that he gives the best shoeshine in the West.
   c. Neither of the above answers is correct.

3. Why does Shoeshine mutter, "These folks of Mudville are whing-dang-dingy"?
   a. He wishes they'd make up their minds about what they want.
   b. He can't believe they don't know what color their buildings are.
   c. He can't believe they like their town so clean.

4. Why do the people buy mud from Shoeshine?
   a. They are used to buying things from traveling salesmen.
   b. He tells them the mud is shine duller, and it will solve their problem.
   c. Shoeshine sells shine duller cheaper than anyone else around.

5. When do you think Shoeshine will most likely visit Mudville again?
   a. When he wants to spend a night in jail.
   b. When he needs more mud to sell.
   c. When he runs out of money and needs more.

Check your answers with your teacher. Give yourself 1 point for each correct answer, and fill in your Strategy score here. Then turn to page 205 and transfer your score onto Graph 1.

Personal
Vocabulary
► Strategy
Comprehension
TOTAL SCORE
✓ T

Check your answers with your teacher. Give yourself 1 point for each correct answer, and fill in your Comprehension score here. Then turn to page 205 and transfer your score onto Graph 1.

Personal
Vocabulary
Strategy
► Comprehension
TOTAL SCORE
✓ T

Extending

Choose one or both of these activities:

PLAN SHOESHINE'S RETURN
Shoeshine Whittaker says he'll probably return to Mudville. With a partner, brainstorm something that he might try to sell during his next visit. Then use a problem-solution frame to plan a story about Shoeshine's visit. If you can, perform your story for the class.

LEARN ABOUT THE OLD WEST
Use some of the reference books listed on this page to learn more about the Old West. Choose a real town or person, and write a brief report. Or choose a legendary fictional hero, and report on what makes him or her so popular.

Resources

Books

Flanagan, Mike, and Carl Waldman. *Complete Idiot's Guide to the Old West.* Alpha Books, 1999.

Green, Carl R., and William R. Sanford. *Buffalo Bill Cody: Showman of the Wild West.* Legendary Heroes of the Wild West. Enslow Publishers, 1996.

Kalman, Bobbie. *Boomtowns of the West.* Life in the Old West. Crabtree Publishers, 1999.

———. *Life on the Trail.* Life in the Old West. Crabtree Publishers, 1998.

Shellenberger, Robert. *Wagons West: Trail Tales 1848.* Heritage West Books, 1991.

The Big Toe Contest

Building Background

Suppose you heard your grandpa say, "Hey, where's the fire?" Would you understand what he meant? Well, if he saw a fire truck racing down the street, he would have meant one thing. But if he saw your little brother rushing happily toward his bike, he would have meant something else.

To understand what your grandpa meant, you would need to use context clues. **Context** is the information surrounding a word or situation that helps you understand it. When you don't have enough context about a word or a situation, misunderstandings often happen. Misunderstandings also happen when information is taken *out* of context. The following exercise will help you understand how context works.

1. Write this sentence at the top of a sheet of paper:
   Felix was in a real jam!
2. Think of one meaning for the sentence. On the top half of the paper, write or draw the context that would help someone understand your meaning.
3. Then think of another meaning for the sentence.
4. On the bottom half of the paper, write or draw the context that would help someone understand that meaning.
5. Explain why someone might misunderstand the sentence if the context was not clear.

Vocabulary Builder

fair

toe

1. Before you begin reading "The Big Toe Contest," use the clipboards or a separate sheet of paper to list all the meanings of *fair* and *toe* that you know. (Use a dictionary or thesaurus if you need help.)

2. Then, as you read the story, decide which of the meanings that you wrote on the clipboards are used in the story. Put a star (★) next to those meanings.

3. Save your work. You will use it again in the Vocabulary Check.

Strategy Builder

Making Predictions While Reading a Story

- When you read, you often make predictions. As you know, a **prediction** is a kind of guess that you make based on information or clues that the author provides. Those clues are often context clues. They help you understand what's happening. They also help you predict what might happen next.

- As you read "The Big Toe Contest," you will pause twice to make predictions. At Strategy Break #1, you will write down your predictions. You also will write which context clues helped you make your predictions.

- At Strategy Break #2, you will check your earlier predictions. Then you will make more predictions, and you will tell which clues helped you make them.

- After you finish reading the story, you will see if any of your predictions matched what happened in the story.

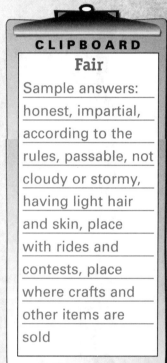

CLIPBOARD

Fair

Sample answers: honest, impartial, according to the rules, passable, not cloudy or stormy, having light hair and skin, place with rides and contests, place where crafts and other items are sold

CLIPBOARD

Toe

Sample answers: part of the foot, part of a stocking or shoe that covers the toes, forepart of a hoof, dance performed on the toes, anything shaped like a toe

The Big Toe Contest

by James Russell

The story you are about to read shows why knowing the right context is important—and how misunderstandings can happen without it.

Hayden Tucker is my best friend, but he gets weird ideas. Like the time my grandpa and grandma took Hayden and me to the county **fair**.

I reached Hayden's house at around seven in the morning and banged on his bedroom door.

"Time to go, sleepyhead," I shouted. "The Gramps-mobile will be here any minute.

Not hearing anything, I opened the door and went in. My friend was sitting on the bed, counting.

" . . . forty-five, forty-six—"

"What are you doing?"

Hayden glanced at me. "Shhh. Don't mess me up, Rick. Forty-eight, forty-nine . . ."

I walked around the bed and stopped short. His right pants leg was rolled up to the knee, and on the end of his big **toe** was a plastic weight from his dad's weightlifting set. Every second or so, Hayden flexed his toe up, then down.

"Get your toe stuck?"

"No," he grunted. "I'm training for an important event."

I laughed. "What event? The Mr. Toeriffic Competition?"

Hayden sighed and stopped counting. He pulled a piece of paper out of his pocket and waved it at me.

"I am preparing for the River County Fair's Big Toe Contest," he announced.

I snatched the paper in mid-wave. Sure enough, in big blue letters it said:

The Big Toe Contest
$50 First Prize

"Nobody's going to give away money for people's toes," I argued.

"They will too. Says so right there. 'Prize money offered by the River County Fair.' "

 Stop here for Strategy Break #1.

Strategy Break #1

Use the information in the story to help you answer these questions:

1. What do you predict will happen next?

   Students' responses will vary but should be supported with clues from

   the text.

2. Why do you think so?

   _____

   _____

3. What clues from the story helped you make your prediction(s)?

   _____

   _____

 Go on reading to see what happens.

He was right. It even had an official-looking logo. "But, Hay, there must be thousands of great toes in River County. How are you going to win?"

"I've been practicing twenty minutes every day, and soaking my toe in orange juice. Vitamin C keeps you healthy."

Hayden and I inspected his big toe. It did look healthy.

Outside, a horn blasted twice. Hayden grabbed his gym bag, and we raced downstairs. The Gramps-mobile sat in the driveway. Grandma and Grandpa grinned and waved at us from the RV's high front seat.

"You boys make yourselves comfortable," said Grandma as we scrambled in. "We'll be there in an hour or so." The inside of the Gramps-mobile was fixed up like a little house, with a kitchen, a living room, and a bedroom. Grandma handed us two glasses of apple juice and a plate of warm blueberry muffins.

For the next few minutes we munched on muffins and stared out the window at the farmland. Then Hayden pulled a bottle from his gym bag. He unscrewed the cap and gave me a sniff. Phew! It smelled like gasoline and flowers mixed together.

"What *is* that?"

Hayden rubbed the liquid on his big toe. "It's supposed to keep your joints from getting stiff. I figure judges like toes that are kind of springy." Finished, he pulled two socks over his foot.

By the time we reached the fairgrounds and Grandpa had bought tickets, Hayden was so excited he was jumping up and down.

"Hold on there," said Grandpa. "Where's the fire?"

"I've got to sign up for the Big Toe Contest," Hayden explained.

Grandma smiled. "Goodness, Hayden, I didn't know you had a big toe. Are you sure yours is ready to be judged?"

Hayden patted his bag. "Of course it is. I've been taking care of it for a whole month."

The other Big Toe contestants were a lot older than Hayden, but he wasn't worried. "I bet *they* haven't been lifting weights," he whispered, climbing onto the stage. He stood between a man wearing overalls and a woman in a red-flowered dress. All the contestants were carrying small bags or boxes.

Two men with badges clipped to their pockets walked onstage.

"We'll get started in a minute," one said, "but first we'd like to say a very special hello to our youngest contestant, eleven-year-old Hayden Tucker."

Hayden grinned as the crowd applauded.

Then the judges announced, "Contestants, display your big toes," and craziness hit the stage like a thunderstorm as people dug into their boxes and bags. I lost sight of Hayden. Then I heard Grandma gasp. A little girl next to me giggled.

 Stop here for Strategy Break #2.

Strategy Break #2

Use the information in the story to help you answer these questions:

1. Do your earlier predictions match what happened? _____ Why or why not?

Students' responses will vary but should be supported with clues from

the text.

2. What do you predict will happen next?

_____

_____

3. Why do you think so?

_____

_____

4. What clues from the story helped you make your prediction(s)?

_____

_____

➡ **Go on reading to see what happens.**

"Mommy, look-it that boy!" she squealed.

I looked. Hayden was sitting on the stage with his right foot stuck high in the air, his naked big toe wiggling like mad. The other contestants still had their shoes on. Each of them was holding up a small pickle. It was a West India gherkin, Grandma told me later. Folks around here called them "big toe" pickles because they grew short and stubby, just like a lot of people's big toes.

At that moment everybody was busy laughing—except Hayden. First his face turned red, then green.

But all of a sudden he must have decided the whole thing was pretty funny because he started grinning. Then he wiggled his toe again. The crowd laughed louder.

Eventually, the judges stopped laughing and started judging. Hayden didn't win the fifty dollars, but he did get a ribbon for having the funniest big toe in River County.

On the trip home, I couldn't resist teasing him.

"Boy, *toe*day was *toe*rrible," I said. "Hope it wasn't *toe* hard on you."

Hayden just grinned. "Wait until next month," he said. "My aunt's dance troupe is looking for toe dancers. I can't wait to try out."

I groaned. Hayden Tucker's big toe in a tutu? It was *toe* horrible to think about! ●

Strategy Follow-up

Go back and look at the predictions that you wrote in this lesson. Do any of them match what actually happened in this story? Why or why not?

_____

_____

_____

_____

_____

_____

_____

_____

_____

_____

_____

_____

_____

_____

✓Personal Checklist

Read each question and put a check (✓) in the correct box.

1. How well do you understand what happened in "The Big Toe Contest"?
    - ☐ 3   (extremely well)
    - ☐ 2   (fairly well)
    - ☐ 1   (not well)

2. How well were you able to use the information in Building Background to figure out the misunderstanding in this story?
    - ☐ 3   (extremely well)
    - ☐ 2   (fairly well)
    - ☐ 1   (not well)

3. How well were you able to use the definitions of *toe* to figure out the misunderstanding in this story?
    - ☐ 3   (extremely well)
    - ☐ 2   (fairly well)
    - ☐ 1   (not well)

4. How well were you able to predict what would happen next in this story?
    - ☐ 3   (extremely well)
    - ☐ 2   (fairly well)
    - ☐ 1   (not well)

5. How well were you able to understand why Hayden won the "funniest big toe" award?
    - ☐ 3   (extremely well)
    - ☐ 2   (fairly well)
    - ☐ 1   (not well)

Vocabulary Check

Look back at the work you did in the Vocabulary Builder. Then answer each question by circling the correct letter.

1. What does Hayden think when he reads "The Big Toe Contest, $50 First Prize"?
    - (a.) He thinks he can win $50 for having the best big toe.
    - b. He thinks he can win $50 for having the best gherkin pickle.
    - c. He thinks he'll have to pay $50 to win first prize.

2. Which meaning of *toe* fits the context of the contest?
    - a. part of the foot
    - (b.) West India gherkin pickle
    - c. dance performed on the toes

3. Which sentence reveals the true meaning of *toe* in the Big Toe Contest?
    - a. On the end of his big toe was a plastic weight.
    - (b.) Folks around here called them "big toe" pickles.
    - c. Hayden Tucker's big toe in a tutu?

4. Which meaning of *fair* fits the context of this story?
    - a. passable
    - b. not cloudy or stormy
    - (c.) place with rides and contests

5. What other meaning of *fair* could be used to describe the outcome of the Big Toe Contest?
    - (a.) according to the rules
    - b. having light hair and skin
    - c. place where crafts and other items are sold

Add the numbers that you just checked to get your Personal Checklist score. Fill in your score here. Then turn to page 205 and transfer your score onto Graph 1.

Check your answers with your teacher. Give yourself 1 point for each correct answer, and fill in your Vocabulary score here. Then turn to page 205 and transfer your score onto Graph 1.

Strategy Check

Look back at what you wrote at each Strategy Break. Then answer these questions:

1. At Strategy Break #1, if you predicted that Hayden would win the contest, which clue would have best supported your prediction?

   a. Hayden is exercising his big toe when his friend Rick arrives.

   b. Hayden's friend says that no one will give away money for people's toes.

   c. Hayden is sitting on his bed counting when he friend Rick arrives.

2. Which meaning of *toe* does Hayden think the paper means?

   a. anything shaped like a foot

   b. part of the foot

   c. part of a stocking or shoe that covers the toes

3. If you first predicted that Hayden might win the contest, which clue might have caused you to change your prediction?

   a. Craziness hit the stage as people dug into their boxes and bags.

   b. "I bet they haven't been lifting weights."

   c. Two men with badges walked onstage.

4. Grandma gasps, and a little girl giggles. What might you have predicted caused their reactions?

   a. While others pull things out of bags or boxes, Hayden pulls off his sock.

   b. It's becoming clear that Hayden had misunderstood "Big Toe Contest."

   c. Both of the above answers are correct.

5. If Hayden tries out for his aunt's dance troupe, what do you predict he will probably do first?

   a. start exercising his big toe again

   b. find out exactly what a toe dancer is

   c. start growing a West India gherkin

Comprehension Check

Review the story if necessary. Then answer these questions:

1. At the beginning of the story, why is Hayden excited about going to the county fair?

   a. He wants to go on the amusement rides.

   b. He wants to ride in the Gramps-mobile.

   c. He wants to win The Big Toe Contest.

2. Why does Hayden say he's been soaking his toe in orange juice?

   a. He wants his toe to be healthy.

   b. He wants his toe to be flexible.

   c. He wants his toe to be strong.

3. Why is Hayden jumping up and down before the contest?

   a. He loves pickles and can't wait to eat one.

   b. He is excited about being in the contest.

   c. He is warming up his toe for the contest.

4. How are a West India gherkin and Hayden's big toe similar?

   a. They are both short and stubby.

   b. They both have their own contest.

   c. They are both green and flexible.

5. Why does the narrator use words such as *toeday, toeribble,* and *toeriffic?*

   a. to show Hayden that he likes his big toe

   b. to make fun of Hayden's big toe

   c. to make fun of Hayden's misunderstanding

Check your answers with your teacher. Give yourself 1 point for each correct answer, and fill in your Strategy score here. Then turn to page 205 and transfer your score onto Graph 1.

Personal
Vocabulary
Strategy
Comprehension
TOTAL SCORE
✓ T

Check your answers with your teacher. Give yourself 1 point for each correct answer, and fill in your Comprehension score here. Then turn to page 205 and transfer your score onto Graph 1.

Personal
Vocabulary
Strategy
Comprehension
TOTAL SCORE
✓ T

Extending

Choose one or both of these activities:

MAKE UP A CONTEST

Work with a partner to think of a multiple-meaning word that you could use in a contest. For example, a Dressing Contest could be for the best-tasting salad dressing, the best-tasting turkey stuffing, or the best-looking outfit on a teddy bear or doll. If you'd like, you can use some of the books listed on this page for ideas. The riddle books might work especially well.

Present your contest orally without giving away the correct context. Have your classmates predict what the contest is really for. Then show a poster for the contest, with a drawing that makes your meaning clear.

EXPLORE COUNTY FAIRS

Find out about an item, an animal, or a performance that is often exhibited at a county fair. Learn what it would take to make your chosen subject a winner. Include some winning facts about your subject, such as the weight of the largest county-fair pumpkin, the speed of a barrel-jumping horse, or the markings on a grand-champion bunny. Report your findings to your class in a booklet about your subject.

Resources

Books

Gallant, Morrie. *Funniest Riddle Book in the World.* Sterling Publications, 1996.

Keller, Charles. *Best Riddle Book Ever.* Sterling Publications, 1998.

Martin, Ann M. *Karen's Cooking Contest.* Baby-Sitters Little Sister. Little Apple, 1998.

Moore, Miriam, and Penny Taylor. *The Kwanzaa Contest.* Hyperion Chapters. Hyperion Press, 1996.

Spinelli, Jerry. *Do the Funky Pickle.* Scholastic, 1995.

Web Sites

http://www.artcontest.com
This site chooses five pictures each week from submissions and enters them in an art contest. Winners are chosen by online voting.

http://www.ocfair.com/2003/CompetitionResults/Contests.asp
The Orange County Fair organizers have thought of a variety of fun contests for kids and adults.

Magazine Articles

"Let's Go to the Fair!" *Countryside and Small Stock Journal* May–June 1998: 71–72.

"Make Up a Joke." *Boys' Life* October 1995: 67.

"Reader Riddles." *Ranger Rick* August 1996: 20–21.

The Trail of Tears

exhaustion

exiles

forced

frightened

heartless

orders

relocate

round up

stockades

Building Background

"The Trail of Tears" describes a cruel time in United States history. During the winter of 1838–1839, the United States government forced thousands of Cherokees living in Tennessee to walk from their homeland in the Great Smoky Mountains across several states to Oklahoma. The map below shows their route.

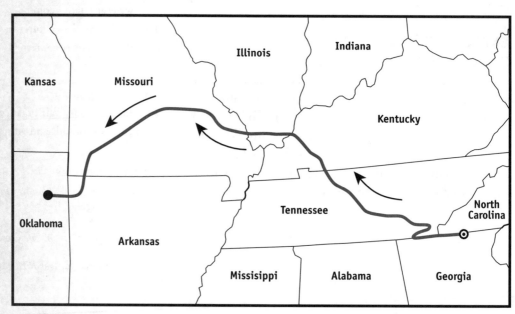

CLIPBOARD 1

Cherokees
exhaustion
exiles
frightened
relocate

CLIPBOARD 2

U.S. Government
forced
heartless
orders
round up
stockades

Vocabulary Builder

1. Read the words in the margin, and think about how they might relate to a forced march across many miles in wintertime.

2. On the first clipboard, write each vocabulary word that describes the Cherokees and what they experienced. On the second clipboard, write the words that describe the United States government and what it did. (Use a dictionary to find words you don't know.) If necessary, revise your choices after you finish reading the selection.

3. Save your work. You will use it again in the Vocabulary Check.

Strategy Builder

Summarizing Nonfiction

- **Nonfiction** is writing that gives facts and information about a particular subject, or **topic**.

- Sometimes when you read nonfiction, you're given a lot of information all at once. To keep the information straight—and to remember it better—it helps to stop once in a while and summarize. When you **summarize** a section of text, you list or retell in your own words just the most important ideas.

- Read the following paragraphs from an article about bamboo. Think about how you might summarize the most important ideas.

Bamboo—What a Bargain!

There are several reasons why bamboo is such a bargain. For one thing, it grows fast. A stalk of bamboo can grow up to three feet per day! So bamboo can be used after only one year of growth. A tree needs to grow for 20 years before it's ready to be used.

Another thing that makes bamboo a bargain is that it is easy to cut. A hacksaw or machete will do the job. And once cut down, bamboo is light enough that it can be carried away by the work crew.

Bamboo is also a bargain because it's simple to use. No machines, no heavy trucks, no sawmill, no steel mill—just ready-to-use bamboo.

- How would you summarize the most important ideas in the paragraphs above? Here is how one student did it:

Bamboo is a bargain because

- it grows fast—up to three feet per day.

- it can be used after only one year of growth.

- it is easy to cut.

- it can be carried away by the work crew.

- it is simple (and ready) to use.

The Trail of Tears

As you begin reading this selection, stop after each section and try to summarize the most important ideas.

A Heartbreaking Discovery

In 1828 gold was found in the Smoky Mountains. This discovery brought heartbreak to the Cherokee Nation. White men wanted the gold. To get it, they wanted the Cherokees to move away. The settlers also wanted the Cherokee land for farming. They hoped to set up their own farms with fields these Native Americans had cleared.

In 1830 the United States government stepped in—to side with the settlers! The government said that the Cherokees would have to **relocate**. They would have to move west to Oklahoma Territory and set up new farms there.

The Cherokees did not want to move away. The Smokies had always been their home. The Cherokees asked President Andrew Jackson to help them, but he said no.

U. S. Troops Arrive

In 1838 United States troops came to the Smokies. They began to **round up** the Cherokees. Only 1,000 Cherokee people got away. They hid deep in the mountains. The rest of the Cherokees were caught.

Soldiers dragged men from their fields. They pulled women and children from their homes. The troops showed no kindness to the **frightened** Cherokees. The soldiers shouted at them in English. It was a language many Cherokees did not understand.

Soldiers **forced** the Cherokees into **stockades** and split up their families. Some children wound up in camps far away from their parents. The soldiers did not care. They had **orders** to move the Cherokee people.

 Stop here for the Strategy Break.

Strategy Break

Did you stop and summarize as you read? If you did, see if your summaries match these:

A Heartbreaking Discovery

- In 1828 gold was found in the Smokies—and whites wanted it.

- To get it, they wanted the Cherokees to move.

- They also wanted Cherokee land for farming.

- In 1830 the U.S. government said the Cherokees would have to relocate to Oklahoma Territory.

- The Cherokees didn't want to move. They asked President Jackson to help them, but he said no.

U.S. Troops Arrive

- In 1838 U.S. troops began to round up the Cherokees.

- Only 1,000 Cherokees got away; the rest were caught.

- The troops showed no kindness to the frightened Cherokees. They had orders to move the Cherokees.

 Go on reading.

A Long, Hard March

When the camps were filled the long march began. Armed soldiers put the Cherokees into 17 large groups and pushed them west. About 15,000 Cherokees set out.

The march was grim from the start. The Cherokees were herded onward like cattle. Some were shoved into wagons. A few rode on horses. Most of the people had to walk. They did not have enough blankets or warm clothes. Many did not even have shoes.

Children cried as they waved good-bye to their mountain homes. Men and women also cried. As one Cherokee said during the farewell, ". . . all look[ed] sad like when friends die."

Oklahoma was a thousand miles away. To get there, the Cherokees had to tramp through mud and dust. They slogged through rain, sleet, and snow. John Burnett was a soldier on the march. He later wrote about that time. "The sufferings of the Cherokee[s] were awful," he said. "The trail of the **exiles** was a trail of death. They had to sleep in the wagons and on the grounds without fire. And I have known as many as 22 of them to die in one night. . . ."

Death on the Trail

Some people died from the cold. They shivered and shook but could not get warm. At last, their bodies ran out of heat. Others, too tired to keep going, died from **exhaustion**. Still others died from disease; they were too weak to fight off sickness.

Hunger was always a problem. The marchers only had the food they could carry with them. Their grain sacks got wet and were soon filled with bugs. No one had enough to eat. They all grew weak. Many Cherokees starved to death.

Cruel Treatment

The soldiers saw the pain and death they were causing. Yet they kept the groups of Cherokees moving anyway. It was hard for old people to keep up the pace. The **heartless** soldiers whipped them to make them move faster.

Mothers with young children struggled along. Burnett told of one woman with three small children. She set out ". . . with a baby strapped on her back and leading a child with each hand." As Burnett told it, "the task was too great for that frail mother. . . . She sank and died with her baby on her back and her other two children clinging to her hands."

There was no time to give the dead funerals or burial. The soldiers forced the groups to keep moving. Bodies of the dead were thrown into ditches dug along the trail.

After about six months, the march ended. The Cherokees had reached Oklahoma. By then 4,000 people had died. More than one fourth of those who set out died on the Trail of Tears. ●

Strategy Follow-up

On a separate sheet of paper, summarize the rest of this selection. Use your own words. Be sure to list only the most important ideas, and skip unnecessary details.

✓Personal Checklist

Read each question and put a check (✓) in the correct box.

1. How well do you understand why the Cherokees' march was named "The Trail of Tears"?
    - ☐ 3 (extremely well)
    - ☐ 2 (fairly well)
    - ☐ 1 (not well)

1. How well were you able to use the map in Building Background to follow the Trail of Tears?
    - ☐ 3 (extremely well)
    - ☐ 2 (fairly well)
    - ☐ 1 (not well)

2. How well do you understand why the Cherokees were forced to move?
    - ☐ 3 (extremely well)
    - ☐ 2 (fairly well)
    - ☐ 1 (not well)

4. By the time you finished reading "The Trail of Tears," how many words were you able to write on the appropriate clipboards?
    - ☐ 3 (7–9 words)
    - ☐ 2 (4–6 words)
    - ☐ 1 (0–3 words)

5. How well were you able summarize the second part of this selection?
    - ☐ 3 (extremely well)
    - ☐ 2 (fairly well)
    - ☐ 1 (not well)

Vocabulary Check

Look back at the work you did in the Vocabulary Builder. Then answer each question by circling the correct letter.

1. Which vocabulary word best describes how the Cherokees felt when the soldiers arrived to round them up?
    - (a.) frightened
    - b. heartless
    - c. exhaustion

2. The selection says that the soldiers had their *orders* to move the Cherokee people. What does orders mean in this context?
    - a. patterns
    - (b.) instructions
    - c. sequences of events

3. Which phrase defines the word *stockade*?
    - (a.) pen built to hold prisoners or animals
    - b. roadblock built to keep people out
    - c. tent that serves as a temporary home

4. Soldier John Burnett called the Trail of Tears the "trail of the exiles." What are exiles?
    - a. people who hide high up in the mountains
    - b. people who willingly move to another place
    - (c.) people forced to leave their home or country

5. Which words could describe the United States government and its actions?
    - a. round up, exhaustion, frightened
    - (b.) heartless, orders, round up
    - c. frightened, forced, exiles

Add the numbers that you just checked to get your Personal Checklist score. Fill in your score here. Then turn to page 205 and transfer your score onto Graph 1.

| Personal |
| Vocabulary |
| Strategy |
| Comprehension |
| **TOTAL SCORE** |

Check your answers with your teacher. Give yourself 1 point for each correct answer, and fill in your Vocabulary score here. Then turn to page 205 and transfer your score onto Graph 1.

| Personal |
| Vocabulary |
| Strategy |
| Comprehension |
| **TOTAL SCORE** |

Strategy Check

Review the summaries that you wrote for the second part of this selection. Then answer these questions:

1. What is an important idea in the section called "A Long, Hard March"?
   a. Soldiers dragged men from their fields and pulled women from their homes.
   b. Soldiers put about 15,000 Cherokees into 17 groups and pushed them west.
   c. Both of the above answers are correct.

2. What is not an important idea in the section called "A Long, Hard March"?
   a. The soldiers saw the pain and death they were causing.
   b. People cried as they said good-bye to their homes.
   c. "The sufferings of the Cherokee[s] were awful."

3. Under which heading would you list the idea that many Cherokees starved to death?
   a. A Long, Hard March
   b. Death on the Trail
   c. Cruel Treatment

4. Under which heading would you list the idea that old people were whipped to make them walk faster?
   a. A Long, Hard March
   b. Death on the Trail
   c. Cruel Treatment

5. In what ways did Cherokees die on the march?
   a. cold and exhaustion
   b. disease and starvation
   c. all of the above

Comprehension Check

Review the selection if necessary. Then answer these questions:

1. Why were the Cherokees forced to move to Oklahoma?
   a. The U.S. government needed to exercise its troops.
   b. Gold was discovered in the mountains where they lived.
   c. There was dry, flat land in Oklahoma.

2. Why were U.S. troops sent in to round up the Cherokees?
   a. to force the Cherokees to leave their homes
   b. to help the Cherokees have a smooth, safe move
   c. to make sure the Cherokees could travel with their families

3. Why was moving to Oklahoma so difficult for the Cherokees?
   a. The walk was long, grim, and cruel.
   b. They had to find a new way to live.
   c. Both of the above answers are correct.

4. What happened to the bodies of people who died on the trail?
   a. They were thrown into ditches.
   b. Funeral services were held for them.
   c. They were given proper burials.

5. By the time they reached Oklahoma, how many Cherokees had died?
   a. 400
   b. 4,000
   c. 40,000

Check your answers with your teacher. Give yourself 1 point for each correct answer, and fill in your Strategy score here. Then turn to page 205 and transfer your score onto Graph 1.

Personal
Vocabulary
Strategy
Comprehension
TOTAL SCORE
✓ T

Check your answers with your teacher. Give yourself 1 point for each correct answer, and fill in your Comprehension score here. Then turn to page 205 and transfer your score onto Graph 1.

Personal
Vocabulary
Strategy
Comprehension
TOTAL SCORE
✓ T

Extending

Choose one or both of these activities:

MAP THE TRAIL OF TEARS

Create a three-dimensional map of the route the Cherokees followed as they walked the Trail of Tears. If you have Internet access, check the first Web site listed on this page to learn more about the Trail of Tears. Also, look up the time line on the Web site, and use it to label the Cherokees' locations at various times during the march. How might weather conditions have affected the Cherokees during those times? Attach symbols such as raindrops or snowflakes to your map to show the kinds of weather they encountered in different places.

FIND OUT WHAT HAPPENED AFTER THE MARCH

Work with a research partner to find out what happened to the Cherokees after they arrived in Oklahoma. Use the resources listed on this page or ones you find yourself. Find out such information as what kinds of homes they built, how they survived, and how life in Oklahoma compared and contrasted with life in Tennessee. Take turns with your partner, and present your findings in an oral report to the class.

Resources

Book

Bruchac, Joseph. *The Trail of Tears.* Step into Reading. Random House, 1999.

Web Sites

http://rosecity.net/tears
Click on "Time Line" to learn about events along the Trail of Tears.

http://www.cherokeeimages.com/culture/photo
Examples of the enduring Cherokee culture can be seen and heard at this Web site, which is produced by Cherokee artist Ken Masters.

http://www.neosoft.com/powersource/cherokee/history.html
Read another account of the Trail of Tears. This site tells about Cherokee history and the reasons behind the march.

At Last I Kill a Buffalo

Building Background

As you read the following paragraph by Chief Luther Standing Bear, try to picture the details in your mind.

Ever since I could remember my father had been teaching me the things that I should know and preparing me to be a good hunter. I had learned to make bows and to string them; and to make arrows and tip them with feathers. I knew how to ride my pony no matter how fast he would go, and I felt that I was brave and did not fear danger. All these things I had learned for just this day when Father would allow me to go with him on a buffalo hunt. It was the day for which every Sioux boy eagerly waited. To ride side by side with the best hunters of the tribe, to hear the terrible noise of the great herds as they ran, and then to help bring home the kill was the most thrilling day of any Indian boy's life.

On a separate sheet of paper, sketch pictures showing what you predict might happen to Standing Bear before, during, and after his first big buffalo hunt.

buffalo hunt

tipi

quivers

rawhide

justified

honesty

herd

fatal wound

praised

Vocabulary Builder

1. Below the pictures that you just drew, write what you think might happen on Standing Bear's first buffalo hunt. Use as many vocabulary words as you can.

2. If you do not know the meanings of some of the words, find them in the story and use context to figure them out. If that doesn't help, look up the words in a dictionary.

3. Save your work. You will use it again in the Vocabulary Check.

Strategy Builder

How to Read an Autobiographical Sketch

- An **autobiography** is the story of a real person's life, written by that person. An **autobiographical sketch** is the story of a part of a real person's life.

- Autobiographical sketches describe events in the order in which they happened. That order is called time order, or **sequence**. To make the sequence as clear as possible, writers often use **signal words**. Examples of signal words are *several days later, early the next morning,* and *in a little while.*

- An autobiographical sketch is always written in the **first-person point of view.** That means that the narrator tells his or her own story using the words *I, me, my,* and *mine.*

- As you read the following paragraph, pay attention to the sequence of events. Use the underlined signal words to help you.

My name is Marissa. I've always loved making faces in front of a camera. So it was no surprise that <u>when my favorite TV show held auditions</u> in our town, I asked my mom to take me. <u>Two days later</u>, we showed up at the studio. Was I ever nervous! We filled out forms <u>for several minutes</u>, and <u>then</u> I waited to be called. <u>After what seemed like hours</u>, they called my name. I gulped and smiled. Mom wished me luck. <u>As I stood up</u>, I found my voice and introduced myself.

- If you wanted to show the sequence of events in the paragraph above, you could use a **sequence chain** like this one:

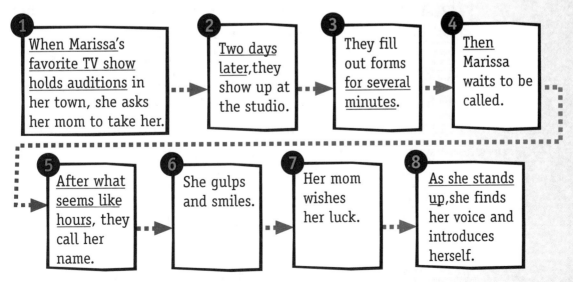

At Last I Kill a Buffalo

by Chief Luther Standing Bear

As you read the first part of this autobiographical sketch, apply the strategies that you just learned. Look for signal words as you read. They will give you a more exact picture of when things happened.

Always the evening before a **buffalo hunt** and when every one was usually in his **tipi**, an old man went around the circle of tipis calling, *"I-ni-la," "I-ni-la,"* not loudly, but so every one could hear. The old man was saying, "Keep quiet," "Keep quiet." We all knew that the scouts had come in and reported buffalo near and that we must all keep the camp in stillness.

That night there would be no calling or shouting from tipi to tipi and no child would cry aloud. Even the horses and dogs obeyed the command for quiet, and all night not a horse neighed and not a dog barked.

The night preceding a buffalo hunt was always an exciting night, even though it was quiet in camp. There would be much talk in the tipis around the fires. There would be sharpening of arrows and of knives. New bow-strings would be made and **quivers** would be filled with arrows.

It was in the fall of the year and the evenings were cool as father and I sat by the fire and talked over the hunt. I was only eight years of age, and I know that father did not expect me to get a buffalo at all, but only to try perhaps for a small calf should I be able to get close enough to one. Nevertheless, I was greatly excited as I sat and watched father working in his easy, firm way.

I was wearing my buffalo-skin robe, the hair next to my body. Mother had made me a **rawhide** belt and this, wrapped around my waist, held my blanket on when I threw it off my shoulders. In the early morning I would wear it, for it would be cold. When it came time to shoot, I should not want my blanket but the belt would hold it in place.

You can picture me, I think, as I sat in the glow of the camp-fire, my little brown body bare to the waist watching, and listening intently to my father. My hair hung down my back and I wore moccasins and breech-cloth of buckskin. To my belt was fastened a rawhide holster for my knife, for when I was eight years of age we had plenty of knives. I was proud to own a knife, and this night I remember I kept it on all night. Neither did I lay aside my bow, but went to sleep with it in my hand, thinking, I suppose, to be all the nearer ready in the morning when the start was made.

We went to bed, my father hoping that tomorrow would be successful for him so that he could bring home some nice meat for the family and a hide for my mother to tan. I went to bed, but could not go to sleep at once, so filled was I with the wonderment and excitement of it all. The next day was to be a test for me. I was to prove to my father whether he was or was not **justified** in his pride in me. What would be the result of my training? Would I be brave if I faced danger and would father be proud of me? Though I did not know it that night I was to be tried for the strength of my manhood and my **honesty** in this hunt. Something happened that day which I remember above all things. It was a test of my real character and I am proud to say that I did not find myself weak.

 Stop here for the Strategy Break.

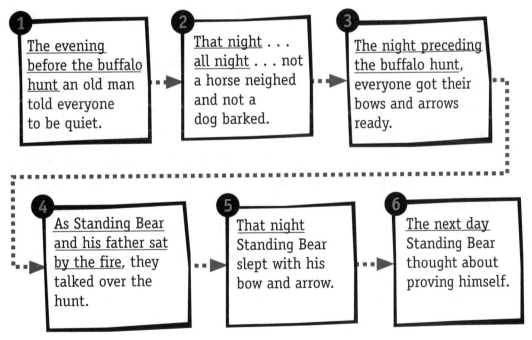

As you continue reading, keep paying attention to the sequence of events. Also keep looking for signal words. At the end of this selection you will use some of them to complete a sequence chain of your own.

 Go on reading.

The next morning the hunters were catching their horses about daybreak. I arose with my father and went out and caught my pony. We were joined with perhaps a hundred or more riders, some of whom carried bows and arrows and some armed with guns.

The buffalo were reported to be about five or six miles away as we should count distance now. At that time we did not measure distance in miles. One camping distance was about ten miles, and these buffalo were said to be about one half camping distance away.

My pony was a black one and a good runner. I felt very important as I rode along with the hunters and my father, the chief. I kept as close to him as I could.

The leaders went ahead until they sighted the herd of grazing buffalo. Then they stopped and waited for the rest of us to ride up. We all rode slowly toward the **herd**, which on sight of us had come together, although they had been scattered here and there over the plain. When they saw us, they all ran close together as if at the command of a leader. We continued riding slowly toward the herd until one of the leaders shouted, *"Ho-ka-he!"* which means, "Ready, Go!" At that command every man started for the herd. I had been listening, too, and the minute the hunters started, I started also.

Away I went, my little pony putting all he had into the race. It was not long before I lost sight of father, but I kept going just the same. I threw my blanket back and the chill of the autumn morning struck my body, but I did not mind. On I went. It was wonderful to race over the ground with all these horsemen about me. There was no shouting, no noise of any kind except the pounding of the horses' feet. The herd was now running and had raised a cloud of dust. I felt no fear until we had entered this cloud of dust and I could see nothing about me, only hear the sound of feet. Where was father? Where was I going? On I rode through the cloud, for I knew I must keep going.

Then all at once I realized that I was in the midst of the buffalo, their dark bodies rushing all about me and their great heads moving up and down to the sound of their hoofs beating upon the earth. Then it was that fear overcame me and I leaned close down upon my little pony's body and clutched him tightly. I can never tell you how I felt toward my pony at that moment. All thought of shooting had left my mind. I was seized by blank fear. In a moment or so, however, my senses became clearer, and I could distinguish other sounds beside the clatter of feet. I could hear a shot now and then and I could see the buffalo beginning to break up into small bunches. I could not see father nor any of my companions yet, but my fear was vanishing and I was safe. I let my pony run. The buffalo looked too large for me to tackle, anyway, so I just kept going. The buffalo became more and more scattered. Pretty soon I saw a young calf that looked about my size. I remembered now what father had told me the night before as we sat about the fire. Those instructions were important for me now to follow.

I was still back of the calf, being unable to get alongside of him. I was anxious to get a shot, yet afraid to try, as I was still very nervous. While my pony was making all speed to come alongside, I chanced a shot and to my surprise my arrow landed. My second arrow glanced along the back of the animal and sped on between the horns, making only a slight wound. My third arrow hit a spot that made the running beast slow up in his gait. I shot a fourth arrow, and though it, too, landed it was not a **fatal wound**. It seemed to me that it was taking a lot of shots, and I was not proud of my marksmanship. I was glad, however, to see the animal going slower and I knew that one more shot would make me a hunter. My horse seemed to know his own importance. His two ears stood straight forward and it was not necessary for me to urge him to get closer to the buffalo. I was soon by the side of the buffalo and one more shot brought the chase to a close. I jumped from my pony, and as I stood by my fallen game, I looked all around wishing that the world could see. But I was alone. In my determination to stay by until I had won my buffalo, I had not noticed that I was far from every one else. No admiring friends were about, and as far as I could see I was on the plain alone. The herd of buffalo had completely disappeared. And as for father, much as I wished for him, he was out of sight and I had no idea where he was.

Every one must know that I, Ota K'te, had killed a buffalo. But it looked as if no one knew where I was, so no one was coming my way. I must then take something from this animal to show that I had killed it. I took all the arrows one by one from the body. As I took them out, it occurred to me that I had used five arrows. If I had been a skillful hunter, one arrow would have been sufficient, but I had used five. Here it was that temptation came to me. Why could I not take out two of the arrows and throw them away? No one would know, and then I should be more greatly admired and **praised** as a hunter. As it was, I knew that I should be praised by father and mother, but I wanted more. And so I was tempted to lie.

I was wondering what to do when I heard my father's voice calling, *"To-ki-i-la-la-hu-wo,"* "Where are you?" I quickly jumped on my pony and rode to the top of a little hill near by. Father saw me and came to me at once. He was so pleased to see me and glad to know that I was safe. I knew that I could never lie to my father. He was too fond of me and I too proud of him.

As he came up, I said as calmly as I could, "Father, I have killed a buffalo." His smile changed to surprise and he asked me where my buffalo was.

I showed my father the arrows that I had used and just where the animal had been hit. He was very pleased and praised me over and over again. I felt more glad than ever that I had told the truth and I have never regretted it. I am more proud now that I told the truth than I am of killing the buffalo. ●

Strategy Follow-up

On a large sheet of paper, create a sequence chain for the second part of this selection. Begin with event 7, and include only the most important events. Some of the chain has been filled in for you.

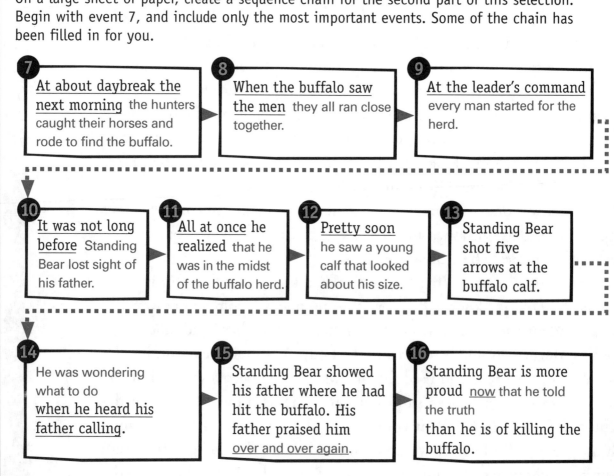

7 <u>At about daybreak the next morning</u> the hunters caught their horses and rode to find the buffalo.

8 <u>When the buffalo saw the men</u> they all ran close together.

9 <u>At the leader's command</u> every man started for the herd.

10 <u>It was not long before</u> Standing Bear lost sight of his father.

11 <u>All at once</u> he realized that he was in the midst of the buffalo herd.

12 <u>Pretty soon</u> he saw a young calf that looked about his size.

13 Standing Bear shot five arrows at the buffalo calf.

14 He was wondering what to do <u>when he heard his father calling</u>.

15 Standing Bear showed his father where he had hit the buffalo. His father praised him <u>over and over again</u>.

16 Standing Bear is more proud <u>now</u> that he told the truth than he is of killing the buffalo.

✓Personal Checklist

Read each question and put a check (✓) in the correct box.

1. How many vocabulary words were you able to use in your prediction about Standing Bear's first buffalo hunt?
   - ☐ 3 (7–9 words)
   - ☐ 2 (4–6 words)
   - ☐ 1 (0–3 words)

2. How well do you understand why Standing Bear was excited about the hunt?
   - ☐ 3 (extremely well)
   - ☐ 2 (fairly well)
   - ☐ 1 (not well)

3. How well do you understand why killing his own buffalo was so important to Standing Bear?
   - ☐ 3 (extremely well)
   - ☐ 2 (fairly well)
   - ☐ 1 (not well)

4. How well do you understand why Standing Bear told his father the truth about the number of arrows he used?
   - ☐ 3 (extremely well)
   - ☐ 2 (fairly well)
   - ☐ 1 (not well)

5. How well were you able to complete the sequence chain in the Strategy Follow-up?
   - ☐ 3 (extremely well)
   - ☐ 2 (fairly well)
   - ☐ 1 (not well)

Vocabulary Check

Look back at the work you did in the Vocabulary Builder. Then answer each question by circling the correct letter.

1. Which vocabulary word describes a container to carry arrows?
   - a. tipi
   - b. herd
   - (c.) quiver

2. Which word or phrase could have helped you predict whether Standing Bear would kill a buffalo?
   - a. buffalo hunt
   - (b.) fatal wound
   - c. justified

3. Standing Bear wants to prove whether his father's pride in him is justified. What does *justified* mean?
   - a. false
   - (b.) deserved
   - c. wrong

4. Standing Bear wears a rawhide belt around his waist. From what is rawhide made?
   - (a.) the skin of an animal
   - b. the teeth of an animal
   - c. the hooves of an animal

5. As he looks back on his first buffalo hunt, of what does Standing Bear say he is most proud?
   - a. his getting lost in the herd
   - b. his fatal wound to the buffalo
   - (c.) his honesty with his father

Add the numbers that you just checked to get your Personal Checklist score. Fill in your score here. Then turn to page 205 and transfer your score onto Graph 1.

Personal
Vocabulary
Strategy
Comprehension
TOTAL SCORE
✓ T

Check your answers with your teacher. Give yourself 1 point for each correct answer, and fill in your Vocabulary score here. Then turn to page 205 and transfer your score onto Graph 1.

Personal
Vocabulary
Strategy
Comprehension
TOTAL SCORE
✓ T

Strategy Check

Review the sequence chain that you completed in the Strategy Follow-up. Then answer these questions:

1. At what time of day did the hunters catch their horses?

    a. at about noon

    b. at about sunset

    c. at about daybreak

2. What did the buffalo do when they saw the men?

    a. they all ran close together

    b. they scattered far apart

    c. they ran straight at the men

3. Which signal words describe when every man started running for the herd?

    a. at the leader's command

    b. all at once

    c. when he heard his father calling

4. What was Standing Bear doing when he heard his father calling?

    a. shooting arrows at the buffalo calf

    b. wondering what to say about the buffalo

    c. realizing he was in the midst of the buffalo herd

5. Which signal words describe how Standing Bear's father praised him?

    a. pretty soon

    b. all at once

    c. over and over again

Comprehension Check

Review the selection if necessary. Then answer these questions:

1. What is the most important reason that Standing Bear wants to go on the buffalo hunt?

    a. He doesn't want to be left behind with all the women.

    b. He wants to get meat and hides for the family.

    c. He wants to prove that his father can be proud of him.

2. Who is Standing Bear's father?

    a. the person scouting the buffalo

    b. the chief of their group

    c. the old man who tells everyone to be quiet

3. Why is Standing Bear surprised when his first arrow hits the buffalo?

    a. He was just taking a chance with that shot.

    b. He is an extremely good shot.

    c. Neither of the above answers is correct.

4. Why does Standing Bear think about lying to his father?

    a. He thinks he should have been able to kill the buffalo with sharper arrows.

    b. He thinks he should have been able to kill the buffalo with more arrows.

    c. He thinks he should have been able to kill the buffalo with fewer arrows.

5. Based on this selection, what conclusion could you draw about Standing Bear's tribe?

    a. They work together very well.

    b. They value honesty over hunting skill.

    c. Both of the above conclusions could be drawn.

Check your answers with your teacher. Give yourself 1 point for each correct answer, and fill in your Strategy score here. Then turn to page 205 and transfer your score onto Graph 1.

Personal
Vocabulary
Strategy
Comprehension
TOTAL SCORE
✓ T

Check your answers with your teacher. Give yourself 1 point for each correct answer, and fill in your Comprehension score here. Then turn to page 205 and transfer your score onto Graph 1.

Personal
Vocabulary
Strategy
Comprehension
TOTAL SCORE
✓ T

Extending

Choose one or both of these activities:

WRITE AN AUTOBIOGRAPHICAL SKETCH

Write an autobiographical sketch about an important learning experience of your own. First use a sequence chain to order the main events. Then write your sketch. Use signal words when appropriate to help clarify the order of events. Put your finished piece together with other classmates' sketches, and bind them into a book.

LEARN ABOUT FAMOUS SIOUX

Use some of the books listed on this page to learn about an important Sioux, such as Crazy Horse, Chief Gall, or Chief Luther Standing Bear. Choose an episode in that person's life, and share it orally with the class. You might want to take notes on index cards. Then you can use the index cards as a sequence chain to help you give your report.

Resources

Books

Bial, Raymond. *The Sioux.* Lifeways. Marshall Cavendish, 1998.

Guttmacher, Peter. *Crazy Horse: Sioux War Chief.* North American Indians of Achievement. Chelsea House, 1994.

Rinaldi, Ann. *My Heart Is on the Ground: The Diary of Nannie Little Rose, a Sioux Girl.* Dear America. Scholastic, 1999.

Sanford, William Reynolds. *Crazy Horse: Sioux Warrior.* North American Indians of Achievement. Enslow Publishers, 1994.

Shumate, Jane, *Chief Gall: Sioux War Chief.* North American Indians of Achievement. Chelsea House, 1995.

Standing Bear, Luther. *My People, the Sioux.* University of Nebraska Press, 1975.

Web Sites

http://www.indigenouspeople.net/buffalo.htm
Many Indian tribes contribute stories, songs, and prayers in honor of the buffalo.

http://www.littlesioux.org/indexx.html
View the history and present-day lives of the Lakota Sioux on the Rosebud Reservation in South Dakota. Drumming and other ceremonial music play in the background.

Two Fat Boys from Venus

Building Background

How do you say hello? Do you wave? shake hands? nod your head? speak a greeting? How you say hello is often influenced by your particular culture. Your **culture** includes the customs, actions, and beliefs of the group of people you belong to. Cultures can exist among people of different age groups, geographic areas, and ethnic groups.

On another piece of paper, draw someone from a particular culture saying hello. That person may be bowing, kissing cheeks, or slapping a "high five." Share your picture with your classmates, and have them guess which culture you are showing.

abundant

courteously

customer

decent

Earth

fainted

gorgeous

haircutters

inhabitants

screamed

Venus

Venusian

Vocabulary Builder

1. Use the words in the margin to answer the questions below. Use as many words as make sense when you answer each question. You can use each word more than once.

   a. Which words might describe the setting of this story?
   Earth, Venus, Venusian
   b. Which words might describe the characters?
   customer, haircutters, inhabitants, Venusian
   c. Which words might describe how the characters act?
   courteously, decent, fainted, screamed
   d. Which words might describe a problem in this story?
   Answers will vary. Students should be able to explain their choices.

2. When you finish reading the story, look at your answers again. Circle the words that you used accurately.

3. Save your work. You will use it again in the Vocabulary check.

Strategy Builder

Identifying Problems and Solutions

- "Two Fat Boys from Venus" is a science fiction story. Like fantasy stories, **science fiction** stories often contain characters, settings, or events that could not exist or happen in real life.

- Although science fiction characters can be "way out," they have **problems** just like other fictional characters do. Throughout a story, the characters will try to solve their problem. Sometimes they try more than one **solution**. But by the end of the story, they usually come up with the solution that works—the **end result**.

- As you read the following paragraphs, notice Strangely Strange's problem and the solutions he tries in order to solve it.

Strangely Strange landed his spaceship on Venus. He shined his flashlight across the surface to find what he had been sent for. Finally he saw it: a blob as big as a boulder and as sticky as a hot fudge sundae. What could it be? Strangely wasn't sure, but he had to find a way to bring a sample home to Mars.

   Strangely tried rolling it, but the blob wouldn't budge. He tried zapping it, but the blob began to melt around his feet. Just before it was all melted, Strangely blasted the blob with his freezer ray. It worked! The blob froze solid. Strangely broke off a sample to take back home to Mars.

- If you wanted to show the problem and solutions, you could create a **problem-solution frame**. It might look like this:

What is the problem?
Strangely Strange has to take a sample of the blob home to Mars.

Why is it a problem?
He doesn't know how to do it.

Solutions		Results
1. Strangely tries rolling it.	➡	**1.** The blob won't budge.
2. He tries zapping it.	➡	**2.** It begins to melt.
3. He blasts it with his freezer ray.	➡	**3.** **END RESULT:** It freezes, and he breaks off a chunk to take home.

Two Fat Boys from Venus

by Jeanne Modesitt

As you read the first part of this story, notice the two boys' problem. (It is circled.) Then notice the solutions they try, and the results of each one. (The solutions are underlined once. The results are underline twice.) Why do the boys keep trying new solutions?

One day, two fat boys from **Venus** landed on planet **Earth**. Now, these boys didn't come to Earth to take over the planet, or to scare its **inhabitants**, or to get some pointers on how to lose weight. (As a matter of fact, *all* boys from Venus are very, very fat, and it suits them just fine, thank you.)

No, the reason these two boys came to planet Earth was to get a **decent** haircut.

You see, for all its beauty and splendor and **abundant** ice-cream shops, Venus doesn't have any good **haircutters**. In fact, the last haircut the boys got was from a partially blind **Venusian** man in his mid-hundreds who fell asleep while cutting the boys' hair. Tired of one lousy haircut after another, the boys decided to come to planet Earth—a planet famous throughout the galaxy for its superb haircuts.

As they stepped out of their spacecraft, Frank, the older boy, turned to Harry.

"Where do you suppose the nearest haircutter is?" he asked.

"I don't know," said Harry. "Probably not in this cornfield. Let's go ask that farmer over there. Maybe he knows."

"Good idea," said Frank.

A moment later, they reached the farmer. "Say there," said Frank. "Could you please direct us to the nearest haircutter?"

"Someone reasonably priced, if at all possible," added Harry.

The farmer took one look at Frank and Harry and **screamed**. Then he **fainted** and fell flat on his back.

"I wonder what that was all about," said Frank.

"I don't know," said Harry. "Maybe it's the way Earth people say 'hi.'"

Just then, the farmer's wife appeared on the scene.

Frank and Harry, being polite boys, immediately greeted her in Earth fashion—a scream followed by a fall on their backs.

The farmer's wife proceeded to do the same.

Frank and Harry sat up and waited for the farmer's wife to wake up.

When she did, Frank said, "<u>Could you please tell us where the nearest haircutter is?</u>"

But <u>all the farmer's wife did was scream and faint again.</u>

 Stop here for the Strategy Break.

Strategy Break

If you were to create a problem-solution frame for this story so far, it might look like this:

What is the problem?
Two boys from Venus (Frank and Harry)
have come to Earth for haircuts.

Why is it a problem?
They can't find anyone who gives decent haircuts on Venus.

Solutions	Results
1. They ask the farmer where the nearest haircutter is.	**1.** The farmer screams and faints.
2. They ask the farmer's wife where the nearest haircutter is.	**2.** She screams and faints twice.

As you continue reading, keep paying attention to what Frank and Harry do to try and solve their problem. Underline each solution once and each result twice. At the end of the story, you will complete the problem-solution frame.

 Go on reading to see what happens.

"Oh dear," said Frank. "I'm afraid this saying 'hi' business is taking up too much time. <u>Maybe we'd better just find a haircutter on our own</u>."

"Good idea," said Harry.

And so they walked across the cornfield, and then across another cornfield, and then still another until they came to a small town.

They began walking down Main Street, saying a quick 'hi' to people (scream only). In return, everyone gave Frank and Harry a full 'hi' (scream and faint).

"These Earth people sure are a friendly bunch," noted Frank.

"Sure are," said Harry.

Finally <u>they came to a shop with a sign that said, "Quick and Cheap Haircuts. No Appointment Needed</u>."

Frank beamed over at Harry.

"Bingo!" he said, and they walked into the shop.

The only customer inside was a young boy. His face lit up when he saw Frank and Harry.

"Wow!" he said. "Where'd you guys come from?"

Just as Frank and Harry were about to respond, the haircutter turned around. He took one look at the two fat boys from Venus and screamed.

Frank and Harry **courteously** let out two short screams, turned to the boy, and said, "We're from Venus."

"Fantastic!" said the boy.

The haircutter had a different opinion.

He let out another scream—this one a little louder—and ran out of the shop, arms flailing and head rolling like a madman.

"Excuse me, sir," Frank called after the man. "When you're done exercising, would you mind cutting our hair?"

The haircutter picked up speed and was soon no longer in sight. Frank and Harry felt a tap on their tails. They turned around, and there stood the boy.

"I hate to tell you this," he said, "but <u>I think Mr. Jones—the haircutter—will be taking the rest of the day off</u>." Upon seeing Frank and Harry's faces drop with disappointment, the boy quickly added, "<u>But don't worry. I'll cut your hair!</u>"

"Would you really?" asked Harry.

"You bet!" said the boy, feeling terribly important. "C'mon over to these two chairs, and I'll have you done in a jiffy."

And so, during the next thirty minutes, Frank and Harry had their hair shampooed, rinsed, combed, cut, and dried. When it was all over, the boy handed Frank and Harry two large mirrors.

"Well?" he said, applying a finishing touch of gel. "What do you think?"

Frank and Harry were speechless. <u>They looked **gorgeous**! Fantastic!</u>
<u>Unbelievably handsome</u>!

"How can we ever thank you?" they said to the boy.

"It was nothing at all," he said, flushed with pride.

Frank and Harry gave the boy their addresses and phone numbers. "If
you ever get to Venus," they said, "please look us up. We'll treat you to a
one-hundred-scoop ice-cream cone." They thanked the boy one more time
and headed back to their spacecraft.

Just before they boarded, Frank said, "You know what, Harry?"

"What?" said Harry.

"That marvelous boy back there sure gave us a lot of good pointers on
how to cut hair. I mean, who would have thought of using scissors to cut
hair instead of yanking it out by hand?"

"Or," said Harry, "using warm water to wash a customer's hair instead of
throwing a bucket of cold water on top of his head?"

"Yes," sighed Frank. "Our haircutters have a lot to learn." Frank paused
for a moment. "Say, Harry, I've just had an idea. <u>When we get back home,</u>
<u>why don't you and I become haircutters? With all these new pointers we've</u>
<u>gotten, we're bound to do a better job than the haircutters we have now.</u>
What do you think?"

"Frank, I think that is a *great* idea!" said Harry.

And so it was that <u>Frank and Harry became Venus's first decent haircutters.</u>
<u>And the whole planet was very, very happy</u>. ●

Strategy Follow-up

Now complete this problem-solution frame for the second part of "Two Fat Boys from Venus." Use a separate sheet of paper if necessary. The problem box has been filled in for you.

What is the problem?
Two boys from Venus (Frank and Harry)
have come to Earth for haircuts.

Why is it a problem?
They can't find anyone who gives decent haircuts on Venus.

Solutions	**Results**
3. They boys decide to find a haircutter on their own.	3. They find a shop with a sign that says, "Quick and Cheap Haircuts. No Appointment Needed."
4. Mr. Jones the haircutter runs out of the shop, so the boy in the shop gives Frank and Harry haircuts.	4. They look gorgeous! Fantastic! Unbelievably handsome!
5. Frank and Harry decide to become haircutters when they get back home.	5. **END RESULT:** They become Venus's first decent haircutters, and the whole planet is happy.

✓Personal Checklist

Read each question and put a check (✓) in the correct box.

1. How well do you understand why everyone screams and faints when they see the two fat boys from Venus?
   - ☐ 3 (extremely well)
   - ☐ 2 (fairly well)
   - ☐ 1 (not well)

2. How well can you explain what makes this story funny?
   - ☐ 3 (extremely well)
   - ☐ 2 (fairly well)
   - ☐ 1 (not well)

3. How well were you able to use the information in Building Background to help you understand cultural differences?
   - ☐ 3 (extremely well)
   - ☐ 2 (fairly well)
   - ☐ 1 (not well)

4. How well were you able to answer the questions in the Vocabulary Builder?
   - ☐ 3 (extremely well)
   - ☐ 2 (fairly well)
   - ☐ 1 (not well)

5. How well were you able to complete the problem-solution frame in the Strategy Follow-up?
   - ☐ 3 (extremely well)
   - ☐ 2 (fairly well)
   - ☐ 1 (not well)

Vocabulary Check

Look back at the work you did in the Vocabulary Builder. Then answer each question by circling the correct letter.

1. The story says that the boys from Venus don't want to scare Earth's inhabitants. Which definition describes *inhabitants*?
   - a. people who visit a place
   - (b.) people who live in a place
   - c. people who scare a place

2. Which question or questions could you have answered with the word Venusian?
   - a. question a
   - b. questions a and d
   - (c.) questions a, b, and d

3. According to the story, Venus has abundant ice cream shops. What does *abundant* mean?
   - (a.) a very large number of
   - b. a very small number of
   - c. none at all

4. Which of the following is an example of the boys trying to act courteously?
   - a. screaming and falling on their backs
   - b. asking politely where they can get a haircut
   - (c.) both of the above

5. They young boy is a customer of Mr. Jones the haircutter. What is another word for *customer*?
   - a. boss
   - (b.) client
   - c. worker

Add the numbers that you just checked to get your Personal Checklist score. Fill in your score here. Then turn to page 205 and transfer your score onto Graph 1.

Check your answers with your teacher. Give yourself 1 point for each correct answer, and fill in your Vocabulary score here. Then turn to page 205 and transfer your score onto Graph 1.

Strategy Check

Review the problem-solution frame that you completed in the Strategy Follow-up. Then answer these questions:

1. What happens when Frank and Harry decide to find a haircutter on their own?
   a. They get lost and never end up finding one.
   b. They finally find a shop, but it is closed.
   c. They find a shop with quick, cheap haircuts.

2. What is the result when the boy in the shop gives Frank and Harry haircuts?
   a. They look gorgeous.
   b. They look ridiculous.
   c. Both of the above answers are correct.

3. What's the end result of the boys' problem?
   a. They stay on Earth and open a shop.
   b. They become haircutters in Mr. Jones's shop.
   c. They become the first decent haircutters on Venus.

4. Why do Frank and Harry become haircutters?
   a. because they got so many good pointers from the boy
   b. because they want to yank their customers' hair out
   c. because they want to throw cold water on customers' heads

5. If Frank and Harry didn't become haircutters themselves, how else might they have solved their problem?
   a. They might have screamed and fainted when they needed haircuts.
   b. They might have returned to Earth when they needed haircuts.
   c. They might have asked Mr. Jones to open a shop on Venus.

Comprehension Check

Review the story if necessary. Then answer these questions:

1. Why do Frank and Harry land on Earth?
   a. to take over the planet
   b. to get decent haircuts
   c. to learn how to lose weight

2. Why does the farmer scream and faint when he sees Frank and Harry?
   a. He is afraid of the boys.
   b. He doesn't like their haircuts.
   c. He thinks they're too fat.

3. What could cause Frank and Harry to think that people are saying "hi" when they scream and faint?
   a. It's the way Venusians say "hi" to each other too.
   b. It's the first thing Frank and Harry do when they see people on Earth.
   c. It's the first thing Earth people do when they see Frank and Harry.

4. Later in the story, why do Frank and Harry decide to scream but not faint?
   a. to say a quick "hi"
   b. to say a full "hi"
   c. not to say "hi" at all

5. Why do Frank and Harry think the haircutter is exercising when he sees them?
   a. because he's counting very loudly as he screams
   b. because he's running and flailing his arms
   c. because he's sweating like a madman

Check your answers with your teacher. Give yourself 1 point for each correct answer, and fill in your Strategy score here. Then turn to page 205 and transfer your score onto Graph 1.

Personal
Vocabulary
Strategy
Comprehension
TOTAL SCORE
✓ T

Check your answers with your teacher. Give yourself 1 point for each correct answer, and fill in your Comprehension score here. Then turn to page 205 and transfer your score onto Graph 1.

Personal
Vocabulary
Strategy
Comprehension
TOTAL SCORE
✓ T

Extending

Choose one or more of these activities:

DRAW AN ALIEN

Draw a picture of an alien that might come from another planet. Label the creature's body parts, items of clothing, or special gear. As you share your drawing with a partner or the class, explain why your alien is linked to a particular planet. For help in getting started, you might use *Drawing Aliens* and some of the books on planets that are listed on this page.

WRITE A SCIENCE FICTION STORY ABOUT YOUR ALIEN

Use a problem-solution frame to create a problem for your alien when it visits Earth for the first time. Then plan a few solutions and results, including the end result. Use your problem-solution frame to write a short science fiction story about your alien's adventures. If you need help getting ideas, you might look for the problems and solutions in some of the books listed on this page.

GIVE A NEWS REPORT

Choose a partner, and become on-the-scene reporters. In a "live" broadcast that you perform for a few classmates, explain what happened when two fat Venusian boys paid a visit to Earth. Give a detailed account of the highlights of the day. If you'd like, include brief interviews with some of the people who saw or spoke with the Venusians.

Resources

Books

Coville, Bruce. *Aliens Ate My Homework.* Bruce Coville's Alien Adventures. Aladdin Library, 1993.

Gaetz, Dayle Campbell. *Night of the Aliens.* Out of This World. Roussan Publishers, 1999.

Peel, John. *Alien Invasion from Hollyweird.* Outer Limits. Tor Books, 1999.

Pike, Christopher. *Aliens in the Sky.* Bt Bound, 1999.

Reinagle, Damon J. *Draw Alien Fantasies.* Peel Productions, 1996.

Ridpath, Ian. *Facts on File: Stars and Planets Atlas.* Facts on File, 2001.

Schloss, Muriel. *Venus.* First Books—The Solar System. Franklin Watts, 1996.

Scieszka, Jon. *2095.* Time Warp Trio. Puffin, 1997.

Learning New Words

VOCABULARY

From Lesson 1
- dirtiest
  muddiest

- gleamed
  sparkled

- speck
  spot

Synonyms

A synonym is a word that means the same thing—or close to the same thing—as another word. For example, author Helen Ketteman uses the synonyms *dirtiest* and *muddiest* to describe the town of Mudville when Shoeshine Whittaker arrives there. She uses *gleamed* and *sparkled* to describe what Mudville looked like after Shoeshine rubbed and scrubbed it.

Draw a line from each word in Column 1 to its synonym in Column 2.

<u>**Column 1**</u>   <u>**Column 2**</u>

doubt   boring
dull   rule
explore   question
law   faithful
loyal   examine

Antonyms

From Lesson 1
- clean
  dusty

- down
  up

- dulling
  shining

An antonym is a word that means the opposite of another word. For example, Helen Ketteman uses the antonyms *dusty* and *clean* to describe Mudville before and after Shoeshine Whittaker's arrival.

Draw a line from each word in Column 1 to its antonym in Column 2.

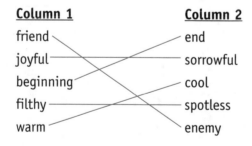

<u>**Column 1**</u>   <u>**Column 2**</u>

friend   end
joyful   sorrowful
beginning   cool
filthy   spotless
warm   enemy

Multiple-Meaning Words

VOCABULARY

From Lesson 2
- fair
- toe

From Lesson 3
- orders

A single word can have more than one meaning. As you learned in Lesson 2, the word *toe* can refer to a part of the foot, a dance performed on the toes, or a West India gherkin pickle. To figure out which meaning of *toe* the author was using, you had to use context. Context is the information surrounding a word or situation that helps you understand it.

When you read "The Big Toe Contest" you used context to figure out that Hayden's meaning for toe was "part of the foot." But in the context of the contest, *toe* referred to a West India gherkin pickle. Then at the end of the selection, Hayden mentioned that his aunt's dance troupe needed toe dancers. In that context, *toe* meant "a dance performed on the toes."

Now use context to figure out the correct meaning of each underlined word. Circle the letter of the correct meaning.

1. Brad and Brenda watched their favorite actress perform in a <u>play</u> last night.
   (a.) dramatic presentation

   b. thing done for sport

2. I replaced the batteries in my alarm clock when it stopped <u>running</u>.
   a. going faster than walking

   (b.) working or operating

3. My mother squeezed our little car into a tight parking <u>space</u>.
   a. length of time

   (b.) spot or place

4. Both sides of the debate team argued their <u>points</u> very well.
   (a.) main ideas

   b. tiny dots

Put the Brolly in the Boot and Let's Go

Building Background

Put the brolly in the boot? You're probably asking yourself, "What does *that* mean?" Believe it or not, the words in the title "Put the Brolly in the Boot and Let's Go" are all in English—British English. You may have noticed that people in various parts of the United States and the world sometimes speak English differently than you do. When you're trying to understand words that you've never heard before—even words spoken in English—you must rely on context to help you break the "language barrier."

Read the following sentences, and see if they provide enough context to help you figure out what a brolly is:

"We'll just put your valise and my brolly in the boot and be on our way. . . ." Uncle Brian stowed the suitcase and the umbrella in the car's trunk.

By using context, you probably figured out that a brolly is either a suitcase or an umbrella. And maybe you noticed that there is some similarity between the words *brolly* and *umbrella.* That probably gave you even more clues. Do you know what a brolly is now?

bangers

biscuits

bonnet

boot

chemist

crisps

loo

lorry

surgery

tea

valise

Vocabulary Builder

1. The words in Column 1 on page 57 are all British terms. Do you know what any of them mean? If you do, draw a line from each one to its definition in Column 2.

2. If you don't know what some of the terms mean, find them as you read the story. Use context to try to figure them out. Then match them to their definitions in Column 2.

3. Save your work. You will use it again in the Vocabulary Check.

COLUMN 1	COLUMN 2
bangers	hood of a car
biscuits	suitcase
bonnet	trunk of a car
boot	truck
chemist	sausages served with mashed potatoes
crisps	snacks served in the late afternoon
loo	doctor's office
lorry	druggist
surgery	cookies
tea	restroom
valise	potato chips

Strategy Builder

Comparing and Contrasting While You Read

- Authors often compare and contrast things when they write. **Comparing** means looking at how two or more things are similar, or alike. **Contrasting** means looking at how two or more things are different.

- Making a **comparison chart** while you read can help you keep track of how things are alike and different. For example, if you were reading an article about soccer and American football, your comparison chart might look like this:

	Soccer	American Football
Equipment	• soccer ball (round)	• American football (oval shaped)
Playing Areas	• outdoor field • indoor stadium	• outdoor field • indoor stadium
Scoring	• goal = 1 point	• touchdown = 6 points • conversion = 1 point • field goal = 3 points • safety = 2 points

- The chart helps you easily compare and contrast the equipment, playing areas, and scoring in each sport. For example, you can see that both football and soccer can be played indoors or outdoors. You also can see that there are four ways to score in football, but there is only one way to score in soccer.

Put the Brolly in the Boot and Let's Go

by Kathryn Slattery

As you read the first part of this story, look for how things in Great Britain compare and contrast with things in the United States. Use context to figure out any unfamiliar words.

Jenny's stomach tightened as she looked around London's Heathrow Airport. She was glad that the airline hostess was there to help. It was her first trip outside the United States. At least her parents had been right about her not having to learn a foreign language. The signs overhead were in English.

Suddenly Jenny saw Uncle Brian waving his umbrella. His eyes twinkled as he shook Jenny's hand. "Welcome to Great Britain," he said.

The air hostess checked Uncle Brian's identification. "Have fun, and eat plenty of **bangers**!" she called as she left.

"Come on. First, we'll grab a trolley; then we can ride the lift down to the ground floor and claim your baggage."

Jenny was confused, and they hadn't even left the airport! She followed Uncle Brian and the luggage cart to the elevator. Soon they had Jenny's suitcase and were outside.

"My car's next to the **lorry**." Uncle Brian pointed to a sedan parked next to a delivery truck. "We'll just put your **valise** and my brolly in the **boot** and be on our way. I checked under the **bonnet** this morning so we'll have a smooth ride."

Uncle Brian stowed the suitcase and the umbrella in the car's trunk. Jenny slid into the front seat. The steering wheel was on the wrong side!

On the drive home, Jenny gripped the edge of the seat. She felt like Alice in Wonderland; everything was just a bit off. "Relax," Uncle Brian said, smiling. "Everyone in England drives on this side. For us it's the right side, even if it is on the left."

"Gee, Uncle Brian," Jenny whispered, "Mom said you would speak English and you do, but not quite."

"Tell you what. Let me know when you don't understand something, and I'll translate."

Jenny nodded.

Stop here for the Strategy Break.

Strategy Break

If you were to make a comparison chart for this story so far, it might look like this:

	Life in Great Britain	Life in the United States
Spoken language	• English	• English
Written language	• English	• English
Transportation	• People drive on the left-hand side of the road. • The steering wheel is on the right-hand side of the car.	• People drive on the right-hand side of the road. • The steering wheel is on the left-hand side of the car.

As you already know, the words for many things are different in each country. Take a look back at the Vocabulary Builder. If you did not correctly match the British terms *bangers, lorry, valise, boot,* and *bonnet* with their American definitions, go back and do that now. Then read the rest of the story. In the Strategy Follow-up, you will continue to compare and contrast life in Great Britain and life in the United States.

 Go on reading to see what happens.

Soon they were driving down a narrow road with houses and shops on each side.

"That's my **surgery**," Uncle Brian said, pointing, "and the **chemist** is right next to it."

Jenny thought her uncle was a regular doctor, but maybe he was a scientist too. "Do you experiment with new medicines and then go next door when you need to operate on your patients?"

Uncle Brian chuckled. "A surgery is a doctor's office in England. And at the chemist's they sell only medicines and such." Uncle Brian turned the car into a gravel drive. "Here we are. Your cousin Heather should be home from cricket practice by now. She's really excited to meet you."

A girl with red hair came running out of the house.

"Heather, slow down," Uncle Brian said.

Heather grinned. She grabbed Jenny's bag. "Come on. You're going to share my room. It'll be brilliant!"

Jenny followed Heather as she bumped the heavy suitcase upstairs.

"My room is right here, past the **loo**," Heather said. She led the way into a bedroom right next to the bathroom.

Even the bathroom has a different name, thought Jenny.

Uncle Brian called from downstairs. "Heather, bring your cousin down. Mum wants to say hello."

Aunt Sylvia greeted Jenny seriously. "Welcome to England," she said. "Are you ready for **tea**?"

"Yes, thank you," Jenny answered, remembering her mother's instructions to be polite. "But could I have something to eat too? I'm really hungry. I didn't eat much on the plane."

Aunt Sylvia smiled. "This is afternoon tea, Jenny," she said, pointing at the dining room table laid with all kinds of food. There were cookies and little sandwiches with the crusts cut off. There were big, fluffy **biscuits**, pots of jam and butter, and a bowl of some kind of dessert topped with whipped cream. "What would you like to eat?" she asked.

"A biscuit, please, and some of those little sandwiches."

Aunt Sylvia served Jenny two triangular sandwiches and passed the plate of cookies.

Jenny took a cookie and asked timidly, "Could I try a biscuit too, please?"

Aunt Sylvia looked puzzled. Heather began to giggle, and Uncle Brian laughed out loud. "Jenny, I'm sorry. I keep forgetting." He turned to Heather. "Jenny is having trouble understanding our English. Lots of things have different names in America. In America biscuits are like our scones. What we call biscuits, they call cookies."

"Just when I think I understand, then someone says something strange," said Jenny. "It's rather like a puzzle."

"I'll help you," Heather offered. "We can make it a game." She got right into the spirit of being a teacher. "That's trifle; under the cream there's cake and custard. For dinner Mum's making my favorite—bangers. That's sausages and mash."

"Speaking of potatoes," added Uncle Brian, "we call French fries chips and what you call potato chips, we call **crisps**."

"When we were in the States when Heather was a baby, I had to learn lots of new words." Aunt Sylvia thought for a minute. "There was the word *diapers* for nappies. A cot was called a crib. The Americans said baby buggy instead of pram. When Heather lost her dummy and we tried to buy a new one, the sales clerk just laughed. 'Call it a pacifier,' she told us."

"I need a pencil and paper," Jenny said. "I'll never remember it all!"

"Come on. Let's go into the living room." Heather was excited. "Jenny can teach me the American words for things we hear on the telly!"

Jenny grinned. "I know what that is—the television."

"Brilliant!" Uncle Brian declared. ●

Strategy Follow-up

Complete the comparison chart below with information from the second part of the story. Go back and skim the story if you need to.

	Life in Great Britain	Life in the United States
What a chemist does	what an American druggist, or pharmacist, does—fills prescriptions	studies different substances and experiments with them
What people have during tea	tea, cookies, sandwiches, biscuits, jam and butter, etc.	tea—and maybe a light snack of cookies, a muffin, or a piece of cake
What baby things are called	nappies, cot, pram, dummy	diapers, crib, baby buggy, pacifier

✓Personal Checklist

Read each question and put a check (✓) in the correct box.

1. How well were you able to use the information in Building Background to understand Jenny's problem?
   - ☐ 3   (extremely well)
   - ☐ 2   (fairly well)
   - ☐ 1   (not well)

2. How well were you able to understand why Jenny felt like Alice in Wonderland on the drive home?
   - ☐ 3   (extremely well)
   - ☐ 2   (fairly well)
   - ☐ 1   (not well)

3. How well were you able to use context to figure out the British terms?
   - ☐ 3   (extremely well)
   - ☐ 2   (fairly well)
   - ☐ 1   (not well)

4. In the Vocabulary Builder, how many British and American terms were you able to match correctly?
   - ☐ 3   (8–11 terms)
   - ☐ 2   (4–7 terms)
   - ☐ 1   (0–3 terms)

5. How well were you able to complete the comparison chart in the Strategy Follow-up?
   - ☐ 3   (extremely well)
   - ☐ 2   (fairly well)
   - ☐ 1   (not well)

Vocabulary Check

Look back at the work you did in the Vocabulary Builder. Then answer each question by circling the correct letter.

1. Which context clue helped you figure out exactly what bangers are?
   a. "Have fun, and eat plenty of bangers!"
   b. "Mum's making my favorite—bangers."
   c. "That's sausages and mash." *(circled)*

2. What is a British dummy called in the States?
   a. diaper
   b. pacifier *(circled)*
   c. crib

3. Which match is correct?
   a. British surgery = American surgery
   b. British surgery = American doctor's office *(circled)*
   c. British surgery = American doctor

4. Which of the following would be served during British tea?
   a. scones and jam *(circled)*
   b. bangers and mash
   c. peanut butter-and-jelly sandwiches

5. What are French fries called in Great Britain?
   a. chips *(circled)*
   b. crisps
   c. potato chips

Add the numbers that you just checked to get your Personal Checklist score. Fill in your score here. Then turn to page 205 and transfer your score onto Graph 1.

Check your answers with your teacher. Give yourself 1 point for each correct answer, and fill in your Vocabulary score here. Then turn to page 205 and transfer your score onto Graph 1.

Strategy Check

Review the comparison chart that you completed in the Strategy Follow-up. Then answer these questions.

1. What does an American chemist do?
   a. studies different substances and experiments with them
   b. studies different patients and operates on them
   c. sells different kinds of medicines

2. Why does Jenny think that her uncle experiments on his patients?
   a. because American chemists do experiments
   b. because he says he's next to a chemist
   c. because of both reasons above

3. What is different about having tea in Britain and having tea in the States?
   a. In Britain you usually have just tea, but in the States you eat lots of food with it.
   b. In the States you usually have just tea, but in Britain you eat lots of food with it.
   c. Nothing—having tea is the same in both countries.

4. How are the names of baby things different in Britain and the States?
   a. An American baby buggy is called a brolly in Britain.
   b. British nappies are called diapers in the States.
   c. Both of the above answers are correct.

5. If you asked for a biscuit in Britain, what would you get?
   a. a scone
   b. a sandwich
   c. a cookie

Comprehension Check

Review the story if necessary. Then answer these questions:

1. Why is Jenny so confused in this story?
   a. Several British terms are unfamiliar to Jenny.
   b. They don't speak English in Great Britain.
   c. Jenny doesn't know a foreign language.

2. Which of the following differences is not related to language?
   a. calling an umbrella a brolly
   b. driving on the other side of the street
   c. saying Mum instead of Mom

3. Why does Jenny ask for something to eat with her tea?
   a. She thinks tea is only something to drink.
   b. She wants a full American dinner with her tea.
   c. She wants to be polite, even though she is full.

4. What does Heather mean when she says, "You're going to share my room. It'll be brilliant!"
   a. It will be great fun to share her room.
   b. Her room will be very shiny.
   c. Sharing a room will be very intelligent.

5. When Jenny arrives, Heather is at cricket practice. In the context of this story, what does cricket mean?
   a. a small, low wooden stool
   b. a leaping insect related to the grasshopper
   c. an outdoor game played with wickets

Check your answers with your teacher. Give yourself 1 point for each correct answer, and fill in your Strategy score here. Then turn to page 205 and transfer your score onto Graph 1.

Personal
Vocabulary
Strategy
Comprehension
TOTAL SCORE
✓ T

Check your answers with your teacher. Give yourself 1 point for each correct answer, and fill in your Comprehension score here. Then turn to page 205 and transfer your score onto Graph 1.

Personal
Vocabulary
Strategy
Comprehension
TOTAL SCORE
✓ T

Extending

Choose one or both of these activities:

PLAN A MENU FOR AFTERNOON TEA

Using some of the resources on this page or ones that you find yourself, find out what foods are typically eaten during afternoon tea in Britain. Then, with a group of classmates, plan a menu for an afternoon tea. If you can, find recipes for some of the foods on your menu. Prepare the foods, and then share them with the class during your own afternoon tea.

READ ALOUD TO YOUNGER STUDENTS

Choose a book written by a British author, such as James Herriot or Michael Bond. Prepare to read the book to a group of younger students. Make sure you understand any unfamiliar words or phrases so that you can explain them as you read. Use the resources listed on this page to help you find British books and terms.

Resources

Books

Bond, Michael. *Paddington at Large.* Houghton Mifflin, 1998.

Butterfield, Moira, and Nicola Wright. *Getting to Know Britain: People, Places.* Getting to Know. Barrons Juveniles, 1994.

Denny, Roz. *A Taste of Britain.* Food Around the World. Thomson Learning, 1997.

Ewart, James, ed. *NTC's Dictionary of British Slang and Colloquial Expressions: The Most Practical Reference for the Informal Expressions of British English.* NTC Publishing, 1996.

Herriot, James. *Oscar, Cat-About-Town.* St. Martin's Press, 1993.

Moore, Margaret E. *Understanding British English: Bridging the Gap Between the English Language and Its American Counterpart.* Citadel Press, 1998.

Steele, Philip. *Great Britain.* Discovering. Crestwood House, 1994.

Web Site

http://www.afternoonteaparty.com
This Web site explores the tradition of the English tea party, shares recipes, and provides further resources.

The Contest

abscess

accompanist

ambitious

aria

flourish

lanced

precious

recitative

trill

unanimous

CLIPBOARD

Descriptive Words

ambitious

precious

unanimous

CLIPBOARD

Medical Words

abscess

lanced

CLIPBOARD

Music Words

accompanist

aria

flourish

recitative

trill

Building Background

Marian Anderson was born in Philadelphia, Pennsylvania, in 1897. She began singing in church choirs when she was just a child. After graduating from high school, she performed in both Europe and the United States.

Because she was black, Marian's career often was affected by racism. For example, in 1939 the Daughters of the American Revolution would not allow Marian to perform at Constitution Hall in Washington, D.C. Things turned out well after all, however: She sang at the Lincoln Memorial instead—to a crowd of more than 75,000 people!

Marian Anderson's talent was so great that the famous conductor Arturo Toscanini praised her voice as one "that comes once in a hundred years." In addition to her many singing accomplishments, Marian wrote her autobiography, *My Lord, What a Morning,* in 1956; became a U.S. delegate to the United Nations in 1958; and won the UN peace prize in 1977. Marian Anderson died in 1993.

Vocabulary Builder

1. Before you begin reading "The Contest," read the vocabulary words in the margin. Write any of the words that you already know on the appropriate clipboards.

2. Later, as you read "The Contest," find the vocabulary words you don't know. Read them in context, and decide what they mean. Then write the words on the appropriate clipboards.

3. If using context doesn't help you figure out what a word means, look it up in a dictionary. If the dictionary gives more than one meaning for the word, be sure to choose the one that is used in the selection.

4. Save your work. You will refer to it again in the Vocabulary Check.

Strategy Builder

How to Read a Biographical Sketch

- A **biography** is the story of a real person's life, written by someone else. A **biographical sketch** is the story of a part of a real person's life. "The Contest" is a biographical sketch that describes what happened to Marian Anderson when she tried out for a chance to sing at Lewisohn Stadium in New York. This biographical sketch is taken from Janet Stevenson's biography of Anderson called *Singing to the World.*

- Biographical sketches describe events in the order in which they happened. That order is called time order, or **sequence**. To make the sequence as clear as possible, writers often use words called **signal words**. Some examples of signal words are *first, then, after that, a few days later,* and *at that moment.*

- A biographical sketch is always written in the **third-person point of view**. That means that the narrator tells the subject's story using words such as *he, she, his, her, they,* and *theirs.*

- The paragraph below is from a biographical sketch about a boy named Jonathan. They describe what he did before school one morning. Notice the signal words, which are underlined.

Jonathan woke up <u>this morning</u> and got out of bed. His dog was waiting for him at the kitchen table. It was wagging its tail and barking. It looked pretty funny. <u>Before breakfast</u> Jonathan watched the news on TV. There was a story about a film being made in his town. <u>After he ate breakfast</u> he brushed his teeth. <u>Next</u> he got dressed and combed his hair. It was picture day at school, and he wanted to look nice. <u>When he left the house</u>, he caught the bus. <u>On the ride to school</u> he studied for a test.

If you wanted to show the sequence of events in the paragraphs above, you could use a **sequence chain** like this one:

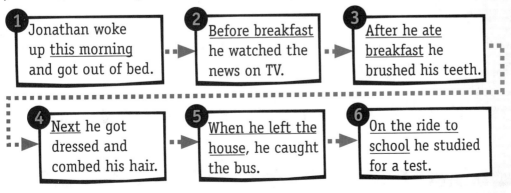

1. Jonathan woke up <u>this morning</u> and got out of bed.
2. <u>Before breakfast</u> he watched the news on TV.
3. <u>After he ate breakfast</u> he brushed his teeth.
4. <u>Next</u> he got dressed and combed his hair.
5. <u>When he left the house</u>, he caught the bus.
6. <u>On the ride to school</u> he studied for a test.

The Contest

by Janet Stevenson

As you read the first part of "The Contest," apply the strategies that you just learned. Notice the underlined signal words. They will give you a more exact picture of when things happened.

Marian Anderson was one of the greatest concert singers of the 20th century. Before achieving worldwide fame, she took part in many voice contests. In 1925 her voice teacher entered her in a contest for an appearance at Lewisohn Stadium in New York City. The biographical sketch you are about to read describes the events leading up to Anderson's final round of tryouts.

Every one of the contestants—and there were 300 of them—had an **accompanist**, and most had a teacher with them too. The crowd filled the whole ground floor of Aeolian Hall.

<u>At the appointed hour</u>, the rules were announced over a public address system from the balcony, where the judges sat—heard but not seen. They explained that there was not time for each contestant to sing all the material he or she had prepared. The judges would listen to what they felt to be a fair sample. Then a clicker would sound. The singer was to stop and leave the stage.

"Pay no attention," Mr. Boghetti whispered in Marian's ear. "If they stop you, pretend you don't hear. Go on to the end. Be sure you get in that final **trill**."

"Go on singing when they tell me to stop?"

Marian was appalled at such boldness, but Mr. Boghetti believed in boldness.

"Not for everybody, maybe. But for you. You must insist that they hear you out."

Marian said nothing, but she didn't believe she could do what he was asking. Hard as it was to disobey her teacher, it would be harder to disobey the unseen judges.

Meanwhile she had drawn a number and was waiting her turn. By the time it came near, several other singers had sung her Donizetti **aria**. Not one of them had got to the final trill. Each time the clicker cut short their song, Marian winced. Each time she winced, Mr. Boghetti glared a warning at her.

"What if I skip the **recitative** and start with the aria itself?" she whispered.

He shook his head. "Sing it all. Make them listen!"

The next contestants got only a minute or two apiece. It was her turn.

She began with the half-spoken recitative, though it seemed a waste of **precious** time. She could feel her teacher's hypnotic eye on her, reminding her of his command. She was expecting at any instant the sound of the clicker and the awful decision—which command to disobey?

But the clicker didn't sound.

Maybe she didn't hear it. (Her ears had felt a little dull since her last ducking in the Y pool.) She was well into the aria now! Singing as if each note might be the last—as indeed it might! On and on to the great final trill! She sang it through to the last beautiful **flourish**!

There was a second of dead silence. Then applause broke out all over Aeolian Hall.

An angry voice on the loud speaker reminded the audience that applause was forbidden. <u>Then</u> it asked Marian whether she had another song.

She sang one of her English songs and went back to her seat.

"Did the clicker sound?" she asked Mr. Boghetti.

"No! You are the only one who has finished the aria! Not to speak of a second song!"

They left soon afterwards to catch the train back to Philadelphia. Mr. Boghetti was elated by her success, but as always he found things that could be improved. He talked about them <u>all the way home</u>, which gave Marian a chance to relax and become aware of something very peculiar about one of her ears.

It was not so much pain as a sort of numbness. She said nothing about it. She had never mentioned the swimming lessons to Mr. Boghetti and she suspected that he was not going to approve. Not if the trouble in her ear had anything to do with them.

Perhaps it would be better to give up swimming.

<u>Two days later</u> Mr. Boghetti called her on the phone.

"You have won!"

"Won?"

"You are one of 16 who will sing in the semifinals. Four will be chosen from them."

 Stop here for the Strategy Break.

Strategy Break

If you were to arrange the main events in this selection so far, they might look like this:

1 <u>At the appointed</u> hour, the rules are announced. → **2** Mr. Boghetti tells Marian to keep singing if they tell her to stop. → **3** Marian makes it through her whole song!

4 <u>Then</u> she is asked to sing another one. → **5** <u>All the way home,</u> she notices a numbness in one of her ears. → **6** <u>Two days later,</u> Marian finds out she has made it to the semifinals.

As you continue reading, keep paying attention to the order of events. Also keep looking for signal words, and underline them. At the end of this selection you will use them to create a sequence chain of your own.

 Go on reading.

So it was back to work in the muggy heat. Marian was almost tempted to go back to the Y pool, just to cool off a little, but her ear still felt strange. She thought once of going to a doctor, but it got no worse, and she really had no time to spare.

On the second trip to New York, Mr. Boghetti was full of **ambitious** hopes. He was talking about how he would coach Marian for the Lewisohn Stadium appearance, assuming that she would win today's round, and go on to win the semifinals. Marian wished she could share his enthusiasm, but she felt wooden beside him.

In fact she felt worse than wooden. Her ear was beginning to hurt.

She had thought when she got up this morning that there was something stuck in it. Perhaps it was one of the little cotton plugs she had used to keep the water out while she swam. She tried pulling it out, first with her fingers, then with tweezers, but working at it made it worse.

By the time they got to Aeolian Hall, she had a real old-fashioned earache. Not unbearable yet, but getting worse.

"It won't be so long today," Mr. Boghetti said cheerfully. "There are only 16 contestants. You may be one of the first."

Marian hoped so. She was not sure now long she could hold out. But Mr. Boghetti was right; she was called after only a half hour's wait.

She had to sing her aria and both her other songs. As soon as she was through, Mr. Boghetti took her back to his studio to rest until train time.

"Why do you look so discouraged?" he asked. "You did well. Very well!"

Marian was tempted to tell him that it was not discouragement he saw on her face. But it had got too bad to talk about at all. She felt as if there were some horrible growth deep inside her ear. Her hearing was affected. What if it turned out to be permanent? Beethoven had gone deaf, and he had gone on composing and conducting, but who ever heard of a deaf singer?

The phone rang and Mr. Boghetti answered it.

"What? . . . Are you sure? . . . All right, all right!"

He turned back to Marian with a dazed look, which could be the shock of joy or the shock of defeat.

"There are to be no finals," he said. "It is **unanimous**. You will sing on August 25th at Lewisohn Stadium!"

At that moment Marian was wondering whether she would ever sing anywhere again.

But the growth in her ear was only an **abscess**. As soon as it was **lanced** and the pressure relieved, the pain began to ease.

"Will I be deaf?" she asked the doctor.

"Not if you take care of yourself, and stay out of swimming pools for the rest of the summer."

Orders she didn't mind obeying for the rest of that summer and several summers to come! ●

Strategy Follow-up

Now create a sequence chain for the second part of this selection. Use a separate sheet of paper if you need to. Don't forget to use (and underline) as many signal words as you can.

7 <u>On the second trip to New York</u>, Marian's ear is beginning to hurt.

8 <u>By the time she gets to Aeolian Hall</u>, Marian has a real earache.

9 Marian is called to sing <u>after only a half-hour's wait</u>.

10 <u>As soon as she is through</u>, Mr. Boghetti takes her back to his studio to rest.

11 The phone rings, and Mr. Boghetti learns that there will be no finals. Marian will sing at Lewisohn Stadium

12 <u>At that moment</u> Marian wonders if she will ever sing again.

13 But as soon as <u>her abscess is lanced</u> the pain begins to ease.

14 The doctor tells Marian to stay out of pools for the rest of the summer.

✓Personal Checklist

Read each question and put a check (✓) in the correct box.

1. How well do you understand what happened in "The Contest"?
    - ☐ 3   (extremely well)
    - ☐ 2   (fairly well)
    - ☐ 1   (not well)

2. How well do you understand the personalities and motivations of Marian and Mr. Boghetti?
    - ☐ 3   (extremely well)
    - ☐ 2   (fairly well)
    - ☐ 1   (not well)

3. How well were you able to use the information in Building Background to help you predict the outcome of Marian's tryouts?
    - ☐ 3   (extremely well)
    - ☐ 2   (fairly well)
    - ☐ 1   (not well)

4. By the time you finished reading "The Contest," how many vocabulary words were you able to write on the appropriate clipboards?
    - ☐ 3   (8–10 words)
    - ☐ 2   (4–7 words)
    - ☐ 1   (0–3 words)

5. How well were you able to complete the sequence chain in the Strategy Follow-up?
    - ☐ 3   (extremely well)
    - ☐ 2   (fairly well)
    - ☐ 1   (not well)

Vocabulary Check

Look back at the work you did in the Vocabulary Builder. Then answer each question by circling the correct letter.

1. On which clipboard did you write the words *ambitious*, *precious*, and *unanimous*?
    - (a.) Descriptive Words
    - b. Medical Words
    - c. Music Words

2. Every contestant in the first round of tryouts has an accompanist. Who or what is an *accompanist*?
    - a. a person who coaches a singer during a contest
    - (b.) a person who plays an instrument to back up a singer
    - c. an instrument that a person uses to back up a singer

3. Which vocabulary word were you able to figure out by using the context clue "half-spoken"?
    - a. trill
    - b. flourish
    - (c.) recitative

4. Which meaning of the word *flourish* fits this selection?
    - (a.) a showy trill or passage of music
    - b. a being in the best time of one's life or activity
    - c. an ornamental curve in one's handwriting

5. The judges' choice of Marian as the contest winner is unanimous. What does *unanimous* mean?
    - (a.) agreed upon by everyone
    - b. agreed upon by no one
    - c. decided by only one judge

Add the numbers that you just checked to get your Personal Checklist score. Fill in your score here. Then turn to page 205 and transfer your score onto Graph 1.

Check your answers with your teacher. Give yourself 1 point for each correct answer, and fill in your Vocabulary score here. Then turn to page 205 and transfer your score onto Graph 1.

Strategy Check

Review the sequence chain that you completed in the Strategy Follow-up. Then answer these questions:

1. Which sentence could you have written for Event 7?

   a. By the time she gets to Aeolian Hall, Marian has a real earache.

   b. Marian is called to sing after only a half-hour's wait.

   c. On the second trip to New York, Marian's ear is beginning to hurt.

2. Which phrase is not an example of signal words?

   a. but it had got too bad

   b. as soon as she was through

   c. at that moment

3. What do Marian and Mr. Boghetti do after Marian finishes her semifinal tryout?

   a. They go back to Mr. Boghetti's studio so Marian can rest.

   b. They go to the train station to wait for the train.

   c. They go to Lewisohn Stadium to prepare for her appearance.

4. When does Marian have her abscess lanced?

   a. before the semifinal round of the contest

   b. during the semifinal round of the contest

   c. after the semifinal round of the contest

5. Which sentence could be the last event on your sequence chain?

   a. Mr. Boghetti tells Marian that there will be no finals.

   b. The doctor tells Marian to stay out of pools for the rest of the summer.

   c. As soon as Marian's abscess is lanced, the pain begins to ease.

Comprehension Check

Review the selection if necessary. Then answer these questions:

1. How many people compete in the first round of the contest?

   a. 30

   b. 100

   c. 300

2. How many people compete in the semifinal round?

   a. 4

   b. 16

   c. 30

3. Why is there no final round to the contest?

   a. The judges all agree after the semifinal round that Marian is the winner of the contest.

   b. Everyone but Marian drops out of the contest, so she wins the final round.

   c. There actually is a final round, but Marian is too ill to compete in it.

4. Why doesn't Marian tell Mr. Boghetti that she is taking swimming lessons?

   a. She doesn't think he will approve of her taking them.

   b. She is afraid he will blame her earache on them.

   c. Both of the above answers are correct.

5. Which words best describe Marian?

   a. happy and carefree

   b. obedient and hard-working

   c. bored and disgusted

Check your answers with your teacher. Give yourself 1 point for each correct answer, and fill in your Strategy score here. Then turn to page 205 and transfer your score onto Graph 1.

Personal
Vocabulary
Strategy
Comprehension
TOTAL SCORE
✓ T

Check your answers with your teacher. Give yourself 1 point for each correct answer, and fill in your Comprehension score here. Then turn to page 205 and transfer your score onto Graph 1.

Personal
Vocabulary
Strategy
Comprehension
TOTAL SCORE
✓ T

Extending

Choose one or more of these activities:

SUMMARIZE THE SELECTION

Use the vocabulary words and your sequence chain to summarize what happened in "The Contest." Try to use as many vocabulary words as possible in your summary. Also use as many signal words as possible to help clarify the order of events. Then share your summary with a partner. Can he or she follow the order of events easily? Make any revisions to your summary that you feel are necessary.

RESEARCH MARIAN ANDERSON'S LIFE

Work alone or with a group of classmates to find out more about Marian Anderson's life and career. Use some of the resources on this page if you'd like. Report your findings orally or in writing.

RESPOND TO ANDERSON'S WORK

Listen to a recording of Marian Anderson's work, and choose the song that most appeals to you. Respond to the song in one of the following ways:

words—write a poem, song, descriptive paragraph, or critique

pictures—work in water colors, oils, or a medium of your choice

shapes—make a sculpture or a three-dimensional scene, using the medium of your choice

music—play or sing a song that you or someone else composed

movement—perform a dance to the song you have chosen

Resources

Books

Ferris, Jeri. *What I Had Was Singing: The Story of Marian Anderson.* Carolrhoda Books, 1994.

Tedards, Anne, and Martina S. Horner. *Marian Anderson.* American Women of Achievement. Chelsea House, 1989.

Web Site

http://www.afrovoices.com/anderson.html
This site includes a brief biography of Anderson as well as a link to pictures, audio/video excerpts, and other resources.

Audio Recording

Great Voices of the Century. Marian Anderson. RCA, 1996.

LESSON 8 The Fabulous Miss Bly

Building Background

In 1890, New York held a parade in honor of Elizabeth Cochrane. Was she a movie star? an astronaut? a visiting princess? No, she was a newspaper reporter. She was about 23 years old. And she had just circled the globe in 72 days. Elizabeth Cochrane changed her name to Nellie Bly when she became a reporter. You will read about her adventurous life and how she tried to help people, especially the mentally ill, in the following selection.

article

editor

editorial

published

reporter

reports

topic

Vocabulary Builder

1. The vocabulary words in the margin are all related to newspaper publishing. Some of the words may be familiar to you. Find those words in the statements below. If a word is used correctly, write **C** on the line beside it. If a word is used incorrectly, write **I**.

2. Then, as you read the selection, use context clues to figure out any of the vocabulary words you don't know. Go back and write **C** or **I** next to those sentences. Double-check your earlier work, and make any necessary changes.

3. Save your work. You will use it again in the Vocabulary Check.

    ___I___ a. James drew an **article** for his daily comic strip.

    ___I___ b. An **editor** is a person who runs a high school.

    ___C___ c. Marcia wrote an **editorial** on her opinion of computers.

    ___C___ d. Mr. Gardner **published** his first book last year.

    ___I___ e. A **reporter** burst into the store to arrest the thief.

    ___C___ f. Sam Hill wrote a series of **reports** on life in big cities.

    ___I___ g. Jason rubbed a **topic** cream on his bruised knee.

Strategy Builder

How to Read a Biography

- In Lesson 7 you learned that a **biographical sketch** tells about a specific time in a real person's life. In this lesson you will read a biography. A **biography** tells about a real person's *entire* life, as written by someone else.

- The events in most biographies are told in the **sequence**, or time order, in which they happened. When you read Marian Anderson's biographical sketch, you used a sequence chain to record the order of events. As you read Nellie Bly's biography, however, you will use a time line. A **time line** is more effective when you are looking at a person's entire life, since it allows you to show a much longer period of time.

- Read the following paragraphs from a biography of Dorthea Dix.

Dorthea Dix was born in 1802 in what is now Maine. Her early life was difficult. This may have led to her later goal of helping others who were unable to help themselves. In 1841 she began to work on improving the treatment of mentally ill people and prisoners. Three years later she moved to New Jersey and worked to build a state asylum for the mentally ill. About a year later, Dix wrote a book about the work she did with prisoners.

   In 1861 Dix was chosen to be the Superintendent of Army Nurses during the Civil War. She was not very good at this job. Five years later she decided to return to her first cause, helping the mentally ill. Dix died in 1887 at the age of 85. The New Jersey State Lunatic Asylum stands as a tribute to her life's work.

- If you wanted to create a time line to show the major events in Dorthea Dix's life, it would look like this:

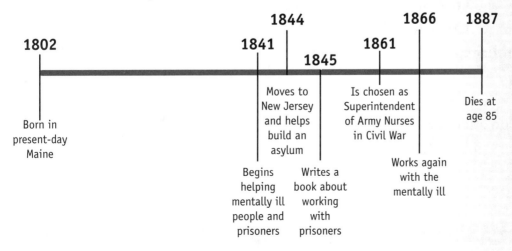

The Fabulous Miss Bly

As you read this biography, note the dates and important events in Nellie Bly's life. Be careful—not all of the dates are presented in order.

In the 1800s, many young women had hard, dull jobs. Their pay was low. Almost all good jobs went to men. After all, people said, a woman's place is in the home. In 1885, the *Pittsburgh Dispatch* printed an **editorial** about working women. It said that women could not do a good job outside the home.

Look Out, World!

Elizabeth Cochrane read the **article**. Elizabeth was born in 1867 in Cochran's Mills, Pennsylvania. In 1885, when she read the article, she was young and eager for adventure. The article made her angry. She wrote to the *Dispatch*. Women, she said, could do many jobs well. It was wrong to waste their talents. The paper printed her letter. Then Cochrane asked for a job as a **reporter.** The **editor** liked her letter. So he gave her a try.

Cochrane wrote under another name. She chose Nellie Bly. "Nellie Bly" is the name of a song by Stephen Foster, an American songwriter who lived in the 1800s.

Travel to Mexico

Nellie Bly's first **reports** told about the hard lives of other working women. She wrote about the slums of Pittsburgh. She wrote about divorce. She got readers excited about her **topics**.

The *Dispatch* saw how popular Bly's work was. So in 1887 the paper sent her to Mexico. For six months, Bly traveled around Mexico. She wrote reports about all that she saw.

In those days, few people saw other countries. There were no movies or TV shows about far-off lands. So almost everything in Bly's reports was new to her readers. They were eager to learn about Mexico. Later, Bly **published** her reports in a book called *Six Months in Mexico*.

Bly Tells All

Soon after Bly came home to Pittsburgh, she moved to New York. She had a new job with a larger paper. She then worked for the *New York World*.

Bly's first big topic in New York was insane asylums. Most often, the city asylums made little news. People with mental illnesses were just "put away" and forgotten. But how well were patients treated? Bly wanted to find out.

Bly knew that visitors are always shown the best things. She wanted to see the worst things too. So she pretended to be insane. She was sent to a New York asylum as a patient.

Inside, Bly learned that patients were often mistreated. Many were dirty and hungry. They were left for long times without care. Instead of getting better, patients got worse.

Two weeks later, Bly was out of the asylum. But the outcome of her daring stunt lasted for years. Her reports about asylums were first printed in the *World*. In 1888, they came out as a book called *Ten Days in a Madhouse*. Readers were shocked by what she wrote. They cried for changes. Because of Bly, life got better for patients in New York asylums.

 Stop here for the Strategy Break.

Strategy Break

If you were to show the main events in Nellie Bly's life so far, they might look like this:

Go on reading.

The Biggest Trip of All

Nellie Bly had proved she was a great reporter. But she still wanted adventure. A book gave her the idea for her greatest success. *Around the World in Eighty Days* was a popular book in 1889. It tells the tale of Phileas Fogg, a noted English gentleman. On a bet, he travels around the world in just 80 days. Few people believed the trip was possible. Bly thought she could make the trip even faster.

At first, the *World* would not let her try. The idea was crazy. No one could go around the world in so few days! And for a woman, there would be added danger. But Bly kept asking. Finally, her boss told her to go ahead. He knew Bly loved adventure. Besides, the trip could make both her and the paper famous.

Bly packed a single bag. Then she set off. On November 14, 1889, at 9:40 A.M., her ship left New Jersey. Bly first landed in England. Then she went on to France. There she met Jules Verne, the writer of *Around the World in Eighty Days*. After Verne wished her good luck, Bly left for Hong Kong.

A Race Against Time

Nellie Bly traveled by ship, train, horse, handcart, and burro. Wherever she went, she wrote. She kept an exact record of what she saw and did. Bly planned to share her adventures with others. She wanted her readers to feel as if they had traveled along with her.

When Bly's ship from Hong Kong reached San Francisco, she was famous. The *World* sent a train to meet her. It would bring her to New Jersey as fast as it could. Even so, crowds met the train at each stop. Everyone wanted to see the young world traveler.

At last, the train reached New Jersey. Bly jumped from it on January 25, 1890, at 3:31 P.M. She had circled Earth in exactly 72 days, 6 hours, and 11 minutes. The waiting crowd cheered. A few days later, New York greeted her. Fireworks went off. Brass bands played. A parade marched down Broadway.

Of course, Bly reported on her trip in the *World*. She also wrote *Nellie Bly's Book: Around the World in Seventy-Two Days* was published in 1890. This was her most popular book.

Other Adventures

Nellie Bly kept up her writing until 1895. Then she married Robert Seaman, a very rich man. After he died, she successfully ran his business. But her gift was for news, not business. By 1920, she was writing again.

Nellie Bly died in 1922. By then, planes carried people over land and seas. Bly's speed record was broken. Yet Bly's boldness is still a model. And her spirit of adventure will never age. ●

Strategy Follow-up

On a wide piece of paper, copy the time line from the Strategy Break. Then continue the time line with dates and information from the second part of this selection.

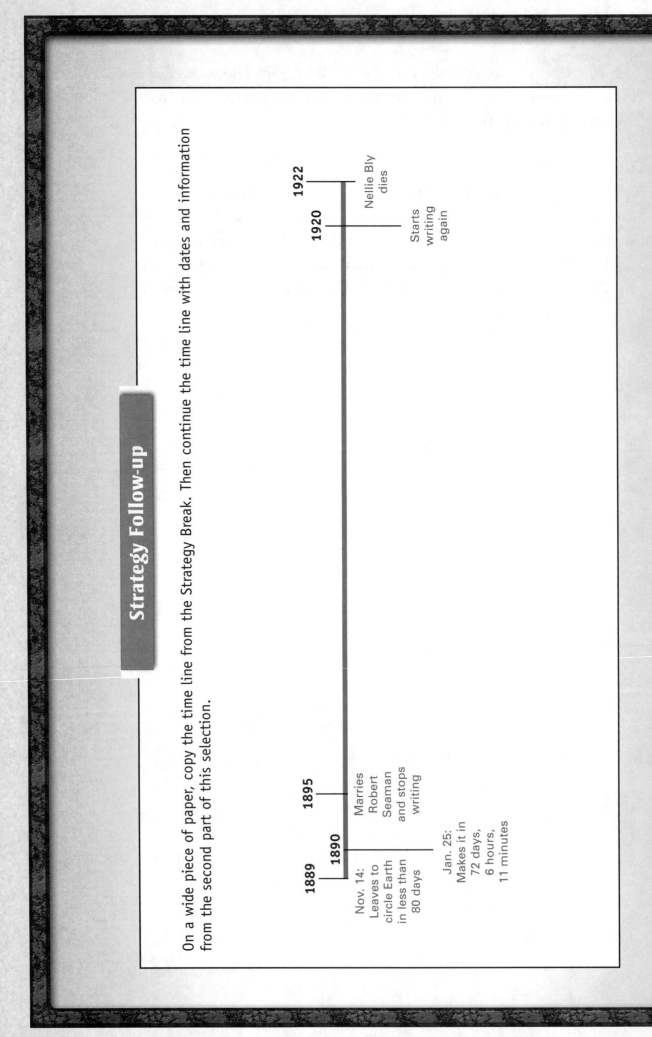

1889

1890

Nov. 14:
Leaves to
circle Earth
in less than
80 days

Jan. 25:
Makes it in
72 days,
6 hours,
11 minutes

1895

Marries
Robert
Seaman
and stops
writing

1920

Starts
writing
again

1922

Nellie Bly
dies

✓Personal Checklist

Read each question and put a check (✓) in the correct box.

1. How well do you understand who Elizabeth Cochrane was?
   - ☐ 3   (extremely well)
   - ☐ 2   (fairly well)
   - ☐ 1   (not well)

2. How well were you able to figure out if the boldfaced words were used correctly in the Vocabulary Builder?
   - ☐ 3   (extremely well)
   - ☐ 2   (fairly well)
   - ☐ 1   (not well)

3. How well do you understand why it was remarkable for Nellie Bly to write for a newspaper and travel?
   - ☐ 3   (extremely well)
   - ☐ 2   (fairly well)
   - ☐ 1   (not well)

4. How well do you understand how Nellie Bly's travels and writings helped people?
   - ☐ 3   (extremely well)
   - ☐ 2   (fairly well)
   - ☐ 1   (not well)

5. How well were you able to complete the time line in the Strategy Follow-up?
   - ☐ 3   (extremely well)
   - ☐ 2   (fairly well)
   - ☐ 1   (not well)

Vocabulary Check

Look back at the work you did in the Vocabulary Builder. Then answer each question by circling the correct letter.

1. What does the word *article* mean in the context of this selection?
   - a. an item of clothing
   - (b.) a piece of writing
   - c. the word *a*, *an*, or *the*

2. Nellie Bly wrote about many topics. Which phrase defines the word *topics*?
   - (a.) subjects that people write about
   - b. creams that people rub on sore body parts
   - c. people in insane asylums

3. What does a reporter do?
   - a. draw cartoons for a newspaper
   - (b.) writes articles for a newspaper
   - c. edits other people's stories

4. Which part of a newspaper is an editorial?
   - a. an article that describes a particular news event
   - b. an advertisement that helps someone find a job
   - (c.) an article that gives an opinion on a subject

5. What does *report* mean in the context of this selection?
   - a. the sound of a shot or an explosion
   - b. a rumor or an item of gossip
   - (c.) a written account of something

Add the numbers that you just checked to get your Personal Checklist score. Fill in your score here. Then turn to page 205 and transfer your score onto Graph 1.

Check your answers with your teacher. Give yourself 1 point for each correct answer, and fill in your Vocabulary score here. Then turn to page 205 and transfer your score onto Graph 1.

Strategy Check

Review the time line that you completed in the Strategy Follow-up. Then answer these questions:

1. How old was Elizabeth Cochrane when she changed her name to Nellie Bly?
   a. about 18
   b. about 20
   c. about 21

2. What did Bly do in 1888?
   a. left to circle the Earth
   b. married Robert Seaman
   c. published *Ten Days in a Madhouse*

3. When did Bly travel through Mexico?
   a. before she published *Ten Days in a Madhouse*
   b. after she circled the Earth
   c. after she married Robert Seaman

4. For about how long did Bly stop writing?
   a. 10 years
   b. 25 years
   c. 30 years

5. About how old was Nellie Bly when she died?
   a. 28
   b. 53
   c. 55

Comprehension Check

Review the selection if necessary. Then answer these questions:

1. Why was Nellie Bly angry when she read an editorial about women in the *Pittsburgh Dispatch*?
   a. It said that many women had hard, dull jobs.
   b. It said that women should not work outside the home.
   c. It said that women could do many jobs well.

2. What topics did Bly first report on for the *Dispatch*?
   a. slums and divorce
   b. insane asylums and mental illness
   c. all of the above

3. Why did Bly enter a New York insane asylum as a patient?
   a. to learn about the treatment of mentally ill patients
   b. to get better help for mentally ill patients
   c. both of the above

4. Why did Bly want to travel around the world?
   a. to see as many countries as she could
   b. to prove she could do it in under 80 days
   c. to report on different parts of Mexico

5. How did Bly's writings and actions help women?
   a. They proved women could do good work outside the home.
   b. They proved that women could be brave and adventuresome.
   c. Both of the above answers are correct.

Check your answers with your teacher. Give yourself 1 point for each correct answer, and fill in your Strategy score here. Then turn to page 205 and transfer your score onto Graph 1.

Check your answers with your teacher. Give yourself 1 point for each correct answer, and fill in your Comprehension score here. Then turn to page 205 and transfer your score onto Graph 1.

Extending

Choose one or more of these activities:

PLAN A TRIP AROUND THE WORLD

Use a world map or a globe to plan a trip around the world. Choose at least six places that you would like to stop. (You might pattern your trip after some of the places that Nellie Bly went. Some of the resources on this page can help, especially the PBS Web site.) Do some research, and write a paragraph telling what you might see on each one of your stops. Include a time line that shows how long you would plan to stay at each stop. Assume this is not a race but an opportunity to see each place.

WRITE A LETTER TO THE EDITOR

Think of a local issue about which you feel strongly. It might be the need to clean up a nearby park, add bike lanes to your neighborhood, or promote a charity. Then write an editorial that you can publish in your class or school newspaper. As another option, read some editorials in your local paper and respond to one of them with your own opinion. Post your letters in the classroom for others to read.

READ THE NEWSPAPER

Read the newspaper, and look for an article written by someone reporting from another country. Make a list of the words and phrases the reporter uses to describe the place. Try to find details that appeal to as many of the five senses as possible (sight, hearing, touch, taste, and sound).

Resources

Books

Bly, Nellie, and Ira Peck, ed. *Nellie Bly's Book: Around the World in 72 Days.* Twenty-First Century Books, 1999.

Emerson, Kathy Lynn. *Making Headlines: A Biography of Nellie Bly.* People in Focus. Dillon Press, 1989.

Verne, Jules. *Around the World in Eighty Days* and *Five Weeks in a Balloon.* Wordsworth Classics. Wordsworth Editions, 1997.

Web Site

http://www.pbs.org/wgbh/amex/world
The map on this PBS site shows each place Nellie Bly stopped on her 72-day world tour. Explore the site to learn more about Nellie Bly and other important women in U.S. history.

Videos/DVDs

Around the World in 72 Days. American Experience. PBS Home Video, 2003.

Around the World in Eighty Days. Adventure Classics. Plaza Entertainment, 1999.

Audio Recording

Around the World in Eighty Days (abridged) by Jules Verne. Nexos Audio Books, 1995.

Bungee Jumping: A Leap of Faith

Building Background

The article you are about to read explains why people try bungee jumping. Some of the information will be new to you. But some of it may be information that you have already heard or read. Before you read this article, think of three things that you already know about bungee jumping. Then think of three questions that you have about it. As you read the article, look for answers to your questions.

cords

courage

daredevil

gorge

plunge

thrill

vines

yo-yo

Vocabulary Builder

1. The words in the margin are all specialized vocabulary words. **Specialized vocabulary** words are related to a particular topic. For example, the words *fungicides, greenhouses, irrigation,* and *pesticides* are all related to growing vegetables.

2. Read the words and phrases below. The words in Column 1 are related to the sport of bungee jumping. Draw a line from each word in Column 1 to its definition in Column 2. Use a dictionary if you need help.

3. Save your work. You will use it again in the Vocabulary Check.

COLUMN 1	COLUMN 2
cords	person who does reckless things for fun
courage	ropes or cables
daredevil	dive
gorge	toy that goes up and down on a string
plunge	long, slender stems of a plant
thrill	excitement
vines	bravery or "guts"
yo-yo	deep, narrow valley

Strategy Builder

Outlining Main Ideas and Supporting Details

- As you know, informational articles give facts and details about a particular **topic**. You also know that most informational articles are organized according to **main ideas** and **supporting details**. These ideas and details help explain or support the topic.

- One way to keep track of main ideas and details as you read is to outline them. Some **outlines** use a system of Roman numerals (I, II, III, IV, V, and so on) and capital letters (A, B, C, D, E, and so on).

- Read the following paragraphs, which describe the Big Dipper. Then read the outline of the paragraphs. Note how the main ideas in the paragraphs are identified with Roman numerals, and the supporting details are shown with capital letters.

The Big Dipper

The Big Dipper is part of the constellation called Ursa Major, or the Great Bear. People see many different things when they look at the Big Dipper. Some Native Americans see the bowl of the Big Dipper as a bear. They see the three stars in the handle as three warriors chasing the bear. Other people see the Big Dipper as a cart. Still other people see it as plow, a bull's thigh, and even the Chinese government!

The Big Dipper had an important part in helping Southern slaves escape to freedom. Because the slaves thought that the Big Dipper looked like a ladle for drinking water, they called it the drinking gourd. They used the drinking gourd's North Star to find their way north to Canada.

The Big Dipper

I. The Big Dipper is part of Ursa Major (the Great Bear).

II. People see many different things when they look at the Big Dipper.
   A. Some Native Americans see a bear with three warriors chasing it.
   B. Other people see a cart.
   C. Others see a plow.
   D. Others see a bull's thigh.
   E. Others see the Chinese government.

III. The Big Dipper had an important part in helping slaves escape.
   A. The slaves called the Big Dipper the drinking gourd.
   B. They used its North Star to find their way to Canada.

Bungee Jumping: A Leap of Faith

Look for the main ideas as you read this article. Stop from time to time and think about how you might summarize them.

Bungee jumping began long ago as a ritual on certain islands in the South Pacific. (These islands form the present-day country of Vanuatu.) Each spring the islanders gathered **vines**. They wove them into a kind of rope. Then young men called "land divers" climbed high towers. They tied the vines to their ankles and jumped. They did it to prove their **courage**. A good jump was also supposed to help ensure healthy crops for the island.

Modern bungee jumping began in England on April 1, 1979. Note the day. It was April *Fool's* Day. The members of the Oxford Dangerous Sports Club were looking for a new **thrill**. They had heard of "land diving" and wanted to try it for themselves. So the men climbed up a high bridge, tied rubber **cords** to their ankles, and jumped. One member later said the jump was "quite pleasurable, really."

But it was a man from New Zealand who made bungee jumping a big sport. His name was Alan John Hackett. Hackett was quite a **daredevil**. He had once jumped off the Eiffel Tower in Paris, France. Now, in 1988, he wanted to give others a chance to try bungee jumping. At this time, though, the sport was illegal. So Hackett made a deal with New Zealand police. Using his own money, he would fix up a dilapidated bridge over a river **gorge**. In return, the police let him open a legal bungee jumping center on the bridge.

The center was a huge success. Hackett gave each jumper a special T-shirt. It became a hot item among daredevils. Everyone wanted one of those shirts. And since the only way to get one was to make a jump, more and more people agreed to do it. Some jumpers did really wild things. They asked to jump with an extralong cord. That way they would dip into the river before the cord pulled them back. One man put shampoo on his head. When he bounced up out of the water, he was washing his hair!

 Stop here for the Strategy Break.

Strategy Break

If you were to outline the main ideas and supporting details in this article so far, your outline might look something like this:

Bungee Jumping

I. Bungee jumping began long ago as a ritual in the South Pacific (present-day Vanuatu).
   A. Each spring "land divers" tied vines to their ankles and jumped to prove their courage.
   B. They also did it to ensure healthy crops for the island.
II. Modern bungee jumping began in England on April 1, 1979.
   A. The Oxford Dangerous Sports Club did it for a new thrill.
   B. They tied rubber cords to their ankles and jumped from a high bridge.
III. In 1988 Alan John Hackett of New Zealand made bungee jumping a big sport.
   A. The sport was illegal, but Hackett made a deal with the police to open a legal bungee jumping center.
   B. Everyone wanted one of Hackett's T-shirts, so more and more people signed up to jump.
   C. The jumpers did wild things, such as jumping with extralong cords and putting shampoo in their hair.

As you continue reading, keep paying attention to the main ideas and supporting details. At the end of this article, you will use some of them to create an outline of your own.

 Go on reading.

Bungee jumping soon caught on in the United States. It was introduced in California and Colorado. Then it spread to other states. At first, only the boldest people did it. But over time, others joined in. All kinds of people took the **plunge**. Even one man who was helped out of a wheelchair jumped. And no jumpers complained about paying $50 or more to do it.

As thrills go, it's hard to beat bungee jumping. The platforms used for the jumps are ten stories high—or higher. That means jumpers fall as far as 150 feet before the cord saves them. First-time jumpers can almost taste their fear. Jay Petrow thought about it for a year before he jumped. He said his palms began to sweat just thinking about it. Emily Trask said, "The first time I jumped, I was terrified." Nora Jacobson said, "My terror [was] cold and rippling."

There is, of course, real danger. There is no margin for error in bungee jumping. One mistake, and you're history. And while most people live to tell the tale, a few don't. In 1989 two French jumpers died when their cords broke. A third died when he slammed into a tower. In 1991 Hal Irish became the first American jumper to die. Somehow his cord became detached as he dove through the air.

So accidents *do* happen. But for many, the danger just adds to the excitement. Besides, bungee jumpers don't talk about the tragedies. They talk about the triumphs. They talk about facing their fears. And they talk about the joy of the fall itself. During a jump, a person hits speeds of sixty miles an hour. Then, when the cord tightens, the jumper springs back up into the air like a rocket. For a short time, he or she is a kind of human **yo-yo**, bounding up and down in the breeze. When the cord loses its bounce, the ride is over.

Even then, though, some of the joy remains. Jumpers feel both happy and relieved when it's over. Most laugh and smile as they are unhooked from the cord. "Hey, look at me! I did it!" many of them shout. It is, as one person said, "a natural high." Bungee jumpers even have a name for this soaring feeling. They call it the post-bungee grin. Maybe someday you'll decide to make that leap of faith and share that grin. All it takes is a little money—and a lot of nerve. ●

Strategy Follow-up

Work with a group of classmates to complete this activity. First, review the second part of this article. Then, on a separate sheet of paper, create an outline that begins with "IV. Bungee jumping soon caught on in the United States." Be sure to include only the most important ideas, and skip unnecessary details. If you can, compare your outline with those of other groups. See if your outlines all contain similar information. Revise your group's outline if necessary.

✓Personal Checklist

Read each question and put a check (✓) in the correct box.

1. In Building Background, how well were you able to think of three questions about bungee jumping?
   - ☐ 3 (extremely well)
   - ☐ 2 (fairly well)
   - ☐ 1 (not well)

2. In the Vocabulary Builder, how well were you able to match the specialized vocabulary words and their definitions?
   - ☐ 3 (extremely well)
   - ☐ 2 (fairly well)
   - ☐ 1 (not well)

3. In the Strategy Follow-up, how well were you able to summarize the second part of the article?
   - ☐ 3 (extremely well)
   - ☐ 2 (fairly well)
   - ☐ 1 (not well)

4. How well do you understand the dangers of bungee jumping?
   - ☐ 3 (extremely well)
   - ☐ 2 (fairly well)
   - ☐ 1 (not well)

5. How well do you understand why people bungee jump in spite of the dangers?
   - ☐ 3 (extremely well)
   - ☐ 2 (fairly well)
   - ☐ 1 (not well)

Vocabulary Check

Look back at the work you did in the Vocabulary Builder. Then answer each question by circling the correct letter.

1. Which vocabulary word best describes a personality trait that all bungee jumpers share?
   - a. thrill
   - b. yo-yo
   - (c.) courage

2. Which vocabulary word describes a person who does reckless things for the thrill of it?
   - a. yo-yo
   - (b.) daredevil
   - b. gorge

3. Alan Hackett set up his bunging jumping center on a bridge over a river gorge. Which phrase describes a gorge?
   - a. mountain with water running down it
   - (b.) deep valley with water running through it
   - c. dry, flat land with water running through

4. Why does the article compare bungee jumpers to human yo-yos?
   - (a.) because they both bounce up and down from a cord
   - b. because they both fly in and out from a cord
   - c. because they both spin in circles as they bounce

5. Which vocabulary word best describes the action of a jumper as he or she dives off a platform or bridge?
   - a. courage
   - (b.) plunge
   - c. thrill

Add the numbers that you just checked to get your Personal Checklist score. Fill in your score here. Then turn to page 205 and transfer your score onto Graph 1.

Personal
Vocabulary
Strategy
Comprehension
TOTAL SCORE
✓ T

Check your answers with your teacher. Give yourself 1 point for each correct answer, and fill in your Vocabulary score here. Then turn to page 205 and transfer your score onto Graph 1.

Personal
Vocabulary
Strategy
Comprehension
TOTAL SCORE
✓ T

Strategy Check

Look back at your summary for the second part of this article. Then answer these questions:

1. Which sentence does not summarize one of this article's main ideas?
    - (a.) At first, only the boldest people did it.
    - b. As thrills go, it's hard to beat bungee jumping.
    - c. Bungee jumping accidents *do* happen.

2. Which sentence *does* summarize one of this article's main ideas?
    - a. Hal Irish became the first American jumper to die.
    - b. Most laugh and smile as they are unhooked from the cord.
    - (c.) As thrills go, it's hard to beat bungee jumping.

3. Which phrase best states the topic of this article?
    - (a.) bungee jumping
    - b. bungee accidents
    - c. bungee jumpers

4. Name one of the dangers of bungee jumping that this article describes.
    - a. bouncing like a yo-yo
    - (b.) having the cord break
    - c. having the cord tighten

5. Which sentence best summarizes this entire article?
    - a. Bungee jumping began long ago as a ritual.
    - b. First-time jumpers can almost taste their fear.
    - (c.) Bungee jumping is a real leap of faith.

Comprehension Check

Review the article if necessary. Then answer these questions:

1. Where did the earliest bungee jumping take place?
    - a. in England
    - b. in California
    - (c.) in the South Pacific

2. Why did modern bungee jumping begin?
    - (a.) A sports club was looking for a new thrill.
    - b. Some islanders wanted to ensure healthy crops.
    - c. A man wanted to bungee jump off the Eiffel Tower.

3. During a jump, what speed can a bungee jumper reach?
    - a. six miles an hour
    - b. sixteen miles an hour
    - (c.) sixty miles an hour

4. How did the first American bungee jumper die?
    - a. He slammed into a tower.
    - (b.) His cord became detached.
    - c. His cord broke.

5. Which quote sums up why some people bungee jump?
    - a. It was "quite pleasurable, really."
    - b. "Hey, look at me! I did it!"
    - (c.) Both of the above answers are correct.

Check your answers with your teacher. Give yourself 1 point for each correct answer, and fill in your Strategy score here. Then turn to page 205 and transfer your score onto Graph 1.

Personal
Vocabulary
Strategy
Comprehension
TOTAL SCORE
✓ T

Check your answers with your teacher. Give yourself 1 point for each correct answer, and fill in your Comprehension score here. Then turn to page 205 and transfer your score onto Graph 1.

Personal
Vocabulary
Strategy
Comprehension
TOTAL SCORE
✓ T

Extending

Choose one or both of these activities:

MAKE A CATALOG

Make a short catalog of some of the equipment necessary for safe bungee jumping. The Web site listed on this page will give you a place to start. Or you can talk to someone at your local sporting goods store. Include your own drawing or a photo with the description of each item. Tell what the item is for and how it is used.

MAKE "STAT SHEETS"

Research the most popular bungee jumping locations in the world. Then write a "stat sheet" for each location that includes the following information:
- the country, state, and/or town in which the jump is located
- its height in both feet and meters
- how many people have made the jump from that location
- the most unusual jump or jumps made from that location

Resources

Book

Glaser, Jim. *Bungee Jumping*. Extreme Sports. Capstone Press, 2000.

Web Site

http://www.fettke.com/bungee
This site includes photos, videos, and information about bungee jumping.

Too-Tall Twyla

Building Background

Have you ever played or watched a basketball game? What words did you use or hear? Think about all of the **specialized vocabulary words** that people use during basketball games, such as *dribble, rebound,* and *fast break.* Add the words to the concept map (web) below. As you read "Too-Tall Twyla" look for more basketball words to add to your web. When you finish reading the story, compare your web with a classmate.

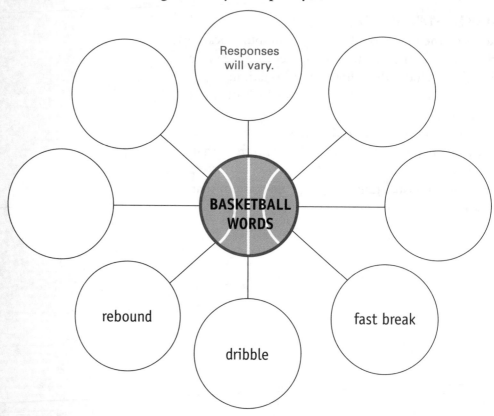

Responses will vary.

BASKETBALL WORDS

rebound

dribble

fast break

coed

forfeit

routines

nickname

MVP

hesitate

accurate

stunned

Vocabulary Builder

1. Read the vocabulary words in the margin, and think about what they mean. Then read the sentences below. On each line, write the vocabulary word in parentheses that best fits the sentence. As you read the story, you may decide to change some of your answers.

   a. If your team has to quit a game before finishing, you must
      _____ forfeit _____ the game. (forfeit, routine)

   b. The _____ MVP _____ of a game is usually the one who played the best. (nickname, MVP)

c. If your ball goes through the hoop every time you shoot, you

are _____accurate_____ . (hesitate, accurate)

d. A team that has a mix of female and male players is a

_____coed_____ team. (coed, stunned)

2. On a separate sheet of paper, write a sentence for each word that you didn't circle. Use story context to help you, or look up the words in a dictionary.

3. Save your work. You will use it again in the Vocabulary Check.

Strategy Builder

Making Predictions While Reading a Story

- While you read, you often make predictions. A **prediction** is a kind of guess. To make a prediction, act like a detective. Use the story's most important information, or clues, to figure out what might happen next.

- The clues in a story are sometimes called context clues. **Context** is the information that comes before or after a word or situation to help you understand it better. In this story some of the context clues are basketball terms. If you don't know a lot about basketball, you might ask a classmate to explain some of the terms.

- As you read "Too-Tall Twyla," you will stop twice to make predictions. At each Strategy Break, you will be asked to write down which context clues helped you make your predictions. Then, after you finish reading the story, you will look back at your predictions and check your work.

Too-Tall Twyla

by Russell Lewis

See if you can use clues that the author provides to help you make predictions while you read.

Shawn and Terry caught the flu, Roland broke his leg, and Jared moved away. Suddenly our Midcity boys' basketball team was down to five players and zero substitutes.

Coach Allens talked to us after school. "League rules require at least one player on the bench. We have two choices. One, we can **forfeit** the championship game with Central this Friday."

"Forfeit? No way!" I exclaimed. "They only beat us by two points last year. This is *our* year to win!"

"Can't we just suit up some kid—any kid?" Mark asked.

Mark was our superstar, the reason we knew this was our year to finally beat Central. He never missed when he had an open shot. He was the league's best shot blocker and rebounder, too. The only time our subs got on the court was when Coach wanted to give Mark a breather!

Well, league rules or not, Coach wasn't about to suit up just any kid. "What if one of our players gets hurt?" he asked. "That sub would have to go into the game, right?"

We all nodded.

"So we need the best player we can get, right?"

We all nodded again.

"So choice number two is..." Coach paused. "The league office said Twyla could play for us."

"Too-Tall Twyla?" everyone exclaimed.

Twyla was my big sister. She was also captain of our girls' basketball team. Twyla had loved to play basketball ever since fourth grade, when she suddenly shot up six inches taller than any boy in the class. That's when she got the nickname "Too-Tall."

She was a pretty good player, too. So when we thought about our choices—either forfeit the game or let Twyla sit on the bench—we didn't **hesitate**. We became the first **coed** basketball team in Midcity's history!

We had one more practice before the big game. Coach had us practice our fast breaks, passing the ball back and forth as we raced down the court.

"Hey, Sis," I yelled. "Don't try to shoot every time you get the ball. Pass the ball to me!"

"But I was open," Twyla yelled back. "Didn't Coach say to shoot if you had an open shot?" Her shot had just swished through the hoop, touching nothing but net.

"Yeah, but he also said to pass the ball around, be a team player!" I was kind of embarrassed. *My* shot had just bounced off the rim, missing badly. Oh well, I thought. It'll be Mark, not Twyla, in the real game.

The real game for the league championship was tomorrow against Central. This was going to be our year, we thought—especially with Mark playing as well as he was.

On Friday the whole school was buzzing. At lunchtime the cheerleaders did their **routines** in the cafeteria. They made each of us players stand up as we were introduced. When Mark's name was called, the whole place went bonkers. Mark was our superstar, and all the kids knew it!

 Stop here for Strategy Break #1.

Strategy Break #1

Use the information in the story to help you answer these questions:

1. What do you predict will happen next?

Students' responses will vary but should be supported with clues from the text.

2. Why do you think so?

_____

_____

3. What clues from the story helped you make your prediction(s)?

_____

_____

Go on reading to see what happens.

After school everyone crowded into the gymnasium. When we ran onto the court to begin our warm-up drills, the cheerleaders jumped up and down, waving their pompons. My heart began pumping like a jackhammer, my mouth felt as if it were stuffed with cotton, and my knees were shaking so hard I thought they would buckle.

After we ran through a few drills, I began to feel a little more normal. Then the warning buzzer sounded, and Coach called us over for a meeting.

"Remember what you've learned," he said as we huddled around him. "Teamwork—passing—look for the open player. If they double-team Mark, that means someone else is open."

We broke out of the huddle with a shout. I was still nervous. It was a good feeling, though, being all pumped up for the game. I knew that this year we were going to win!

We jumped off to an early six-point lead, then held our own until halftime. Mark shot 80 percent from the floor and had five rebounds. No one on Central's team could even come close to matching up with him.

They must have talked it over during halftime. When the second half started, they had two players guarding Mark. That stopped us for a little while, but not for long.

"Look for the open player!" someone yelled from our bench. It was Twyla. She was standing on the sidelines screaming at us as we raced down the court. "You can do it!" she yelled. "Yea, Midcity! Yea, team!"

I had to admit she was right. Every time they put two defenders on Mark, one of us was always left open. But our shooting wasn't as **accurate** as Mark's. Central slowly crept back to within one basket of tying the game.

Then disaster struck. Cutting between two Central players, Mark tripped and fell. The referees stopped play when they saw him rolling on the floor in pain, holding his left ankle.

"It's a bad sprain," Coach announced. "Mark's out for the rest of the game." His face was grim as he turned to Twyla. "Report to the scoring table, Twyla. You're going in for Mark."

Twyla looked scared. She looked at Coach with a frozen expression on her face.

I knew just how she felt. I remembered my jackhammer heart, my cottony mouth, my shaking knees. "You'll do O.K., Twyla," I said. "Just remember what Coach says. Look for the open man . . . er, uh, person!"

Everyone laughed at that. Even Twyla. Then the buzzer sounded, and we took our places on the floor again.

 Stop here for Strategy Break #2.

Strategy Break #2

Use the information in the story to help you answer these questions:

1. Do your earlier predictions match what happened? _____ Why or why not?
   Students' responses will vary but should be supported with clues from the
   text.

2. What do you predict will happen next?
   _____
   _____

3. Why do you think so?
   _____
   _____

4. What clues from the story helped you make your prediction(s)?
   _____
   _____

 Go on reading to see what happens.

"Look what we've got!" shouted the Central players. "The Midcity *girls'* team!" They cracked up laughing. They thought the game was all wrapped up now.

That's the way it looked to me, too. Twyla was scared stiff and not playing well. It was as if we only had four players instead of five. The Central team didn't even bother guarding her. They put the extra player on whichever one of us had the ball.

With three minutes to go, the score was tied. Soon we were down by one basket, then by two. By the time Central pulled into a ten-point lead, we began to play as if we had just about given up.

Even when Sis blocked a shot, we didn't really pay much attention. After all, her **nickname** wasn't "Too-Tall" for nothing! But the next time she blocked a shot, she rebounded the ball herself, dribbled the length of the floor, and sank an easy lay-up.

That got everyone's attention. It jarred Twyla out of her frozen state, too. She blocked shot after shot, rebounded at both ends of the court, and passed the ball to the open player on our fast breaks. She swished nearly every one of her own shots.

The Central team was **stunned** and confused. They weren't laughing now.

Then, with the score tied and only seconds left on the clock, Twyla blocked another Central shot. Expecting another fast break, I started to run up the floor.

"Double-team her!" someone on their team shouted. Two Central players trapped Twyla in the corner.

Twisting her head left and right, she spotted me in the lane, wide open. With a quick head fake, Twyla drew one of the Central players out of position, then pushed a two-handed bounce pass to me under his outstretched arms.

I took the pass, made an easy lay-up as the buzzer sounded—and it was all over.

Final score—Midcity 48, Central 46. We had won! We were the new league champions!

We hugged and laughed and slapped high-fives. Mark had a big grin on his face. So did Coach. Everyone was slapping Twyla on the back. She was grinning, too.

"We're a girl's team, all right," Mark said, "and her name is Twyla! But 'Too-Tall' isn't the right nickname for our **MVP**."

I laughed. "I know her new nickname. It's what Central's probably calling her right now—'Too-Much' Twyla!" ●

Strategy Follow-up

Go back and look at the predictions that you wrote in this lesson. Do any of them match what actually happened in the story? Why or why not?

✓Personal Checklist

Read each question and put a check (✓) in the correct box.

1. How well were you able to understand the basketball terms in this story?
   - ☐ 3 (extremely well)
   - ☐ 2 (fairly well)
   - ☐ 1 (not well)

2. In the Vocabulary Builder, how many words were you able to use correctly in sentences?
   - ☐ 3 (6–8 words)
   - ☐ 2 (3–5 words)
   - ☐ 1 (0–2 words)

3. How well were you able to use context clues to predict what would happen next in this story?
   - ☐ 3 (extremely well)
   - ☐ 2 (fairly well)
   - ☐ 1 (not well)

4. How well do you understand why Twyla was chosen to play on the team?
   - ☐ 3 (extremely well)
   - ☐ 2 (fairly well)
   - ☐ 1 (not well)

5. How well do you understand why no one guarded Twyla when she first began to play?
   - ☐ 3 (extremely well)
   - ☐ 2 (fairly well)
   - ☐ 1 (not well)

Vocabulary Check

Look back at the work you did in the Vocabulary Builder. Then answer each question by circling the correct letter.

1. Why does Mark call Twyla the MVP of the game?
   a. because she came in off the bench and played
   (b.) because she did the most to help the team win
   c. because she was a girl on a boys' team

2. What does the word *hesitate* mean?
   (a.) wait
   b. move
   c. decide

3. Why was Central's team stunned during the game?
   a. They didn't expect Mark to hurt himself.
   (b.) They didn't expect Twyla to play as she did.
   c. They didn't expect to win the game.

4. Which of the following is not a routine?
   a. eating a donut after school every day
   (b.) giving one person a special nickname
   c. practicing lay-ups and free throws

5. The narrator says that his team's shooting isn't as accurate as Mark's. What is another word for *accurate*?
   a. poor
   b. imperfect
   (c.) exact

Add the numbers that you just checked to get your Personal Checklist score. Fill in your score here. Then turn to page 205 and transfer your score onto Graph 1.

Personal
Vocabulary
Strategy
Comprehension
TOTAL SCORE

Check your answers with your teacher. Give yourself 1 point for each correct answer, and fill in your Vocabulary score here. Then turn to page 205 and transfer your score onto Graph 1.

Personal
Vocabulary
Strategy
Comprehension
TOTAL SCORE

Strategy Check

Look back at what you wrote at each Strategy Break. Then answer these questions:

1. At Strategy Break #1, if you had predicted that Twyla's team would win the game, which clue would have best supported your prediction?

   a. Shawn and Terry caught the flu.

   b. "This is our year to win."

   c. "Too-Tall Twyla?" everyone exclaimed.

2. If you had predicted that Twyla would have to join the game, which clue would have best supported your prediction?

   a. "What if one of our players gets hurt?"

   b. Twyla was my big sister.

   c. "Too-Tall Twyla?" everyone exclaimed.

3. At Strategy Break #2, which prediction would not have fit this story?

   a. Twyla will get hurt too.

   b. Twyla will play for the other team.

   c. Twyla will make many baskets.

4. At Strategy Break #2, if you had predicted that the narrator's team would win, which clue would have best supported your prediction?

   a. She was a pretty good player, too.

   b. Mark was our superstar.

   c. Twyla look scared.

5. Which clue helped you know that Twyla was a good basketball player?

   a. She had a nickname.

   b. She loved to play basketball.

   c. Her shots didn't even touch the net.

Comprehension Check

Review the story if necessary. Then answer these questions:

1. Why is this game so important to both teams?

   a. It is the league championship.

   b. It is the first game of the year.

   c. It is the first game Twyla will play.

2. Why is it so unusual for Twyla to play on this team?

   a. Mark never got hurt before.

   b. Twyla was a girl on a boys' team.

   c. Twyla never passed the ball.

3. Why does Twyla have to play in the second half?

   a. Mark fouls out of the game.

   b. Mark is tired and leaves the game.

   c. Mark gets hurt and leaves the game.

4. What happens to make Twyla and her team start playing better?

   a. Mark gets hurt.

   b. Twyla makes a lay-up.

   c. The buzzer sounds.

5. Why might Central call Twyla "Too-Much Twyla?"

   a. because she has so much skill

   b. because she doesn't pass the ball enough

   c. because she is gaining weight

Check your answers with your teacher. Give yourself 1 point for each correct answer, and fill in your Strategy score here. Then turn to page 205 and transfer your score onto Graph 1.

Check your answers with your teacher. Give yourself 1 point for each correct answer, and fill in your Comprehension score here. Then turn to page 205 and transfer your score onto Graph 1.

Extending

Choose one or both of these activities:

MAKE BASKETBALL CARDS OR POSTERS

Make basketball cards or posters for your school's or league's team. Include a picture of each player, information about the position he or she plays, average points scored per game, and other important statistics. Use the resources listed on this page for ideas about what to include. Display the cards during every game.

CREATE "PLAYERS WANTED" POSTERS

Learn about the Women's National Basketball League and what it takes to become a player. Create a "wanted" poster for a particular WNBA team. Include all the requirements and personal characteristics that a player would need for this league. You can use one of the resources listed on this page for ideas and information.

Resources

Books

Dixon, Tamecka, Judith Love Cohen, and Janice J. Martin. *You Can Be a Woman Basketball Player.* Cascade Pass, 1999.

Herman, Gail. *WNBW: We Got Next!* Grosset & Dunlap, 1998.

Owens, Thomas S. *Collecting Basketball Cards.* Millbrook Press, 1998.

Rosenthal, Bert. *Alonzo Mourning.* Chelsea House, 1998.

Web Site

http://www.wnba.com
Here is the place to get up-to-the-minute information on the WNBA.

Videos/DVDs

60 Minute Basketball Skills Workout. Fast Forward Market, 1994.

Defense: Basketball for Women. Tapeworm, 1998.

Game Smart: How to Watch Basketball. Lute Olson, narr. Tapeworm, 1997.

Let's Play Basketball with Mike Krzyewski (1994). ESPN Video, 2000.

Teaching Kids Basketball with John Wooden (1984). ESPN Video, 1998.

Learning New Words

VOCABULARY

From Lesson 9
• daredevil

Compound Words

A compound word is made up of two words put together. In Lesson 9 you read about daredevil bungee jumpers. *Daredevil* is made of the words *dare* and *devil*. *Daredevil* is a name given to a person who does recklessly daring things for fun and thrills.

Fill in each blank with a compound word by combining a word from Row 1 with a word from Row 2.

Row 1:   suit   cook   tear   table   wrist

Row 2:   ware   cloth   watch   jerker   case

1. very sad movie or book = _____tearjerker_____

2. bag used to hold things while traveling = _____suitcase_____

3. clock that's worn on the arm = _____wristwatch_____

4. pots and pans = _____cookware_____

5. covering for an eating surface = _____tablecloth_____

Suffixes

From Lesson 8
• reporter

A suffix is a word part that is added to the end of a root word. When you add a suffix, you often change the root word's meaning and function. For example, the suffix *-ful* means "full of," so the root word *pain* changes from a noun to an adjective meaning "full of pain."

-er

The suffix *-er* is a special kind of suffix. It turns a verb into a noun that means "a person who _____." In Nellie Bly's biography you learned that a *reporter* is a person who writes reports, or articles, for a newspaper.

Write the word that describes each person below.

1. a person who builds houses   _____builder_____

2. a person who writes books   _____writer_____

3. a person who leads others   _____leader_____

4. a person who designs things   _____designer_____

-or

The suffix *-or* does the same thing as *-er:* It turns a verb into a noun that means "a person who _____." Besides learning about reporters in Nellie Bly's biography, you learned about editors. In that selection, the *editor* was the person who ran the newspaper. However, an editor also can be a person who edits articles or books.

Write a description for each person below.

1. decorator   a person who decorates houses

2. sculptor   a person who sculpts things

3. actor   a person who acts in movies

4. creator   a person who creates things

5. visitor   a person who visits others

-ist

The suffix *-ist* has a similar function to *-er* and *-or.* It, too, turns words into nouns that mean "a person who _____." For example, in Lesson 7 you learned that Marian Anderson's *accompanist* was the person who accompanied her, or played the piano with her, while she sang.

Now write the word that describes each person below.

1. a person who plays the piano   pianist

2. a person who makes or performs art   artist

3. a person who tours a place   tourist

4. a person who's an expert in chemistry   chemist

5. a person who terrorizes others   terrorist

VOCABULARY

From Lesson 8
• editor

From Lesson 7
• accompanist

Dava's Talent

Building Background

"Dava's Talent" is a story set in Morocco, a country in the northwestern tip of Africa, where raising sheep has always been a way of life. People who work in the deserts of Morocco often wear long-sleeved, hooded robes called djellabahs (jə lä′ bə). Djellabahs help protect people from the scorching sun and drifting sand.

bleat

flock

herd

lambs

sheared

sheepcote

shepherd

Vocabulary Builder

1. The words in the margin are all related to sheep and their care. Read the words and see if you recognize any of them.

2. Before you read "Dava's Talent," try to match as many of the words in Column 1 to their definitions in Column 2 by drawing lines between them.

3. Then, as you read, find the rest of the words in context and try to figure out their meanings. Match the rest of the words, and change any of your earlier matches.

4. Save your work. You will use it again in the Vocabulary Check.

COLUMN 1

sheared
shepherd
herd
sheepcote
bleat
flock
lambs

COLUMN 2

baby sheep
cut the wool from a sheep
group of sheep
person who cares for sheep
small fenced yard where sheep are kept
sound a sheep makes
move sheep as a group

Strategy Builder

Identifying Cause-and-Effect Relationships in Stories

- Stories are often built on a framework of **cause-and-effect relationships**, similar to real life. For example, picture yourself asleep in bed, happily dreaming away. You hear a loud buzz as your alarm goes off (cause), and you wake up (effect). If you were to ask yourself, "What happened?" you would realize that you woke up. If you asked, "Why did it happen?" the answer would be "because the alarm sounded."

- Pay attention to the causes and effects as you read the following paragraph.

> Mighty Pup is my favorite puppy in the litter. But he's not my mom's favorite. One day he was bouncing around so much that he knocked over his water bowl. That got the floor *and* his paws all wet. Next he put his wet paws in the food bowl and then bounded around the room. He made paw marks all over the furniture! All of Mighty Pup's noise caused Mom to come into the room. When she saw what he had done, she exclaimed, "Oh no! That's a Mighty *Messy* Pup!"

- If you wanted to track the causes and effects in the paragraph, you could put them on a **cause-and-effect chain**. It might look like this:

Dava's Talent

by Lee Ebler

As you read the first part of this story, you can apply the strategies that you just learned. To find the causes and effects, keep asking yourself, "What happened?" and "Why did it happen?"

Dava loved sheep. He loved their cries and their thick coats. He loved to play with the **lambs** and he especially loved to fill the woolsack when Papa **sheared**. Dava's papa was a **shepherd**, and his family lived near a river and mountains in a small village in Morocco.

Dava thought sheep were wonderful, but he could not **herd** them very well. When he wanted them to go right, they went left. When he wanted them to go uphill, they went downhill. And when he wanted them to drink, they stood in the brook and splashed while Dava got wet and sneezy.

"All your forefathers have been shepherds," said Uncle Eban. "Why won't the sheep obey you?"

"I don't know," said Dava sadly.

"Maybe if you wear Papa's clothes," suggested his sister Leah, "the sheep will think you're Papa and mind you."

So Dava put on Papa's djellabah. The sleeves covered his hands, and the hem dragged on the ground. When he walked toward the sheep, he tripped and fell. The sheep were not fooled. While Dava struggled out of the djellabah, they got into the garden and ate the melons.

"Perhaps you should walk slower when you lead the sheep," said Mama. "Sheep do not like bouncy shepherds."

So Dava walked slowly. But he was so slow that the sheep thought he was a tree. They chewed on his sash, leaving it sticky and shredded. Dava decided that walking slowly wasn't the answer.

"Every shepherd has a talent to offer," said Papa. "When you find yours, the sheep will obey. Uncle Eban plays the flute. My talent is singing. We both lead the herd with our music."

"Maybe I'm a singer like Papa," said Dava to Bright Eyes, the smallest sheep. He began to sing in a loud voice about streams and green grass. He thought he had found his talent until Leah chased him away from the house.

"Your music sounds like rocks falling!" she said, slamming the door.

"I will loan you my flute," said Uncle Eban. "It's clear that you are not a singer."

So Dava played the flute. He practiced inside the **sheepcote** until Uncle Eban stuck wool in his ears and the sheep began to **bleat**. They did not like his flute playing.

"You screech like a hawk!" said Uncle Eban, taking back the flute. "You're scaring the sheep."

"I will never be a good shepherd," said Dava to Bright Eyes.

 Stop here for the Strategy Break.

Strategy Break

If you were to create a cause-and-effect chain for this story so far, it might look like this:

CAUSES	EFFECTS
Dava puts on his Papa's djellabah.	The sheep are not fooled. They go into the garden and eat the melons.
Dava walks more slowly.	The sheep think he is a tree and chew on his sash.
Dava sings in a loud voice.	Leah chases him away and says his music sounds like rocks falling.
Dava plays Uncle Eban's flute.	He scares the sheep, and they begin to bleat.

 Go on reading to see what happens.

One day a terrible thing happened. Papa and Uncle Eban were repairing the stone wall. They were working fast because a storm was coming. Suddenly one of the rocks fell on Papa's foot. Dava could see that it hurt. He started toward Papa, but Uncle Eban stopped him.

"I'll take your papa home, but you must lead the sheep back by yourself. Take them slowly, as you have learned."

"But I can't," said Dava. "The sheep won't listen to me."

"Please try," said Uncle Eban.

Dava watched Papa and Uncle Eban leave. The sky was getting dark, and the wind was rising. The sheep began to bleat.

Dava picked up the staff and swished it around. "Hoy!" he shouted. "Hoy, Trud and Bright Eyes. Hoy, Spots!"

But the sheep did not listen. Thunder echoed over the mountains, and the frightened sheep moved toward the broken wall. If Dava didn't stop them, they would run into the desert.

Almost without thinking, Dava began to whistle softly. The sheep didn't hear it, but the whistle calmed Dava. So he whistled louder. Beside him, Bright Eyes stopped trembling.

Then Dava had an idea. He stood in the center of the herd and whistled. He whistled a hopeful tune, a cheerful tune, an everything's-all-right tune. And the sheep understood. They grew calm, because Dava was calm. Still whistling, Dava led them toward the sheepcote. He knew the sheep trusted him now. He felt as if he were part of the **flock**.

I am a whistler, thought Dava, smiling.

The sheep came safely home that day, and Papa was soon feeling well enough to hear Dava's story. ●

Strategy Follow-up

Complete this cause-and-effect chain for the second part of the story. Copy it onto another sheet of paper if you need more room to write.

CAUSES

- A rock falls on Papa's foot.
- Dava swishes the staff around and calls to the sheep.
- Dava begins to whistle softly.
- Dava whistles louder.
- Dava whisltes a cheerful tune.
- Dava leads the sheep safely home.

EFFECTS

- Dava must lead the sheep back by himself
- They do not listen. They move toward the wall.
- The sheep don't hear it, but it calms Dava.
- Bright Eyes stops trembling.
- The sheep understand and grow calm.
- He realizes he is a whistler.

✓Personal Checklist

Read each question and put a check (✓) in the correct box.

1. How well do you understand why people wear djellabahs in Morocco?
   - ☐ 3   (extremely well)
   - ☐ 2   (fairly well)
   - ☐ 1   (not well)

2. How well were you able to match the words and definitions in the Vocabulary Builder?
   - ☐ 3   (extremely well)
   - ☐ 2   (fairly well)
   - ☐ 1   (not well)

3. How well do you understand why Dava has trouble getting the sheep to follow him?
   - ☐ 3   (extremely well)
   - ☐ 2   (fairly well)
   - ☐ 1   (not well)

4. How well do you understand why the sheep are in danger when the wall is broken?
   - ☐ 3   (extremely well)
   - ☐ 2   (fairly well)
   - ☐ 1   (not well)

5. How well were you able to complete the cause-and-effect chain in the Strategy Follow-up?
   - ☐ 3   (extremely well)
   - ☐ 2   (fairly well)
   - ☐ 1   (not well)

Vocabulary Check

Look back at the work you did in the Vocabulary Builder. Then answer each question by circling the correct letter.

1. What is a sheepcote?
   - (a.) a small fenced yard where sheep are kept
   - b   a robe that protects from the sun and sand
   - c. a tool that is used to cut off a sheep's coat

2. What do you call a group of sheep?
   - a. a bleat
   - (b.) a flock
   - c. a sheepcote

3. What is most similar to a sheep being sheared?
   - (a.) a person getting a haircut
   - b. a person having an operation
   - c. a dog walking on a leash

4. What might someone herd besides sheep?
   - a. birds
   - b. cats
   - (c.) cattle

5. What are baby sheep called?
   - a. sheep
   - b. flocks
   - (c.) lambs

Add the numbers that you just checked to get your Personal Checklist score. Fill in your score here. Then turn to page 205 and transfer your score onto Graph 1.

Personal	
Vocabulary	
Strategy	
Comprehension	
TOTAL SCORE	

✓ T

Check your answers with your teacher. Give yourself 1 point for each correct answer, and fill in your Vocabulary score here. Then turn to page 205 and transfer your score onto Graph 1.

Personal	
Vocabulary	
Strategy	
Comprehension	
TOTAL SCORE	

✓ T

Strategy Check

Look back at the cause-and-effect chain that you completed in the Strategy Follow-up. Then answer these questions:

1. What effect does Dava's father's injury have?
   a. The sheep follow Dava's father to the wall.
   b. Dava must lead the sheep back by himself.
   c. The sheep understand and grow calm.

2. Dava swishes the staff around and calls to the sheep. What effect does this have on them?
   a. The sheep do not listen and move toward the wall.
   b. The sheep grow very frightened.
   c. The sheep understand and grow calm.

3. What causes Bright Eyes to stop trembling?
   a. A rock falls on Papa's foot.
   b. Dava calls to the sheep.
   c. Dava begins to whistle louder.

4. What is the effect when Dava begins to whistle softly?
   a. The sheep begin bleating very loudly.
   b. The sheep don't hear it, but it calms Dava.
   c. The sheep begin moving toward the wall.

5. What causes Dava to realize he is a whistler?
   a. His whistling calmed down the sheep.
   b. His whistling led the sheep safely home.
   c. Both of the above answers are correct.

Comprehension Check

Review the story if necessary. Then answer these questions:

1. What is Dava's problem at the beginning of the story?
   a. Dava thinks sheep are awful, but he must herd them all the time.
   b. Dava thinks sheep are wonderful, but he can't herd them very well.
   c. Dava thinks sheep are wonderful, and they go just where he wants them to.

2. Why does Dava wear his father's djellabah?
   a. so the sheep will think Dava is his father and will listen to him
   b. so the sheep will think Dava is funny and will listen to him
   c. so the sheep will be afraid of Dava and will listen to him

3. Why does Dava sing to the sheep?
   a. He loves to sing, and he wants to entertain the sheep.
   b. Leah and Uncle Eban ask Dava to sing them a song.
   c. He's trying to find his talent so the sheep will obey him.

4. What makes Dava feel as if he is part of the flock?
   a. He can bleat just like the sheep can.
   b. He knows the sheep trust him now.
   c. Both of the above answers are correct.

5. What does Dava's talent turn out to be?
   a. whistling
   b. singing
   c. shouting

Check your answers with your teacher. Give yourself 1 point for each correct answer, and fill in your Strategy score here. Then turn to page 205 and transfer your score onto Graph 1.

Personal
Vocabulary
Strategy
Comprehension
TOTAL SCORE
✓ T

Check your answers with your teacher. Give yourself 1 point for each correct answer, and fill in your Comprehension score here. Then turn to page 205 and transfer your score onto Graph 1.

Personal
Vocabulary
Strategy
Comprehension
TOTAL SCORE
✓ T

Extending

Choose one or both of these activities:

LEARN ABOUT MOROCCO

Work with a small group of classmates to find information about Morocco. Use the resources listed on this page or ones that you find yourselves. Divide up the following topics, and share your findings in an oral or written report: history, government, agriculture, land and climate, people, customs, foods.

HOLD A CONTEST

Here's a contest for you to try: Form teams of three or four students each. Have a referee set a timer for a certain amount of time. When the referee says, "Go," brainstorm a list of stories or songs in which a shepherd, a sheep, or a lamb plays a role. When the referee says, "Stop," compare lists. Which team has the most stories or songs? How many stories or songs did both teams list? If you'd like, repeat the same procedure with stories or songs that have to do with whistling or singing.

Resources

Books

Blauer, Ettagale, and Jason Laure. *Morocco.* Enchantment of the World. Children's Book Press, 1999.

Harmes, Jules M. *The Children of Morocco.* Turtleback, 1995.

Seward, Pat. *Morocco.* Cultures of the World. Benchmark Books, 1995.

Sheridan, Noel. *Morocco in Pictures.* Visual Geography. Lerner Publications, 1996.

LESSON 12 Feeling Sleepy?

Building Background

How much sleep do you usually get each night? People need different amounts of sleep at different ages. Study the chart and answer the questions below it to decide if you get enough sleep.

Age	Actual Hours of Sleep*	Hours of Sleep Needed**
9 and under	9 ¼	10 ¼
10–11	9	9 ¾
12	8 ¼	9 ¼
13 and older	7 ¾	9

* Source: *Zillions* Opinion Poll, January/February 1998.
** Source: The Center for Pediatric Sleep Disorders at Boston Children's Hospital.

1. What time do you usually go to bed? _____ Students' responses

2. What time do you usually wake up? _____ will vary.

3. How much sleep do you usually get each night? _____

4. According to the chart, how much sleep *should* you be getting?

   _____

5. At what age will your sleep requirements change? _____

catnaps

functions

internal "clock"

reaction time

readjusting

Vocabulary Builder

1. The words in Column 1 on page 115 are from "Feeling Sleepy?" They are all related to sleep and its effects on the body.

2. Draw a line from each word in Column 1 to its definition in Column 2. If you're not sure of any of the words, guess for now. Then come back and check or change your answers as you find the boldfaced terms in the article.

3. Save your work. You will use it again in the Vocabulary Check.

COLUMN 1
catnaps
functions
internal "clock"
reaction time
readjusting

COLUMN 2
how long it takes you to respond to something
short periods of rest
changing
actions or purposes
the part of the brain that controls different
body activities

Strategy Builder

Outlining Main Ideas and Supporting Details

- You already know that most informational articles describe a particular **topic**, or subject. You also know that most informational articles are organized according to **main ideas** and **supporting details**. These ideas and details help explain or support the topic.

- There are many ways to keep track of main ideas and details as you read. In Lesson 3 you learned to summarize them. In Lesson 9 you learned to use an outline. An outline can be helpful when you do research, plan your own writing, or study for a test. Some outlines use a system or Roman numerals (I, II, III, IV, V, and so on) and capital letters (A, B, C, D, E, and so on).

- Read the following paragraphs, which tell why salt is important. Then read the outline of the paragraphs. Note how the main ideas are identified with Roman numerals, and the supporting details are shown with capital letters.

Salt

Salt is important for many reasons: It is a mineral that we need in order to say healthy. For thousands of years, we've used salt to season food. And before refrigerators were invented, salt was used to preserve food.

In the first century A.D., Roman soldiers were paid in salt. Our word *salary* comes from *sal,* which means "salt" in Latin.

   I. Salt is important for many reasons.
      A. It's a mineral needed for staying healthy.
      B. It is used for seasoning food.
      C. It was used for preserving food.
      D. It was used to pay Roman soldiers.

Feeling Sleepy?

As you read this article, notice how it is organized. Think about how you might show the main ideas and supporting details in an outline.

"I have to be dragged out of bed," says Paul, 9. "It would take 20 alarm clocks to get me up."

Paul is not alone. Mara, 8, says her dad drags her out of bed, too. In fact, when we talked to kids, we discovered that the one thing you hate more than going to bed is getting up in the morning.

The reason: You need more sleep! The kids we surveyed get anywhere from 45 to 75 minutes too little sleep each night.

Zombie Zone

Missing Z's can create big problems. "When I'm sleepy, I can't do much," says Rosalie, 9. "I walk with my eyelids drooping."

Scientists aren't exactly sure why sleep is so important. Many think sleep helps our muscles repair themselves and gives our brains time to store "data" received during the day. Sleep may also help us fight disease. (That could explain why having a cold makes you feel like snoozing all day.)

One thing is certain. "Not getting enough sleep affects every part of your life," says Dr. Mary Carskadon, a scientist who studies snoozers. Sleepy kids have difficulty concentrating on school, friends—even on baseballs zooming past their noses.

Drooping Grades

"Sometimes during school, I put my head on my desk and drift off," says Elizabeth, 11. Desktop **catnaps** might make you feel better. But they might also show up on your report card. According to Dr. Carskadon's research, kids who earn mainly A's and B's go to bed earlier than those who get D's and F's. In one study, kids who got bad grades slept about 35 minutes less each night than their honor-roll classmates.

Friendship Fumbles

Losing sleep may also mean losing friends. Why? Because sleep may help kids control their emotions, says sleep researcher Carol Leotta. Lack of slumber can lead to more fights with friends, family, teachers, and others.

 Stop here for the Strategy Break.

Strategy Break

If you were to outline the main ideas and supporting details in this article so far, your outline might look something like this:

Feeling Sleepy?

I. Missing Z's (sleep) can create big problems—when you're sleepy, you can't do much.
II. Scientists aren't sure why sleep is so important.
    A. It may help our muscles repair.
    B. It may give our brains time to store "data" received during the day.
    C. It may help us fight disease.
III. Not getting enough sleep affects every part of kids' lives.
    A. They may have trouble concentrating on school.
    B. They may have trouble concentrating on friends.
    C. They may have trouble concentrating on sports.
IV. Desktop catnaps might make you feel better, but they might show up on your report card.
    A. According to research, kids who get mainly A's and B's go to bed earlier than kids who get D's and F's.
    B. In one study, kids who got bad grades slept 35 minutes less than kids on the honor roll.
V. Losing sleep may also mean losing friends.

 Go on reading.

Sports Strikeout

If you want to be a high scorer on your basketball team, you can forget catching the "Late Show." Dr. Carskadon says, "Not getting enough sleep slows your **reaction time**." That's how long it takes you to respond to something in your environment, like an opening on the court or a clear shot for the basket. To speed up your reactions and improve your game, take a tip from the pros: Go to bed early the night before the game.

Double Whammy

But the kids we talked to say it's not that easy: After-school sports practices, TV, and loads of homework make it tough to get to bed on time. "And when I spend the night at a friend's, we usually stay up until about 2 A.M.," added Pat.

These "social" reasons for staying awake are only half the problem, says Dr. Carskadon. Her research shows that as your body matures, your brain waits until later at night to release a chemical that makes you sleepy. In other words, it's natural for teens and almost-teens to crawl into bed and fall asleep later.

Pulling the Plug

Staying up later would be no big deal if you could wake up later, too. You'd just be resetting your **internal "clock"** (the part of your brain that controls your body's **functions**) to run on a later schedule. But if you drag yourself out of bed for an early-morning soccer game or to catch the school bus, you can expect to feel like a zombie.

That's because all sleep is not equal. The last hour of sleep, like the highest level on a video game, is worth more. But getting to that high level requires sleeping through all the lower levels first. Waking up too soon is like pulling the plug in the middle of the game.

Sleep Solutions

One way to make sure you get enough sleep is to stick to a regular schedule. It will be easier to fall asleep—and get up—if you go to bed at the same time every night.

Elizabeth tried to end her school-day snoozes by going to bed earlier—at 8:30 instead of 9:45. The change wasn't an immediate success, however. "Last night, I was in bed by 8:30," she reported. "But I finally got to sleep at about 11 o'clock."

If you want to reset your bedtime, Dr. Carskadon says, you need to be patient. Your internal clock is easy to set to a later sleep time—but **readjusting** to an earlier schedule is more challenging. For the best results, try moving your bedtime 15 minutes earlier each night.

Soothing music may also help. Max, 12, puts on a CD and says, "I'm usually asleep halfway through." Scientists also say to avoid exercise right before bed. And stay away from sugary foods; the energy boost might make you think you're not tired.

Afternoon naps can also help you feel well rested. Just make sure you don't nap too close to bedtime. That can make falling asleep at night harder.

The good news: You won't always need as much sleep as you do now. Most adults would be happy with an eight-hour snooze. So enjoy your Z's while you can! ●

Strategy Follow-up

Work with a group of classmates and create an outline for the second part of this article. Be sure to include only the most important ideas, and skip unnecessary details. If you can, compare your outline with those of other groups. See if your outlines all contain similar information. Change your group's outline if necessary.

✓Personal Checklist

Read each question and put a check (✓) in the correct box.

1. How well were you able to use the chart in Building Background to decide if you get enough sleep?
   - ☐ 3 (extremely well)
   - ☐ 2 (fairly well)
   - ☐ 1 (not well)

2. By the time you finished reading this article, how well were you able to match the vocabulary words and their definitions?
   - ☐ 3 (extremely well)
   - ☐ 2 (fairly well)
   - ☐ 1 (not well)

3. How well do you understand how sleep helps your body?
   - ☐ 3 (extremely well)
   - ☐ 2 (fairly well)
   - ☐ 1 (not well)

4. How well do you understand the effects of not getting enough sleep?
   - ☐ 3 (extremely well)
   - ☐ 2 (fairly well)
   - ☐ 1 (not well)

5. In the Strategy Follow-up, how well were you able to help your group outline the second part of the article?
   - ☐ 3 (extremely well)
   - ☐ 2 (fairly well)
   - ☐ 1 (not well)

Vocabulary Check

Look back at the work you did in the Vocabulary Builder. Then answer each question by circling the correct letter.

1. What does your internal "clock" do?
   - (a.) controls your body's functions
   - b. lets you know how old you're getting
   - c. lets you know what time it is

2. Which phrase best defines a catnap?
   - a. a body function
   - (b.) a short period of rest
   - c. the time it takes to respond to something

3. Which word best describes what you are doing when you move your bedtime 15 minutes earlier each night?
   - a. functioning
   - (b.) readjusting
   - c. catnapping

4. Which of these body functions are affected by sleep?
   - a. concentration and memory
   - b. coordination and muscle tone
   - (c.) all of the above

5. What is an example of good reaction time?
   - a. not hitting a ball that has been pitched to you
   - (b.) catching a glass of milk before it spills
   - c. both of the above

Add the numbers that you just checked to get your Personal Checklist score. Fill in your score here. Then turn to page 205 and transfer your score onto Graph 1.

Personal
Vocabulary
Strategy
Comprehension
TOTAL SCORE
✓ T

Check your answers with your teacher. Give yourself 1 point for each correct answer, and fill in your Vocabulary score here. Then turn to page 205 and transfer your score onto Graph 1.

Personal
Vocabulary
Strategy
Comprehension
TOTAL SCORE
✓ T

Strategy Check

Review the outline that your group completed during the Strategy Follow-up. Then answer these questions:

1. Which detail describes how to speed up your reaction time when you play sports?

    a. Go to bed early the night before a game.

    b. Move your bedtime 15 minutes earlier each night.

    c. Make sure you don't nap too close to bedtime.

2. Which section of the article includes details about resetting your bedtime?

    a. "Sports Strikeout"

    b. "Double Whammy"

    c. "Sleep Solutions"

3. Which main idea can be found in the section called "Double Whammy"?

    a. There are many reasons why kids don't get to bed on time.

    b. If you want to be a high scorer, you've got to get enough sleep.

    c. Staying up late would be no big deal if you could wake up later, too.

4. Which section of the articles includes details about the importance of the last hour of sleep?

    a. "Double Whammy"

    b. "Pulling the Plug"

    c. "Sleep Solutions"

5. What would *not* be a main idea in the section called "Sleep Solutions"?

    a. One way to get enough sleep is to stick to a regular schedule.

    b. If you want to reset your bedtime, you need to be patient.

    c. Waking up too soon is like pulling the plug in the middle of a video game.

Comprehension Check

Review the article if necessary. Then answer these questions:

1. In what way does sleep affect relationships?

    a. It improves reaction times.

    b. It helps control emotions.

    c. It resets your internal clock.

2. Why is it hard for teens and almost-teens to fall asleep early?

    a. Their brain waits until later at night to release a chemical that makes them sleepy.

    b. Their brain releases a chemical that makes them want to stay awake all night.

    c. Their brain waits until early in the morning to release a chemical that makes them sleepy.

3. How would you reset your internal clock so you could get to sleep earlier?

    a. Stay up until 2:00 A.M. one night, and go to bed at 9:00 P.M. the next night.

    b. Go to bed 15 minutes earlier each night until you reach your desired bedtime.

    c. Keep your bedtime routine exactly the same every night.

4. Which of the following statements is true?

    a. Your last hour of sleep doesn't provide any benefits.

    b. Your last hour of sleep provides the least benefits.

    c. Your last hour of sleep provides the most benefits.

5. After reading this article, what might you do before bed to help you fall asleep?

    a. Eat some chocolate chip cookies.

    b. Listen to some soothing music.

    c. Play a fast game of basketball.

Check your answers with your teacher. Give yourself 1 point for each correct answer, and fill in your Strategy score here. Then turn to page 205 and transfer your score onto Graph 1.

Check your answers with your teacher. Give yourself 1 point for each correct answer, and fill in your Comprehension score here. Then turn to page 205 and transfer your score onto Graph 1.

Extending

Choose one or both of these activities:

CHART YOUR SLEEP FOR A WEEK

Make a chart to track how much sleep you get in one week. For seven days in a row, record what time you went to sleep and what time you woke up. At the end of the seven days, determine the amount of sleep you got each night, and then average the number of hours. Use the chart in Building Background to help you decide if you are getting the amount of sleep that you need for your age.

RESET YOUR INTERNAL CLOCK

If you aren't getting enough sleep, consider using the suggestions in "Feeling Sleepy?" to reset your own internal clock. Plan the changes that you want to make and how you want to make them. Some of the resources listed on this page might help you get started. As you go through the process of readjusting your schedule, record any noticeable effects in a "sleep log" that you keep by your bed.

Resources

Books

Kelly, Kevin, and Erin Jaeb. *Sleep on It!* World of Difference. Children's Book Press, 1996.

Shapiro, Colin H. *Who Needs to Sleep Anyway!* How Animals Sleep. Black Moss Press, 1996.

Audio Recordings

Beethoven: Key to the Quartets. Emerson String Quartet. Polygram Records, 1997.

Maiden of Mysteries: Music of Enya. Taliesin Orchestra and tribute by Enya. Intersound Records, 1998.

The Mozart Effect: Music for Children, vols. 1–3. Children's Group, 1997.

Mozart for Morning Meditation: Serene Serenade for the Soul. Philips, 1998.

White Stones. Secret Garden. Universal/Mercury, 1999.

How to Be a Super Sorter: Five Steps for Managing the Mess

Building Background

"Clean your room!" How many times have you heard *that* before? Work with a small group to brainstorm and share ideas for how to clean your room. Have one person record your ideas on a large concept map, or web. When you finish reading "How to Be a Super Sorter," return to your web and compare your ideas with those presented in the article.

keepsakes

monumental

tackle

tidy

train

whirlwind

Vocabulary Builder

1. Before you read "How to Be a Super Sorter," read the vocabulary words in the margin. If you do not know what any of the words mean, look them up in a dictionary.

2. Then underline the word or phrase in each row that is a synonym of the boldfaced vocabulary word. (Reminder: A **synonym** is a word that has the same meaning as another word.)

keepsakes	bits of trash	souvenirs
monumental	huge	small
tackle	show off	take on
tidy	sloppy	neat
train	teach	forget
whirlwind	flood	tornado

3. Save your work. You will use it again in the Vocabulary Check.

Strategy Builder

Following the Steps in a Process

- A **"how-to" article** is an article that tells readers how to do or make something. An author's purpose for writing a how-to article is always to **inform**. How-to articles include steps for doing or making things. These steps are written in a particular order, or **sequence**. It is important to follow the steps in their exact order. Otherwise you could end up doing things incorrectly.

- Read the following paragraphs, which explain how to arrange your CDs. Pay attention to the sequence of the steps.

Can you find your favorite compact disc? It's probably in your CD player! But what about all of your other CDs? Follow these steps to organize your CDs, and you'll be moving to the music like never before!

1. **Put CDs in their jewel cases.** Begin by finding all of the jewel cases. Then put each CD in its correct case. Broken or missing jewel cases? You can buy extras at a computer or music store.

2. **Decide where to keep your CDs.** Use the space you have to decide how will you organize and display your CDs. Try to find a box or shelf that will hold them all in one place. Most music stores have inexpensive CD holders.

3. **Put your CDs in order.** Alphabetize your CDs by title or artist. Or organize them by type of music.

Now you can enjoy *all* of your music because you will be able to find whatever you're in the mood to listen to!

- You can show the steps in this process on a **sequence chain**. It would look like this:

1 Put CDs in their jewel cases.	**2** Decide where to keep your CDs.	**3** Put your CDs in order.
• Put each CD in its correct jewel case. • If cases are broken or missing, buy extras at a computer or music store.	• Decide how you will organize and display your CDs. • Try to find a box or shelf that will hold them all in one place.	• Alphabetize your CDs by title or artist. • Or organize them by type of music.

How to Be a Super Sorter: Five Steps for Managing the Mess

By Edith H. Fine and Judith P. Josephson

As you read the beginning of this article, apply the strategies that you just learned. Think about how you could show the steps in this process on a sequence chain.

So your room is a pile of unfinished projects, unsorted papers, a soccer jersey from last fall, and—beneath it all—puzzle pieces and hamster food. You catch a whiff of old banana peel and dirty socks every time you walk in the door, and you can't see the top of your bed. "No baseball until your room is clean!" your parents say.

Some kids seem to be born tidy. But if you were not, you probably hear "clean your room" and think "cram piles under the bed and into the closet." You also know, though, that this kind of cleaning is just a quick fix.

Wouldn't you like to clean up your room for good? A *real* clean-up job is not such a monumental task if you learn a few timesaving "tricks of the trade."

If you share a room, get your brother or sister to help. Then collect a pile of big boxes, haul them and a kitchen timer into your room, and you're ready for the five easy steps that will turn *you* into a super sorter!

1 Do a "Big Sort."
Think about what's in that tangle of stuff in your room:
- clothes
- toys and games
- school supplies
- big stuff
- books and magazines
- sports equipment
- important papers
- not-so-important papers
- candy wrappers that never quite got thrown away

A big job seems smaller when it's broken into chunks. Label the empty boxes with the above big group names (or whatever categories fit the contents of your room). Write "Give Away" on one box for things you don't want. Draw a big "?" on another box for those things that don't belong anywhere else.

Set the timer for 60 minutes. Working for just an hour at a time, you won't feel as if you're climbing a mountain of messiness. Ready, set, *GO*! Put letters from friends and unsorted school papers into a "Papers" box. Stash shin guards in with "Sports Equipment." Throw stinky socks and dirty sweatshirts in a laundry basket. Hang up clothes that belong in the closet. Keep going! Pair your shoes and line them up next to your bed (or in your closet, if there's room). Put dirty dishes in the hall to take to the kitchen later. Take a look around. There's your bed! Dad's missing hammer! Tuesday's homework assignment! Things are getting neater. Toss trash into the wastebasket.

Depending on how messy your room is, this Big Sort could take several sessions. Keep at it!

2 Plan where things should live.

Tackle one of your Big Sort groups at a time. Do the items in your groups already have a home, and they just aren't in it? Or do they need "a place to call home"?

Dirty clothes, for example: If you usually toss them on the floor, put a clothes basket behind your door. Ready, aim . . . shoot your clothes into the basket. Score!

Store similar supplies in one place. Desk supplies can go into the bottom and lid of an empty egg carton. Put puzzle pieces in small empty gift boxes. Stash hobby supplies in labeled plastic bags or tubs.

Draw a map of your room to figure out where to put things. Once everything has a home, you can train yourself to put items in their place as soon as you're done with them. That makes it much easier to keep your room neat.

 Stop here for the Strategy Break.

Strategy Break

If you wanted to begin a sequence chain to show the steps in the process of cleaning your room, it might look like this:

1 Do a "Big Sort."

- Label boxes with categories that fit the contents of your room.
- Set the timer for 60 minutes.
- Sort things into the boxes, and put things away as you go.
- Take as many sessions as you need to do the Big Sort.

2 Plan where things should live.

- Tackle one Big Sort group at a time, and give the items in each group a home.
- Draw a map of your room to figure out where to put things.
- Train yourself to put things in their homes as soon as you are done with them.

To be continued . . .

 Go on reading.

3 Decide what to keep or toss.

Do you really want the poster you bought two summers ago? The ticket stub from last week's movie? The sweatshirt you wore in kindergarten? Start a box for "Keepsakes"—things you'd like to keep but never use.

For "I don't know" papers, put a future date (perhaps six months from now) in the corner and put them to one side on your desk. If you haven't looked at the papers by that date, toss them.

4 Make cleaning a habit.

Every day for at least three weeks, practice putting things in their "homes" after you've used them. As soon as you come in from school, for example, drop off your lunch box in the kitchen, hang your jacket on a hook, and put your homework on your desk. After you've done your homework, put away books and pencils, and sort papers into neat stacks.

In addition to daily cleaning, work like a whirlwind on your Big Sort boxes for 30 minutes each Saturday until you have gone through the contents of each one.

5 **Take it one step at a time.**

Don't be discouraged if your room gets messy again. It takes time to develop a new habit.

But once things are in place, you'll be able to vacuum and dust much faster. Things will be easier to find. Mom and Dad will be very impressed. And visitors won't catch a whiff of banana-and-gym-sock perfume as they approach your room. ●

Strategy Follow-up

First, look back that the concept map that your group created in Building Background. How do your ideas for cleaning your room compare with the ones in the article?

Next, work with a partner to finish the sequence chain for this article. Begin by copying Steps 1 and 2 onto a large sheet of paper. Add boxes for Steps 3–5, and then take turns filling in the information.

1

Do a "Big Sort."

- Label boxes with categories that fit the contents of your room.
- Set the timer for 60 minutes.
- Sort things into the boxes, and put things away as you go.
- Take as many sessions as you need to do the Big Sort.

2

Plan where things should live.

- Tackle one Big Sort group at a time, and give the items in each group a home.
- Draw a map of your room to figure out where to put things.
- Train yourself to put things in their homes as soon as you are done with them.

3

Decide what to keep or toss.

- Toss anything you don't really want to keep.
- Start a box for "Keepsakes" (things you'd like to keep but never use).
- Make a box for "I don't know" papers, and put a date on it. Toss anything you haven't looked at by that date.

4

Make cleaning a habit.

- Every day for at least three weeks, practice putting things into their homes after you've used them.
- Also work on your Big Sort boxes for 30 minutes every Saturday until you've gone through each box.

5

Take it one step at a time.

- Don't be discouraged if your room gets messy again. (It takes time to develop a new habit.)
- Once things are in place, you'll be able to do and find things much faster.

✓Personal Checklist

Read each question and put a check (✓) in the correct box.

1. In Building Background, how well were you able to come up with ideas for how to clean your room?
   - ☐ 3 (extremely well)
   - ☐ 2 (fairly well)
   - ☐ 1 (not well)

2. In the Vocabulary Builder, how well were you able to find the synonym of each vocabulary word?
   - ☐ 3 (extremely well)
   - ☐ 2 (fairly well)
   - ☐ 1 (not well)

3. Now that you've read this article, how well could you follow the steps in it to clean your own room?
   - ☐ 3 (extremely well)
   - ☐ 2 (fairly well)
   - ☐ 1 (not well)

4. How well do you understand the importance of "finding a home" for all of your things?
   - ☐ 3 (extremely well)
   - ☐ 2 (fairly well)
   - ☐ 1 (not well)

5. How well were you able to complete the sequence chain in the Strategy Follow-up?
   - ☐ 3 (extremely well)
   - ☐ 2 (fairly well)
   - ☐ 1 (not well)

Vocabulary Check

Look back at the work you did in the Vocabulary Builder. Then answer each question by circling the correct letter.

1. What is a synonym for the word *tidy*?
   - a. dirty
   - (b.) neat
   - c. sloppy

2. Which of these things would you describe as monumental?
   - a. a tiny ant
   - (b.) a huge mountain
   - c. a minivan

3. Which of these might you put into a box of keepsakes?
   - (a.) pictures
   - b. trash
   - c. paper clips

4. When might a person act like a whirlwind?
   - a. when he or she is falling asleep
   - (b.) when he or she is in a big hurry
   - c. when he or she is taking a bath

5. What is another way of saying, "tackle a job"?
   - (a.) take on a task
   - b. take a break
   - c. knock down a box

Add the numbers that you just checked to get your Personal Checklist score. Fill in your score here. Then turn to page 205 and transfer your score onto Graph 1.

Check your answers with your teacher. Give yourself 1 point for each correct answer, and fill in your Vocabulary score here. Then turn to page 205 and transfer your score onto Graph 1.

Strategy Check

Review the sequence chain that you completed in the Strategy Follow-up. Then answer these questions:

1. What is one of the things that Step 3 suggests for deciding what to keep or toss?
   a. Practice putting things into their homes.
   b. Start a box for "Keepsakes" that you never use.
   c. Don't be discouraged if your room gets messy again.

2. In which step would you find the suggestion to make a box for "I don't know" papers?
   a. Step 3
   b. Step 4
   c. Step 5

3. Which step suggests working on your Big Sort boxes for 30 minutes every Saturday?
   a. Step 3
   b. Step 4
   c. Step 5

4. What does Step 5 suggest?
   a. Decide what to keep or toss.
   b. Make cleaning a habit.
   c. Take it one step at a time.

5. Why is it important to follow the steps in this article in the exact order that they are given?
   a. The process won't work if the steps are out of order.
   b. It's not important—you can follow the steps in any order.
   c. It will take you much longer if you do the steps out of order.

Comprehension Check

Review the article if necessary. Then answer these questions:

1. Why do the authors suggest setting a timer while you clean your room?
   a. Working for an hour at a time makes a big job seem smaller.
   b. An hour is all the time it will take to clean your entire room.
   c. Whatever you haven't cleaned in an hour isn't worth keeping.

2. What do the authors say will help you "find homes" for all of your things?
   a. vacuuming your rug
   b. drawing a map of your room
   c. throwing away boxes

3. How often do the authors say you should clean in order to get into the habit?
   a. every day for at least one week
   b. every day for at least two weeks
   c. every day for at least three weeks

4. What do the authors say you should you do every Saturday?
   a. clean your entire room
   b. find new homes for things
   c. empty the Big Sort boxes

5. Why shouldn't you get discouraged if your room gets messy again?
   a. Cleaning it is a waste of time anyway.
   b. It takes time to develop a new habit.
   c. It will never stay clean, so why bother?

Check your answers with your teacher. Give yourself 1 point for each correct answer, and fill in your Strategy score here. Then turn to page 205 and transfer your score onto Graph 1.

	Personal	
	Vocabulary	
	Strategy	
	Comprehension	
TOTAL SCORE		
✓ T		

Check your answers with your teacher. Give yourself 1 point for each correct answer, and fill in your Comprehension score here. Then turn to page 205 and transfer your score onto Graph 1.

	Personal	
	Vocabulary	
	Strategy	
	Comprehension	
TOTAL SCORE		
✓ T		

Extending

Choose one or more of these activities:

WRITE A HOW-TO ARTICLE

Think of something that you know how to do well. Create a sequence chain that shows all of the steps in the process. Then use your sequence chain to write a how-to article. Read your article aloud, and if possible, demonstrate the process for the class.

LEARN A NEW SKILL

Use one of the how-to books listed on this page, and follow the steps to make or do something new.

WATCH A HOW-TO VIDEO

Use the how-to video listed on this page, or videotape someone making or doing something on a TV show. Write down the steps involved in the process. You might need to pause, rewind, or watch the tape several times to make sure you get all the steps. Then put the steps on a sequence chain, and let someone else read it. Can that person follow the sequence clearly? Why or why not?

USE THIS ARTICLE TO CLEAN AND SORT YOUR ROOM

Take a "before" picture of your room, or draw one. Then use the sequence chain that you created for this article to sort and clean your room. Keep a log of what you did for each step. Then take or draw an "after" picture. Include the pictures in your log, as well as any additional tips that you come up with for sorting and cleaning. Share your log with a classmate or classmates.

Resources

Books

Baker, Camy. *Camy Baker's How to Be Popular in the Sixth Grade.* Camy Baker's Series. Skylark, 1998.

Beard, Daniel Carter. *The American Boy's Handy Book: What to Do and How to Do It.* Nonpareil Books. David R. Godine, 1998.

Francis, John. *Bicycling: How to Play the All-Star Way.* Raintree/Steck-Vaughn, 1998.

McQuinn, Conn. *Chess for Kids: How to Play (And How to Win!)* Troll Discovery Kit. Troll Associates, 1998.

Terban, Marvin, and John O'Brien (illustrator). *Funny You Should Ask: How to Make Up Jokes and Riddles with Wordplay.* Clarion Books, 1992.

Video/DVD

Kids Make Puppets: Easy Scarf Marionettes. Jim Gamble Puppets. Blackboard Entertainment, 1999.

Go on reading to see what happens.

Scene 6

Narrator 2: A month later, the maid finds Mina in her bed, very sick. Dr. Seward examines Mina and writes his findings in his journal.

Seward's Journal: The patient is very pale and weak. She looks like she has lost a lot of blood. But where did it go? The only marks on her body are two tiny holes, like pinpricks, on her neck.

Narrator 1: Over the next few days, Mina becomes even sicker.

Seward's Journal: I have sent for my mentor from medical school, Professor Van Helsing of Amsterdam.

Narrator 2: Van Helsing arrives and examines Mina. Then he calls Dr. Seward into the next room.

Van Helsing: You were right to call me. I know exactly what troubles the young woman.

Seward: What a relief! What is it?

Van Helsing: She is the victim of a vampire.

Seward: A vampire? Are you insane? With all due respect, Professor, there must be some other explanation. Vampires don't exist!

Van Helsing: Young man, there are many things on this earth that exist without our knowledge. You must find a way to open your mind to the possibility of this vampire, or Mina will die.

Seward: I will if I can. What kind of creatures are you talking about?

Van Helsing: Vampires are persons who exist somewhere between life and death. They have been robbed of their souls. The only way they can remain on this earth is to drink the blood of innocent people, through two tiny holes in the victim's throat.

Seward: Mina has two little red marks on her neck!

Van Helsing: Worse still, vampires' victims do not merely die. They themselves become vampires, and must spend **eternity** drinking the blood of others.

Seward: But how could this happen to Mina behind our backs?

Van Helsing: Vampires can do almost anything to accomplish their goal. They can turn themselves into bats or wolves or dogs. They can **hypnotize**

their victims and control their minds, beckoning them in their sleep. It's possible that Mina herself doesn't even know it's happening to her.

Seward: How can we stop this villain?

Van Helsing: Vampires sleep in the ground during the day, and only wake to do their evil deeds once the sun goes down. So we only need to worry about Mina during the night. I know of several things that will protect her from the vampire, such as garlic flowers.

Seward: But we can't protect her forever.

Van Helsing: Quite right. We must kill the vampire. There's only one way to do it: We must drive a wooden **stake** through his heart. Only then will he rest.

Seward: If his victims become vampires, does that mean that Mina is now a vampire?

Van Helsing: No, as long as she is still alive, she won't become a vampire. But if he takes too much of her blood and her body dies, her soul will depart, and then all is lost.

Scene 7

Van Helsing's Journal: Tonight we lined the windows and doors of Mina's room with foul-smelling garlic blossoms. Then I constructed a wreath of them for the girl to wear around her neck. This should keep her safe for the night.

Narrator 1: But a few hours later, when the doctors come to check on Mina, they find a maid putting all the flowers outside in the hall.

Maid: When I checked on my mistress, I saw a huge bat pounding against the window. He scared me. I thought maybe he was attracted to the flowers, so I threw them away.

Van Helsing: Dr. Seward, brace yourself for anything we may find in there!

Narrator 2: They burst through the door to find Mina lying in her bed with a tall, thin old man bending over her. When he lifts his head, blood trickles down his chin.

Dracula: Good evening, gentlemen. My name is Dracula. I'll forgive this one **intrusion,** but let me warn you. Do not try again to fool me with garlic flowers. You are no match for the powers of Dracula. I have come to this country because my own land is too empty of souls. Yours is deliciously full of people, and I intend to stay and make them mine.

Seward: Old man, leave that woman alone!

Dracula: Silence, fool! You try my patience. I am talking about issues too large for your tiny mind to grasp. Trifle me no more.

Seward's Journal: What happened next was so fast, I almost didn't see it. Dracula flew at Professor Van Helsing like a giant bird. But at the last moment, Van Helsing produced a gold **crucifix** and held it in front of him. This seemed to scare the vampire, who evaporated into a mist, and floated out of the room through a crack under the door.

Scene 8

Narrator 1: Van Helsing and Seward revive Mina, but others are not so lucky. The next morning, an old couple down the road are found dead, drained of all of their blood. Professor Van Helsing realizes that if he doesn't find the vampire, all of Whitby could be in danger.

Narrator 2: Late the next afternoon, Seward and Van Helsing are talking in Seward's den when the attendant knocks on the door.

Attendant: Sorry to disturb you, Dr. Seward, but there is a man here to see you. He says his name is Jonathan Harker, and that he is Miss Murray's fiancée.

Narrator 1: Doctor Seward and Professor Van Helsing meet Harker in the hallway. He is very thin and pale.

Harker: Sirs, I have been on a terrible journey to a place of unimaginable horror. Somehow I managed to escape with my life and have returned to look for my fiancée. I am told that she is ill. What is wrong with her?

Van Helsing: You would not believe us if we told you. But let me ask you: Does the name Dracula mean anything to you?

Narrator 2: A look of terror crosses Harker's face, and he faints. A few minutes later, they are able to revive him.

Harker: I know Count Dracula very well. He is a vampire from Transylvania. And he's just bought the Carfax estate!

Narrator 1: Thirty minutes later, as the sun sets, Seward, Van Helsing, and Harker head cautiously down the cellar stairs of the Carfax estate. As they reach the bottom, they see a large, coffin-like box in the middle of the floor.

Harker: That's it. Be very careful. He's very clever.

Narrator 2: They open the lid of Dracula's coffin.

Van Helsing: There lies the monster, neither alive nor dead. The fresh blood of the innocent Mina is still on his hideous lips. Time is of the essence. Hand me the wooden stake and the mallet.

Renfield: Not so fast, Doctor!

Narrator 1: The mental patient, Renfield, stands in the shadows with a pistol aimed at the men.

Seward: Renfield! What are you doing here?

Renfield: The Master knew you would come. He summoned me to protect him.

Seward: So that's what all your antics have been about. Dracula is controlling your mind. Don't you understand? He's evil! He'll destroy your soul!

Renfield: The sunlight will be all gone in a few minutes. Then the Master will rise and you can discuss it with him.

Van Helsing (*whispering*): He's right. This is our only chance.

Narrator 2: Harker tackles Renfield and takes his gun. At that moment, Dracula begins to stir.

Harker: Do it now, Professor, while he is still weak from sleep.

Narrator 1: Van Helsing pounds the stake into Dracula's heart. A terrible scream comes from the monster's lips, as bloody foam forms around them. Moments later, Dracula's entire body turns to sand, and disappears.

Van Helsing: It is over, gentlemen. The curse is lifted.

Narrator 2: They all return to check on Mina.

Seward: She's barely awake. But she looks better already, and the wounds are gone from her neck.

Mina: Jonathan, is that you? You're alive!

Harker: It's all over, Mina. We're together, and we're free! ●

Strategy Follow-up

Look back at the examples of foreshadowing that you underlined. Now that you know the ending, do you see even more examples? Get together with a partner or a small group to share the passages that you underlined.

✓Personal Checklist

Read each question and put a check (✓) in the correct box.

1. How well do you understand what vampires are supposed to be?
   - ☐ 3 (extremely well)
   - ☐ 2 (fairly well)
   - ☐ 1 (not well)

2. In the Vocabulary Builder, how many words did you correctly match with their synonyms?
   - ☐ 3 (6–7 words)
   - ☐ 2 (3–5 words)
   - ☐ 1 (0–2 words)

3. How well do you understand what happens to Mina in this play?
   - ☐ 3 (extremely well)
   - ☐ 2 (fairly well)
   - ☐ 1 (not well)

4. How well do you understand why Harker says that he and Mina are free at the end of the play?
   - ☐ 3 (extremely well)
   - ☐ 2 (fairly well)
   - ☐ 1 (not well)

5. How well were you able to use foreshadowing to predict what might happen next in this play?
   - ☐ 3 (extremely well)
   - ☐ 2 (fairly well)
   - ☐ 1 (not well)

Vocabulary Check

Look back at the work you did in the Vocabulary Builder. Then answer each question by circling the correct letter.

1. Which word is a synonym for *eternity*?
   - (a.) forever
   - b. never
   - c. ending

2. Which word might describe a haunted castle?
   - a. closed
   - b. dusty
   - (c.) spooky

3. Which word means the same as *intrusion*?
   - (a.) invasion
   - b. separation
   - c. reunion

4. Which word means "observer"?
   - a. stake
   - (b.) witness
   - c. hypnotize

5. What letter does a crucifix look most like?
   - a. an *X*
   - (b.) a *T*
   - c. a *Z*

Add the numbers that you just checked to get your Personal Checklist score. Fill in your score here. Then turn to page 205 and transfer your score onto Graph 1.

Check your answers with your teacher. Give yourself 1 point for each correct answer, and fill in your Vocabulary score here. Then turn to page 205 and transfer your score onto Graph 1.

Strategy Check

Review the examples of foreshadowing that you underlined in the play. Then answer these questions:

1. Which detail from the newspaper might have helped you predict that Dracula was in England?

    a. a storm causes a ship to run aground

    b. a dead man is tied to the ship's wheel

    c. a large dog emerges from the ship

2. Fifty large wooden boxes of dirt are labeled for delivery to the Carfax estate. Now that you've read the whole play, what do you think Dracula might have intended to do with the boxes?

    a. use them to store the bodies of the people he kills

    b. use the dirt to bury the bodies of the people he kills

    c. use the dirt to plant garlic flowers in his garden

3. At the beginning of Scene 6, if you had predicted that Dracula had gotten to Mina, what clue would have best supported your prediction?

    a. She looks like she has lost a lot of blood.

    b. She has two tiny holes on her neck.

    c. Both clues would have supported the prediction.

4. What does the line, "They can turn themselves into bats or wolves or dogs" foreshadow?

    a. Dracula will kill a bat, or wolf, or a dog.

    b. Dracula will turn into one of these creatures.

    c. Dracula will turn into sand and disappear.

5. Dr. Van Helsing tells Dr. Seward to brace himself for anything they may find in Mina's room. What would have been a logical prediction for what they might find?

    a. Dracula vanishing for good

    b. Dracula drinking Mina's blood

    c. Dracula driving a stake through Mina's heart

Comprehension Check

Review the selection if necessary. Then answer these questions:

1. Why is Mina worried at the beginning of Scene 4?

    a. Their wedding date is set, and Jonathan is going to miss it.

    b. It is not like Jonathan to be out of touch for so long.

    c. Mina thinks Jonathan is working way too hard.

2. Why do you think Mr. Renfield eats bugs?

    a. He is probably a vampire.

    b. The hospital doesn't feed him.

    c. He likes to scare Mina.

3. Why do you think Mina keeps getting sicker?

    a. She can't sleep at night because Dracula keeps scaring her.

    b. Dracula keeps visiting her and taking more of her blood.

    c. She can't sleep at night because she misses Jonathan.

4. Why was there a huge bat pounding against Mina's window?

    a. It was trying to get to the garlic flowers.

    b. It was Dracula trying to get to the maid.

    c. It was Dracula trying to get to Mina.

5. According to Dr. Van Helsing, what is the one way to kill a vampire?

    a. Put a stake through the vampire's heart.

    b. Hold a crucifix out to the vampire.

    c. Show the vampire a mirror.

Check your answers with your teacher. Give yourself 1 point for each correct answer, and fill in your Strategy score here. Then turn to page 205 and transfer your score onto Graph 1.

Check your answers with your teacher. Give yourself 1 point for each correct answer, and fill in your Comprehension score here. Then turn to page 205 and transfer your score onto Graph 1.

Extending

Choose one or more of these activities:

WRITE A NEW DIARY OR JOURNAL ENTRY

The diary and journal entries are an important part of this play. Choose one of the characters (Harker, Mina, Seward, or Van Helsing), and write what that character might have written on the day after Dracula vanishes.

CASTING CHARACTERS

Think about the characters of Dracula, Harker, Mina, and Renfield. What is unique about each character? With a partner or small group, brainstorm a list of the personality traits and physical features that someone playing each of these character should have. Then use your lists to write descriptions that you would use to advertise for actors to play these parts.

LEARN ABOUT VAMPIRE BATS

Vampire bats really do exist! But do they really suck other creatures' blood? Learn more about vampire bats by using one of the resources listed on this page. Or use sources that you find yourself. Present your findings in an oral or written report. Try to include pictures in your report too.

Resources

Books

Anscombe, Roderick. *The Secret Life of Laszlo, Count Dracula.* DIANE Publishing, 1994.

Aylesworth, Thomas G. *Movie Monsters.* Harpercollins Juvenile Books, 1990.

Dadey, Debbie. *Dracula Doesn't Drink Lemonade.* Little Apple, 1995.

Web Sites

http://www.seaworld.org/AnimalBytes/vampire_batab.html
Read some fun facts about vampire bats.

http://www.thewildones.org/animals/bat.html
This site contains general information about bats and specific information about fruit bats and vampire bats.

Learning New Words

VOCABULARY

From Lesson 11
• readjusting

Prefixes

A prefix is a word part that is added to the beginning of a root word. (*Pre-* means "before.") When you add a prefix, you often change the root word's meaning and function. For example, the prefix *un-* means "not," so adding *un-* to the root word *tied* changes *tied* to its antonym, *untied.*

re-

The prefix *re-* means "do over" or "do again." In Lesson 12 you learned that if you wanted to *readjust* your sleep habits, you would have to adjust them again.

Write the definition for each word below.

1. reappear   appear again
2. rebuild   build again
3. rediscover   discover again
4. redraw   draw again
5. reunite   unite again

trans-

The prefix *trans-* can mean "across," "over", or "through." In Lessons 14 and 15 Dracula transforms himself into a wolf, a bat, and a dog. *Transform* means "change over to another form."

Complete each sentence with one of the words below.

transcontinental   translator   transparent   transfused

1. When a person's blood is removed and passed over to someone else, it is being ___transfused___.

2. A plane that travels across a continent is making a ___transcontinental___ flight.

3. When you can easily see through a window, that window is ___transparent___.

4. A ___translator___ is a person who changes a person's words into another language.

From Lesson 14
• transforms

Compound Words

A compound word is made up of two words put together. For example, in "Dava's Talent" the sheep are kept in a sheepcote. A *cote* is a shelter or shed in which animals are kept. So a *sheepcote* is a shelter or shed for keeping sheep.

Fill in each blank with a compound word by combining a word from Row 1 with a word from Row 2.

Row 1: rain road tooth week

Row 2: runner end bow ache

1. mouth pain caused by a cavity = _____toothache_____

2. arch of colorful light = _____rainbow_____

3. speedy desert bird = _____roadrunner_____

4. Saturday and Sunday = _____weekend_____

Multiple-Meaning Words

You know that a single word can have more than one meaning. To figure out which meaning an author is using, you have to use context. Context is the information surrounding a word or situation that helps you understand it.

Use context to figure out the correct meaning of each underlined word. Circle the letter of the correct meaning.

1. I have an important homework assignment that I need to <u>tackle</u> this weekend.
   a. take on or deal with
   b. knock down

2. Harry is in <u>training</u> to become the store's new manager.
   a. making fit for a sport
   b. teaching a skill

3. These new glasses have really improved my <u>vision</u>.
   a. thing seen in the mind
   b. ability to see

VOCABULARY

From Lesson 11
- sheepcote

From Lesson 12
- catnaps

Lesson 13
- keepsakes
- whirlwind

From Lesson 13
- tackle
- train

From Lesson 14
- vision

When Disaster Strikes . . .

Building Background

If water were overflowing a river near your home, how would you stop it? One way people try to stop floodwaters is by sandbagging. A sandbag is made by taking a bag made of burlap or some other strong material and filling it with sand. The bag is then sealed and stacked to make a wall—or dike—which changes the flow of water. When communities are forced to sandbag, many volunteers work together. They make an assembly line in which some people make the bags, some people pass the bags, and some people stack them to build the dike.

copilot

life jackets

rope ladder

navigated

submerged

controls

hovered

Vocabulary Builder

1. Before you read this story, read the vocabulary words in the margin. Then talk with a partner about what might happen during a helicopter rescue. Use as many of the vocabulary words as possible in your discussion. If you don't know what any of the words mean, find them in context or look them up in a dictionary.

2. Sketch pictures or takes notes on your discussion. You will use your ideas again in the Vocabulary Check.

Strategy Builder

Using Foreshadowing to Make Predictions

- In Part 2 of *Dracula* you looked for examples of foreshadowing, and you used them to **predict** what would happen in the play. In this lesson, you will use foreshadowing to predict what might happen in "When Disaster Strikes . . ."

- Remember that **foreshadowing** is when an author drops clues about what might happen later in the story.

- As you read "When Disaster Strikes . . ." you will stop twice to make predictions. At each Strategy Break, you will write down which clues helped you make your predictions. Then, after you finish reading the story, you will look back at your predictions and check your work.

When Disaster Strikes . . .

by Cindy Trebus

As you read, look for examples of foreshadowing. They will help you predict what might happen next.

Stacey brushed the sand off her navy blue T-shirt revealing the words, I SURVIVED THE FLOOD OF SUMMER '93. She grabbed another bag for her dad to fill with sand and glanced toward the backyard. It was completely under water now. It's a good thing they'd decided to help sandbag, she thought. She could go for a ride in her dad's helicopter anytime.

"I'm afraid that's it for my back." Stacey's dad straightened up and groaned as a radio blared in the background. "Let's rest and let that busload of people do some sandbagging."

"We interrupt this broadcast to bring you a special news bulletin. The Meramec River is rising a foot an hour. Sandbaggers are desperately needed at . . ."

"I thought the water was rising fast," Stacey exclaimed. "Dad, why don't we go over to the airport and take the helicopter for a ride along the Meramec? That way we can check for people and animals that might be trapped by the rising waters."

Forty minutes later Stacey found herself sitting in the **copilot**'s seat. "Remember. Half an hour. That's it," her dad shouted. Stacey shook her head in agreement. She disliked trying to talk above the noise of the helicopter.

"Wait!" Stacey jumped out of the helicopter and ran into a nearby shed. After scrambling back into the cockpit, she held up two **life jackets** and a **rope ladder.** "Just in case," she yelled.

 Stop here for Strategy Break #1.

Strategy Break #1

Use the information in the story to help you answer these questions:

1. What do you predict will happen next?

Students' responses will vary but should be supported with clues from

the text.

2. Why do you think so?

_____

_____

3. What clues from the story helped you make your prediction(s)?

_____

_____

 Go on reading to see what happens.

Stacey gazed at the churning waters from the helicopter. Just imagine all those flooded towns, homes, schools, and trailer parks. She had hoped to practice flying her dad's helicopter more this summer, but they'd been busy sandbagging and helping people move. Now summer was almost over. Hey! What was that up ahead?

"I'm turning around. It's been half an hour, and I haven't seen anything," her dad said.

"Let's keep going. I see something over there," Stacey shouted.

Her dad leaned forward. "That's a roof sticking up out of the water."

"I see something on the roof," Stacey hollered. Her dad shrugged and **navigated** the helicopter toward the **submerged** roof. "I see dots. Three dots. And they're moving! It's three people, Dad!"

"What are they doing out here? They should've already left this area!" Grabbing the radio's microphone, her dad said, "This is 2360 Q. Our helicopter is about 10 miles south of Weiss Airport. We've spotted three people on a rooftop surrounded by the Meramec. The river is rising a foot an hour. Emergency equipment needed immediately."

"Where on the Meramec are you?" a voice crackled over the radio.

"Between the Arnold and Telegraph bridges where the Meramec divides St. Louis County and Jefferson County."

"The closest helicopter is 45 minutes away. Do you have the equipment and manpower necessary for a rescue attempt?" the voice asked, anxiously.

After a brief pause, her dad said, "Yes. There are two of us and a rope ladder, but we'll need specific directions. We've never done this before."

Stacey turned away and stared at the river. Just a few days ago four people were rescued by the State Water Patrol after hanging onto tree branches for eight hours. Six people had died in Cliff Cave due to flash flooding. Four of them were kids her age. The cave was 10 minutes away from her house!

It all seemed like a horrible nightmare, but it wasn't. Now she was in a helicopter above the Meramec watching helplessly as the river threatened to claim three more lives.

"Stacey, here's the plan. I'm going to circle the helicopter above them. When I'm ready, come here and take the **controls**," her dad said.

"But, Dad, I've only flown . . ." Stacey began.

"Stacey, you can do this. You know where the controls are and what they do. I have to attach the rope ladder to the cargo tiedown rings in the back."

As the helicopter began to circle above the three dots on the river, Stacey closed her eyes. She felt as if she'd gotten on a roller coaster ride too soon after eating. Her stomach was queasy, and her palms were sweaty.

 Stop here for Strategy Break #2.

Strategy Break #2

Use the information in the story to help you answer these questions:

1. Do your earlier predictions match what happened? _____ Why or why not?

Students' responses will vary but should be supported with clues from

the text.

2. What do you predict will happen next?

_____

_____

3. Why do you think so?

_____

_____

4. What clues from the story helped you make your prediction(s)?

_____

_____

➡ **Go on reading to see what happens.**

"Come take the controls, Stacey," her dad shouted.

Stacey licked her lips and tried to swallow. She took a couple of deep breaths and stood up. Even though her legs felt like Jell-O, she made it to the pilot's seat.

Her dad hurried to the back of the helicopter. After what seemed like a long time, he grabbed the life jackets and rushed back to his seat, unfolding the ladder as he went. "OK. The ladder's secure."

As the helicopter **hovered** directly above the people, Stacey found herself back in the copilot's seat putting on her life jacket. She kicked the door open and let the ladder fall toward them. She could see their faces now. The man and woman appeared to be old and tired. The girl looked as if she was younger than Stacey.

Stacey looked anxiously at her dad. "It doesn't reach. We need to get closer."

"Tell me when I'm close enough," her dad shouted.

Looking back over her shoulder, Stacey yelled, "Lower. There's a girl down there about my height. Lower. Just a little lower. Stop!"

First came the girl. Then the woman. Stacey helped the woman into the helicopter. She crawled over, sat down, and put her arms around the girl. The man slowly climbed up the ladder. Stacey peered down at his weary face. Just then the man slipped. Still holding on, he managed to regain his footing.

"There are only a few more rungs. Then I'll be able to help you. Can you make it?" Stacey shouted. The man nodded and continued climbing. "There. Nice and easy. That's it. I've got you!" She grabbed the man's hand and pulled him into the helicopter.

As they were getting ready to leave for Weiss Airport, a helicopter came into view. Stacey glanced down where the roof had been and gulped. Her dad put his hand on her shoulder. "It's a good thing you wanted to take a ride along the Meramec—not to mention thinking of bringing life jackets and a rope ladder!" ●

Strategy Follow-up

Go back and look at the predictions that you wrote in this lesson. Do any of them match what actually happened in the story? Why or why not?

_____

_____

_____

_____

_____

_____

_____

_____

✓Personal Checklist

Read each question and put a check (✓) in the correct box.

1. How well do you understand why sandbagging is important during a flood?
   - ☐ 3 (extremely well)
   - ☐ 2 (fairly well)
   - ☐ 1 (not well)

2. How many vocabulary words were you and your partner able to use in your discussion about a helicopter rescue?
   - ☐ 3 (6–7 words)
   - ☐ 2 (3–5 words)
   - ☐ 1 (0–2 words)

3. How well were you able to use foreshadowing to predict what would happen next in this story?
   - ☐ 3 (extremely well)
   - ☐ 2 (fairly well)
   - ☐ 1 (not well)

4. How well do you understand why the people were on the roof of their house?
   - ☐ 3 (extremely well)
   - ☐ 2 (fairly well)
   - ☐ 1 (not well)

5. How well do you understand why the timing of the rescue was so important?
   - ☐ 3 (extremely well)
   - ☐ 2 (fairly well)
   - ☐ 1 (not well)

Vocabulary Check

Look back at the work you did in the Vocabulary Builder. Then answer each question by circling the correct letter.

1. Which phrase best defines the job of a copilot?
   - a. flies the aircraft
   - (b.) helps fly the aircraft
   - c. rides in the aircraft

2. For what are life jackets used?
   - a. to help people climb rope ladders
   - b. to help people learn to swim
   - (c.) to help people stay afloat in water

3. If you navigated a helicopter, what would you have done?
   - (a.) steered the helicopter
   - b. watched the helicopter
   - c. landed the helicopter

4. The roof of a house is submerged in this story. What does *submerged* mean?
   - (a.) The roof is covered with water.
   - b. The roof is covered with sand.
   - c. The roof is high in the air.

5. What would you say a helicopter was doing if it hovered over your house?
   - a. It moved in a big circle.
   - (b.) It hung in one place.
   - c. It flew past your house.

Add the numbers that you just checked to get your Personal Checklist score. Fill in your score here. Then turn to page 205 and transfer your score onto Graph 1.

Personal

Vocabulary

Strategy

Comprehension

TOTAL SCORE

✓ T

Check your answers with your teacher. Give yourself 1 point for each correct answer, and fill in your Vocabulary score here. Then turn to page 205 and transfer your score onto Graph 1.

Personal

Vocabulary

Strategy

Comprehension

TOTAL SCORE

✓ T

Strategy Check

Look back at what you wrote at each Strategy Break. Then answer these questions:

1. At Strategy Break #1, if you predicted that Stacey and her dad would find someone, which clue would have helped?

   a. Stacey and her dad are filling sandbags.

   b. "I'm afraid that's it for my back."

   c. Stacey runs back for life jackets and a ladder.

2. What does the news bulletin that "the Meramec River is rising a foot an hour" suggest?

   a. Someone is likely to get caught in the river.

   b. The river will stop rising very soon.

   c. The volunteers can all go home soon.

3. Which clue best foreshadows the fact that Stacey and her dad will perform the rescue themselves?

   a. "Where on the Meramec are you?"

   b. "Between the Arnold and Telegraph bridges where the Meramec divides."

   c. "Do you have the equipment and manpower necessary for a rescue attempt?"

4. At Strategy Break #2, what would have been a likely prediction?

   a. Stacey will be afraid when she goes to fly.

   b. She will have no idea how to fly.

   c. She will decide to never fly again.

5. Why do you think the author might have written, "But, Dad, I've only flown . . ."?

   a. to suggest that Stacey has taken over the controls as the pilot

   b. to suggest that Stacey has never taken over the controls as the pilot

   c. to suggest that Stacey has never flown in a helicopter before

Comprehension Check

Review the story if necessary. Then answer these questions:

1. How does the special news bulletin about the rising waters affect Stacey?

   a. She doesn't care about it and would rather be having fun in the helicopter.

   b. She thinks about taking the helicopter out to try and find trapped people.

   c. She thinks about how much her back will hurt from all the sandbagging.

2. Which words best describe Stacey?

   a. thoughtful and brave

   b. selfish and lazy

   c. shy and afraid

3. Why don't Stacey and her dad wait for the rescue helicopter?

   a. Stacey and her dad are too interested in being heroes.

   b. The water will cover the house by the time the rescue team arrives.

   c. They've never rescued anyone before, and they want to try it.

4. How does the author increase suspense?

   a. She includes the fact that others have been killed by this flood.

   b. She includes the fact that Stacey has not had time to practice flying.

   c. Both of the above answers are correct.

5. Why does Stacey gulp when she looks down after the rescue helicopter arrives?

   a. She thinks that she and her dad might be in the rescuers' way.

   b. See sees that the roof of the house is now completely underwater.

   c. She wants to alert the rescue helicopter to the trouble below.

Check your answers with your teacher. Give yourself 1 point for each correct answer, and fill in your Strategy score here. Then turn to page 205 and transfer your score onto Graph 1.

Check your answers with your teacher. Give yourself 1 point for each correct answer, and fill in your Comprehension score here. Then turn to page 205 and transfer your score onto Graph 1.

Extending

Choose one or more of these activities:

LEARN ABOUT MAJOR FLOODS
Find out about some of our country's major floods by reading one or more of the books listed on this page. Use a map, and make a poster to show and describe where the damage was.

COMPARE FLOODS
Choose two or more rivers that have flooded in the past few years, either near your home or in one of the books listed on this page. Compare how fast and how high the waters rose. Also compare the damage done to property and the number of lives lost in each flood. Use a comparison chart to compare the results of each flood.

LEARN ABOUT DISASTER ASSISTANCE PROGRAMS
Find out about how the American Red Cross and the Salvation Army help out in a disaster. Interview someone who works for one of these nonprofit agencies, or write a letter to your local or regional office. Decide which questions to ask in advance. For example:
- Who calls you when there is a disaster?
- In what ways do you give help?
- Where do you get the food and money that you give to people in disasters?

Resources

Books
Bennett, Paul. *Flood*. The World Reacts. Smart Apple Media, 1999.

Bredeson, Carmen. *The Mighty Midwest Flood: Raging Rivers*. American Disasters. Enslow Plublishers, 1999.

Sipiera, Paul. *Floods*. Bt Bound, 2001.

Vogel, Carole G. *The Great Midwest Flood*. Little Brown, 1995.

Web Site
http://www.crh.noaa.gov/arx/93flood.html
Compare flood crests of the 1993 and the 1997 floods in Midwestern towns.

Building Background

In this lesson you will read about how seeds travel. You know that seeds need sunlight, air, water, and food to grow. Talk with a group of classmates about why and how seeds might travel to find these things.

glide

hitchhike

launch

nourishes

parachutes

pods

species

whirls

Vocabulary Builder

1. Before you read "Seed Travel," read the vocabulary words in the margin. If you don't know what any of the words mean, find them in the selection and use context to figure them out.

2. If that doesn't help, discuss them with a classmate or look them up in a dictionary. Then match the vocabulary words in Column 1 to their definitions in Column 2.

3. Save your work. You will use it again in the Vocabulary Check.

COLUMN 1	COLUMN 2
glide	catch a ride with someone or something else
hitchhike	provides food for
launch	move smoothly and easily
nourishes	type or class
parachutes	shells or coverings around seeds
pods	send off or send forth
species	spins or twirls
whirls	things used to fall slowly through the air

Strategy Builder

Comparing and Contrasting While You Read

- Authors often compare and contrast things when they write. **Comparing** means telling how two or more things are alike. **Contrasting** means telling how two or more things are different.

- Read the following passage. It compares and contrasts some different kinds of flowers.

If you have a garden plot, think about growing these great flowers. A morning glory grows on a vine, so choose a sunny place where you can provide a fence or a trellis for it to climb. It blooms from summer through early fall with beautiful blue, pink, or white flowers.

Impatiens are the perfect choice for a shady garden or border. A variety of colors, including coral, orange, pink, red, and white will bloom all summer long! Just remember to pinch back the early buds to get full, bushy plants.

Another pretty flower is the sweet pea, which also grows on a vine. Plant it next to a fence in full sun, and watch the blue, pink, rose, and white flowers bloom from early spring to early summer.

The sunflower can also be an exciting addition to your flower garden. As its name suggests, this tall plant loves the sun. It blooms with a head full of seeds and leaves of yellow and red in the late summer.

- If you wanted to show how these flowers are alike and different, you could create a **features chart**. It would look something like this:

	needs a sunny area	has summer blooms	includes white blossoms	grows on a vine
morning glory	yes	yes	yes	yes
impatiens	no	yes	yes	no
sweet pea	yes	yes	yes	yes
sunflower	yes	yes	no	no

Seed Travel

by Ann Ackroyd

As you read this article, apply the strategies that you just learned. Notice how the author compares and contrasts the ways in which seeds travel.

We like to think only humans use rockets, helicopters, **parachutes**, and gliders, but that's not true. Other travelers used such methods long before we did. These travelers are seeds! But why would a seed need to travel?

Seeds need to get away from their parent plants. If they remain too close, young plants starve. Their bigger, stronger parents overshadow them, hogging sunlight and water. It's also a seed's job to claim new living space for its **species**.

Have you ever watched a toy rocket take off with a small explosion? The Mediterranean squirting cucumber behaves like a rocket—without the fire. The little cucumber fills with juice until it's so full, it bursts off its stalk. A trail of slime follows it as it shoots through the air. This slime contains the seeds.

Plants with **pods launch** their seeds using another kind of explosion. When broom seeds are ready, the sun warms one side of the pod and dries it. The other side remains in shadow and dries more slowly. The sides pull against each other until the pod splits, hurling the seeds away from the parent plant. A Brazilian tree called the monkey's dinner bell does the same. It pops so loudly, strangers think they are under attack. The seeds can travel 40 feet, so it's best not to be in the way.

Many seeds use parachutes. Think of dandelion puffs—they contain hundreds of tiny seeds, each with its own silky parachute for riding the wind. Milkweed seeds come in pods instead of blowballs. If you open a ripe milkweed pod, you will see a packaging miracle. Hundreds of seed heads overlap neatly, while their closed parachutes lie flat, resembling hair.

 Stop here for the Strategy Break.

Strategy Break

If you were to begin a features chart for the article so far, it might look like this:

	launches like a rocket	pod splits	uses parachutes
Mediterranean squirting cucumber	yes	no	no
broom	no	yes	no
monkey's dinner bell	no	yes	no
dandelion	no	no	yes
milkweed	no	no	yes

 Go on reading.

Some seeds have wings to help them **glide** away from their parent plants. The simplest designs have one wing. Have you ever seen pine seeds leave an open cone? If so, you know that each seed sits at the base of a paper-thin wing. As the seed falls, it **whirls** through the air like a helicopter blade. The seeds of the alsomitra, an Asian creeper, also have one wing, but instead of spinning like helicopter blades, they sail like gliders. This is because the seed sits in the middle of the wing.

The Asian anisoptera has seeds with two wings instead of one. They spin because one wing is shorter than the other. If you live near maples or sycamores, you might think their seeds have two wings. Actually, each seed has one wing, and the seeds grow in pairs.

Some seeds travel in water by floating. The coconut is one example. Air spaces between its outer shell and the hairy inner seed keep it from sinking. A sweet, milky liquid in the center **nourishes** the seed.

The sea bean provides its seeds with wooden cases that can stay afloat for a year. These seeds ride the Gulf Stream and sometimes land in Europe—4,000 miles away from their parents in the Caribbean.

Many seeds **hitchhike**. Some use hooks to grab an animal's fur or a person's clothing. The next time you pull cockleburs from your socks, remember that you are helping the burdock plant expand its territory.

Other hitchhiking seeds ride inside the animals that eat them. They do this by hiding in fruits like strawberries and raspberries. All such hitchhikers have the advantage of landing in a pile of fertilizer!

A number of plants use only one seed carrier. Oaks and hickories belong to this group. The armor around their seeds is so thick, only a squirrel can break it. However, a squirrel collects more acorns and hickory nuts than it can eat. It hides the extras to eat later. But the extras aren't always needed, and sometimes a squirrel forgets its hidden treasure. The uneaten seeds grow into new trees far from their parents.

Look around and see if you can find more seedy rockets, helicopters, parachutes, hitchhikers, and floaters. Or what about seeds that travel in other ways? Look at a poppy, for instance. It acts like a salt shaker, shaking out its seeds. Once you start noticing how seeds travel, you'll want to make your own list. ●

Strategy Follow-up

Now fill in this features chart for the second part of "Seed Travel." Go back and skim the article for information when you need to.

	glides (by whirling, sailing, or spinning)	floats in water	hitchhikes	shakes
pine	yes	no	no	no
alsomitra	yes	no	no	no
Asian anisoptera	yes	no	no	no
maple	yes	no	no	no
sycamore	yes	no	no	no
coconut	no	yes	no	no
sea bean	no	yes	no	no
burdock	no	no	yes	no
oak	no	no	yes	no
hickory	no	no	yes	no
poppy	no	no	no	yes

✓Personal Checklist

Read each question and put a check (✓) in the correct box.

1. In Building Background, how well were you able to brainstorm why and how seeds travel?
   - ☐ 3   (extremely well)
   - ☐ 2   (fairly well)
   - ☐ 1   (not well)

2. In the Vocabulary Builder, how many words were you able to match with their definitions?
   - ☐ 3   (6–8 words)
   - ☐ 2   (3–5 words)
   - ☐ 1   (0–2 words)

3. How well do you understand the different ways in which seeds travel?
   - ☐ 3   (extremely well)
   - ☐ 2   (fairly well)
   - ☐ 1   (not well)

4. How well do you understand the reasons why seeds travel?
   - ☐ 3   (extremely well)
   - ☐ 2   (fairly well)
   - ☐ 1   (not well)

5. How well were you able to complete the features chart in the Strategy Follow-up?
   - ☐ 3   (extremely well)
   - ☐ 2   (fairly well)
   - ☐ 1   (not well)

Vocabulary Check

Look back at the work you did in the Vocabulary Builder. Then answer each question by circling the correct letter.

1. Which word is most related to how a plant gets food?
   - a. hitchhikes
   - (b.) nourishes
   - c. species

2. Which method of travel is most closely related to the word *launch*?
   - (a.) rocket
   - b. helicopter
   - c. airplane

3. What do you call the shells or coverings around seeds?
   - a. glides
   - (b.) pods
   - c. wings

4. Which word means "type or class"?
   - a. pods
   - b. parachutes
   - (c.) species

5. Which two words describe how seeds travel?
   - a. *species* and *whirls*
   - b. *nourishes* and *parachutes*
   - (c.) *glide* and *hitchhike*

Add the numbers that you just checked to get your Personal Checklist score. Fill in your score here. Then turn to page 205 and transfer your score onto Graph 1.

	Personal	
	Vocabulary	
	Strategy	
	Comprehension	
TOTAL SCORE		

✓ T

Check your answers with your teacher. Give yourself 1 point for each correct answer, and fill in your Vocabulary score here. Then turn to page 205 and transfer your score onto Graph 1.

	Personal	
	Vocabulary	
	Strategy	
	Comprehension	
TOTAL SCORE		

✓ T

Strategy Check

Review the features charts for both parts of this selection. Then use them answer these questions:

1. What do oak and hickory seeds have in common?
   a. They both glide by spinning.
   b. They both shake like salt shakers.
   c. They both hitchhike. *(circled)*

2. How are pine and burdock seeds different?
   a. pines travel by whirling, burdocks travel by shaking
   b. pines travel by whirling, burdocks travel by hitchhiking *(circled)*
   c. pines travel by hitchhiking, burdocks travel by floating

3. Which seeds get shaken out as if from a salt shaker?
   a. poppy seeds *(circled)*
   b. hickory seeds
   c. alsomitra seeds

4. Which seeds travel by using parachutes?
   a. broom and monkey's dinner bell
   b. dandelions and milkweeds *(circled)*
   c. oaks and hickories

5. How do coconut and sea bean seeds travel?
   a. by launching like a rocket
   b. by shaking
   c. by floating in water *(circled)*

Comprehension Check

Review the article if necessary. Then answer these questions:

1. Why do seeds need to travel?
   a. so they do not starve
   b. to get sunlight and water
   c. both of the above *(circled)*

2. When a seed travels, what is it doing for its species?
   a. providing new colors
   b. providing new spaces to live *(circled)*
   c. providing more food

3. Which tree has seeds that pop very loudly and travel 40 feet?
   a. the monkey's dinner bell *(circled)*
   b. the Mediterranean squirting cucumber
   c. the Asian anisoptera

4. Why is floating a good way for sea bean seeds to travel?
   a. The seeds are nourished by the water.
   b. They can travel up to 4,000 miles in the water. *(circled)*
   c. They can land right in piles of fertilizer.

5. What happens to the acorns and hickory nuts that squirrels hide but don't eat?
   a. They grow into new trees. *(circled)*
   b. They dry up and die.
   c. They grab onto animals' fur.

Check your answers with your teacher. Give yourself 1 point for each correct answer, and fill in your Strategy score here. Then turn to page 205 and transfer your score onto Graph 1.

Personal
Vocabulary
Strategy
Comprehension
TOTAL SCORE
✓ T

Check your answers with your teacher. Give yourself 1 point for each correct answer, and fill in your Comprehension score here. Then turn to page 205 and transfer your score onto Graph 1.

Personal
Vocabulary
Strategy
Comprehension
TOTAL SCORE
✓ T

Extending

Choose one or both of these activities:

LIST WAYS THAT YOU'VE SEEN SEEDS TRAVEL

Work alone or with a partner to create a list of other ways that seeds travel. Think back to your ideas in Building Background about *why* seeds travel to help you think of *how* they travel. Use some of the resources listed on this page if you need help getting started.

COMPARE AND CONTRAST SEEDS IN YOUR NEIGHBORHOOD

Work with the whole class or in a small group, and collect a variety of seeds from your neighborhood. Take some time to study and compare the seeds. Then create a features chart that compares and contrasts what the seeds look like and how they travel. (Don't forget to compare the seeds' insides too.)

Resources

Books

Burton, Jane, and Kim Taylor. *The Nature and Science of Seeds.* Exploring the Science of Nature. Gareth Stevens, 1999.

Lauber, Patricia. *Seeds: Pop-Stick-Glide.* Crown Books for Young Readers, 1991.

Simon, Seymour. *Ride the Wind: Airborne Journeys of Animals and Plants.* Browndeer Press, 1997.

Web Site

http://www.chestnut-sw.com/seedhp.htm
Learn all about planting and starting seeds for your garden.

Vegetables

Building Background

The selection you are about to read explains what vegetables are and how they are grown. Draw a concept map, or web, on a separate sheet of paper. In the center of the web, write the name of your favorite vegetable. In the surrounding ovals, write what you know about the vegetable, including how it looks, smells, tastes, and feels—and maybe even sounds.

As you read "Vegetables," find out what part of a plant your favorite vegetable is, how it is grown, and whether or not it is really a vegetable. When you finish reading, add to the web any new information that you learned about your vegetable.

fertilizers

fungicides

greenhouses

irrigation

pesticides

produce

truck farms

Vocabulary Builder

1. "Vegetables" uses several specialized vocabulary words. As you know, **specialized vocabulary** words are all related to a particular topic, such as basketball or figure skating.

2. Think about how the words in the margin might relate to vegetables. Then use the words to complete the word map below. (If you need help with any of the words, look them up in a dictionary.)

3. Save your work. You will use it again in the Vocabulary Check.

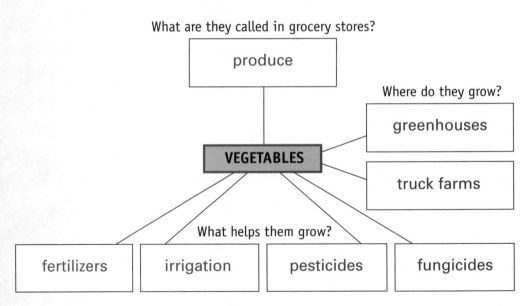

What are they called in grocery stores?

produce

Where do they grow?

greenhouses

VEGETABLES

truck farms

What helps them grow?

fertilizers   irrigation   pesticides   fungicides

Strategy Builder

Summarizing Nonfiction

- Sometimes when you read **nonfiction**, you're given a lot of information all at once. To keep it straight—and to remember it better—it helps to stop once in a while to summarize. When you **summarize** a section of text, you list or retell in your own words the most important ideas.

- Think about how you might summarize these paragraphs:

> When vegetables are harvested, some are sold to be eaten fresh, but a large part of the crop will be eaten later in the year. Fresh vegetables will eventually begin to rot, so they must be preserved in order to be eaten later.
>
> Freezing is a widely used method of preserving vegetables. Freezing must be done very quickly so that the vegetables will remain fresh. Vegetables are cleaned and blanched, or boiled briefly, before they are frozen. Blanching preserves the taste of the vegetables and keeps nutrients from being lost. Frozen vegetables are the most nutritious type of preserved vegetables.
>
> Drying is an ancient way of preserving food. It is also a good method of keeping in nutrition. Vegetables are washed and blanched before dried. Then they are placed in insulated cabinets, and hot air is blown over them until they are completely dry. Dried vegetables may be used in soup mixes or packaged meals.
>
> Canning vegetables is another way of preserving them. Some nutrition is lost in the canning process, but canned vegetables are popular and convenient.

- Here is how one student summarized the paragraphs:

When vegetables are harvested, some are eaten fresh, but some will be eaten later. To keep them from rotting, the ones to be eaten later need to be preserved.

1. Freezing is one way of preserving. (Frozen vegetables are the most nutritious preserved vegetables.)

2. Drying is another way. (Dried vegetables are good for soup mixes and packaged meals.)

3. Canning is another way. (Some nutrition is lost in this process, but it's popular and convenient.)

Vegetables

by Susan Wake

As you read the first part of this selection, try to summarize the most important ideas.

What Is a Vegetable?

A vegetable is the part of a plant that we eat. It may be the root, stem, leaf, seeds, or even the flowers and buds of the plant. Some vegetables are eaten raw, others are cooked, and many can be eaten either way.

Some of the vegetables we eat grow wild, but most are specially raised. Some vegetables, such as potatoes, are easy to grow and are found in many countries. Others, such as yams, only grow in tropical climates. Certain vegetables, such as cabbages, thrive in cool conditions.

Vegetables can now be produced all over the world, even in places where they do not grow naturally. Plants that need warmth to thrive can be raised in enclosed buildings called **greenhouses**. **Irrigation** brings extra water to dry areas so crops can grow. Because of these and other farming methods, the vegetables in our stores may come from almost any part of the world.

 Stop here for the Strategy Break.

Strategy Break

If you summarized the first part of this selection, your summary might look like this:

What Is a Vegetable?

- A vegetable is the part of the plant that we eat. It could be the root, stem, leaf, seeds, flowers, or buds.
- Vegetables can be eaten raw or cooked.
- Some vegetables are easy to grow and are found in many countries.
- Others grow only in tropical climates or cool conditions.
- With greenhouses, irrigation, and other farming methods, vegetables can now be produced all over the world.

As you read the rest of this selection, keep thinking about how you might summarize each section.

Go on reading.

Different Types of Vegetables

All vegetables come from some part of a plant. Root vegetables come from plants that store food in their roots. The roots swell, and the swollen roots are the vegetables that we eat. Carrots, beets, and radishes are all root vegetables.

Some plants store food in special underground stems. These stems swell to form tubers, which we dig up and eat. Potatoes, yams, and Jerusalem artichokes are all tubers.

We may eat the leaves, stems, flowers, or buds of some plants. Asparagus and leeks are stems; Brussels sprouts, cabbages, and lettuces are leaves. Cauliflower and broccoli are clusters of flower buds.

Peas and some types of beans are seeds. When we eat green beans, we are eating both seeds and pods. Corn kernels are also seeds.

There are several different varieties of each vegetable. Next time you go shopping, look at the selection available in the grocery store.

Fruits or Vegetables?

Some foods that we call vegetables are in fact fruits. The fruit is the part of the plant that contains the plant's seeds. If you can see the seeds inside a "vegetable," it is really a fruit. For example, tomatoes, peppers, and cucumbers are all fruits. We call them vegetables because we tend to think of fruits as sweet. Some foods that we think of as fruits, such as watermelons, are actually considered vegetables by scientists who study plants.

Vegetables in the Past

Vegetables have been an important part of people's diets for thousands of years. In early times, vegetables were not thought to be necessary for a healthy diet, but today we know that they are.

The first humans ate the fruit and roots of wild plants. Later, people collected seeds and planted them to grow food. They made primitive tools to help farm these plants. Eventually, as people migrated, they brought their plants to other parts of the world.

Onions and beans have been found in ancient Egyptian tombs. The ancient Egyptians believed that the dead would need these vegetables in their next lives.

The ancient Romans ate leeks, onions, lettuce, cauliflower, olives, celery, beans, and peas. They brought these plants to many parts of the world as they conquered more and more countries.

Vegetables for Health

It is important to have a balanced diet. We need to eat a variety of foods to give us the important carbohydrates, proteins, fats, minerals, and vitamins we need.

Although vegetables contain a great deal of water, they are an excellent source of vitamins and minerals. Vegetables also provide fiber, which helps our digestive systems to function properly. Most vegetables contain very little fat.

When vegetables are overcooked, the minerals and vitamins in them are lost. Vegetables that are raw or lightly cooked are more nutritious than those that are cooked for a long time.

Processes such as freezing, canning, and drying can also destroy some of the nutrition in vegetables.

Growing Vegetables

Many people grow vegetables in home gardens, but most vegetables are grown on **truck farms**, farms which produce only vegetables.

Vegetable growers often add **fertilizers** to the soil to help plants grow. Growing plants are often sprayed with **pesticides** and **fungicides** to protect them from pests and diseases. Some farmers prefer not to use these chemicals because they can be harmful.

Many truck farms have greenhouses. Greenhouses are used in cool climates to protect growing plants from frost, which can kill them.

Farmers often plant seeds in batches so their vegetables will ripen at different times. This way, there are several harvests instead of just one. Once harvested, the crops are sorted, graded according to quality, and packed. This **produce** is then shipped to factories to be canned or frozen, or to markets and stores to be sold. ●

Strategy Follow-up

Now work with a partner to summarize the rest of this selection. Stop after each main section, and take turns recording the summary. Write the summaries in your own words, and be sure to list only the most important ideas.

✓Personal Checklist

Read each question and put a check (✓) in the correct box.

1. In Building Background, how well were you able to fill in the concept map with details about your favorite vegetable?
   - ☐ 3   (extremely well)
   - ☐ 2   (fairly well)
   - ☐ 1   (not well)

2. How well were you able to complete the word map in the Vocabulary Builder?
   - ☐ 3   (extremely well)
   - ☐ 2   (fairly well)
   - ☐ 1   (not well)

3. Now that you've read this selection, how well could you explain what a vegetable is?
   - ☐ 3   (extremely well)
   - ☐ 2   (fairly well)
   - ☐ 1   (not well)

4. How well could you explain the importance of vegetables?
   - ☐ 3   (extremely well)
   - ☐ 2   (fairly well)
   - ☐ 1   (not well)

5. How well were you able to help your partner summarize the second part of this selection?
   - ☐ 3   (extremely well)
   - ☐ 2   (fairly well)
   - ☐ 1   (not well)

Vocabulary Check

Look back at the work you did in the Vocabulary Builder. Then answer each question by circling the correct letter.

1. What are vegetables sometimes called in grocery stores?
   a. fungicides
   (b.) produce
   c. truck farms

2. Which word does not describe what helps vegetables grow?
   a. fungicides
   b. irrigation
   (c.) produce

3. When vegetables are not usually found in a certain climate, how can people grow them there?
   a. They can grow them on truck farms.
   (b.) They can grow them in greenhouses.
   c. They can grow them using both of the above.

4. Which of the following best protects vegetables from diseases?
   a. irrigation
   b. fertilizer
   (c.) fungicides

5. How is water brought to vegetables in dry areas?
   a. through truck farms
   (b.) through irrigation
   c. through pesticides

Add the numbers that you just checked to get your Personal Checklist score. Fill in your score here. Then turn to page 205 and transfer your score onto Graph 1.

Check your answers with your teacher. Give yourself 1 point for each correct answer, and fill in your Vocabulary score here. Then turn to page 205 and transfer your score onto Graph 1.

Strategy Check

Review the summaries that you and your partner completed. Then answer these questions:

1. What's the most important idea to include in a summary of "Different Types of Vegetables"?

    a. When we eat green beans, we are eating both seeds and pods.

    b. Cauliflower and broccoli are clusters of flower buds.

    (c.) All vegetables come from some part of a plant.

2. Which detail should not be included in a summary of "Fruits or Vegetables?"

    a. Some "vegetables" are really fruits.

    (b.) The first humans ate wild plants.

    c. If you can see the seeds, it is really a fruit.

3. Vegetables have been an important part of people's diets for thousands of years. In which section does this main idea belong?

    (a.) "Vegetables in the Past"

    b. "Vegetables for Health"

    c. "Growing Vegetables"

4. Which detail should be included in a summary of "Vegetables for Health"?

    (a.) Vegetables are an excellent source of vitamins and minerals.

    b. Onions and beans have been found in tombs.

    c. Growers often add fertilizers to the soil to help plants grow.

5. What is the most important idea to include in a summary of "Growing Vegetables"?

    a. Farmers often plant seeds in batches so vegetables ripen at different times.

    b. Growers often add fertilizers to the soil to help plants grow.

    (c.) Most vegetables are grown on truck farms, which produce only vegetables.

Comprehension Check

Review the selection if necessary. Then answer these questions:

1. What parts of vegetables can we eat?

    a. We can eat everything but the seeds.

    b. We can eat everything but the skin.

    (c.) It all depends on the vegetable.

2. Which part of a potato plant do we eat?

    (a.) the tubers

    b. the seeds

    c. the leaves

3. How can you tell the difference between a fruit and a vegetable?

    a. Fruits taste very sweet.

    b. Vegetables taste sour.

    (c.) Fruits contain the plant's seeds.

4. How were early plants brought to other parts of the world?

    a. They were buried with people in ancient tombs.

    (b.) People brought their plants as they migrated to other countries.

    c. People drove their truck farms around from country to country.

5. In what ways are vegetables good for our health?

    a. They provide needed vitamins and minerals.

    b. They help us have balanced diets.

    (c.) Both of the above answers are correct.

Check your answers with your teacher. Give yourself 1 point for each correct answer, and fill in your Strategy score here. Then turn to page 205 and transfer your score onto Graph 1.

Personal

Vocabulary

Strategy

Comprehension

TOTAL SCORE

✓ T

Check your answers with your teacher. Give yourself 1 point for each correct answer, and fill in your Comprehension score here. Then turn to page 205 and transfer your score onto Graph 1.

Personal

Vocabulary

Strategy

Comprehension

TOTAL SCORE

✓ T

Extending

Choose one or both of these activities:

LEARN MORE ABOUT YOUR VEGETABLE

Learn more about the favorite vegetable that you named in Building Background. Find out as much as you can about your vegetable, and make a presentation to your class. Include some recipes or samples of dishes that are made with your vegetable. You might find some ideas in the Web site listed on this page.

DEBATE PESTICIDES

Pesticides have been shown to save crops from pests. However, studies have shown that certain pesticides can be damaging to our health. Work in two teams. Choose a position and learn more about your side of the issue. Write summaries from the resources that you choose to use in the debate. Then hold a debate in which each team presents its position. Allow time to ask questions of the other side, and then give a final statement. You might have the audience discuss whether they were swayed from their original opinions.

Resources

Books

Hughes, Meredith Sayles. *Stinky and Stringy: Stem and Bulb Vegetables.* Plants We Eat. Lerner Publications, 1998.

Landau, Elaine. *Tomatoes.* True Books—Food and Nutrition. Children's Book Press, 2000.

Urban, Victoria Bellett, and Alayna Maria Morgan. *Children's Veggies on Parade.* Vantage Press, 1998.

Web Site

http://www.farmfreshtoyou.com/recipes
Hundreds of great recipes for fruits and vegetables are given on this site.

LESSON ⓳ The Magic Bowl

Building Background

The story you are about to read is a folktale. A **folktale** is a kind of traditional tale. **Traditional tales** are stories have been retold through the ages by word of mouth. At some point, people retell these stories in writing, just as Robert San Souci has done with "The Magic Bowl."

Most folktales have certain common elements. For example, the characters' personalities are usually "flat," or one-sided. This means that they are based on one trait, such as stubbornness, kindness, or selfishness. The problem in a folktale is usually a simple one, so the plot moves along quickly as the characters try to solve the problem.

greedy

jealous

wisely

Vocabulary Builder

1. Read the words in the margin, and then think about folktales or traditional tales that you have read or heard. Can you think of characters from those tales that act greedy, jealous, or wisely?

2. On the following chart, list the names of two or three characters that fit each description. Later on, you can add the names of characters from this story.

3. Save your work. You will use it again in the Vocabulary Check.

Greedy Characters	Jealous Characters	Wise Characters
1. King Midas	1. the witch in "Sleeping Beauty"	1. Cinderella's fairy godmother
2. the troll in " The Three Billy Goats Gruff"	2. Cinderella's stepsisters	2. Merlin the magician
3. the wolf in "The Three Little Pigs"	3. the witch in "Snow White"	3. Little Wong and his mother in "The Magic Bowl"
4. the master in "The Magic Bowl"	4. the neighbors in "The Magic Bowl"	4.

Strategy Builder

Identifying Causes and Effects in Stories

- In Lesson 11 you learned that a **cause-and-effect relationship** tells what happened and why it happened. In "The Magic Bowl" you will read about a series of cause-and-effect relationships in which one event causes another.

- As you read the following paragraph, think about what happens and why.

> Joey was really hungry, so he made himself a big turkey sandwich. Just as he was about to eat it, his dog Sly walked up and gave Joey his paw. Joey broke off a corner of this sandwich and gave it to Sly. Sly gobbled the sandwich and rolled over twice. Joey gave Sly another piece of his sandwich. Sly gobbled it up and howled as if he were singing. Joey gave Sly another piece of his sandwich. Suddenly Joey realized he had given Sly all of his sandwich! Joey got up and made another sandwich.

If you wanted to track the causes and effects in this paragraph, you could put them on a **cause-and-effect chain**. It might look like this:

CAUSES

- Joey was really hungry.
- Just as Joey was about to eat, Sly walked up and gave Joey his paw.
- Sly gobbled the sandwich and rolled over twice.
- Sly gobbled it up and howled as if he were singing.
- Joey realized he had given Sly all of his sandwich!

EFFECTS

- He made himself a big turkey sandwich.
- Joey broke off a corner of his sandwich and gave it to Sly.
- Joey gave Sly another piece of his sandwich.
- Joey gave Sly another piece of his sandwich.
- Joey got up and made another sandwich.

The Magic Bowl

retold by Robert D. San Souci

As you read the first part of this tale, apply the strategies that you just learned. To find the causes and effects, keep asking yourself "What happened?" and "Why did it happen?"

Once a poor boy named Little Wong lived with his mother. The two made a scant living working for a rich farmer. The woman sewed and did the laundry; she also fed the ducks and pigs. Little Wong spent his days in the hills, cutting fresh grass to feed the farmer's horses.

Because he had to cut so much grass from the area around the farm, Little Wong had to go farther and farther into the fields to find enough grass to satisfy his employer.

But the grass on the hillside grew thin. The boy climbed higher yet, afraid to go back without full bundles on each end of his carrying pole. "Surely my master will beat me," he said aloud, "if his horses go hungry."

Suddenly, around a bend in the path, he discovered a meadow of ripe green grass. The wind rippled through it so that it looked like ocean waves. Eagerly, Little Wong began to cut the grass. As fast as his sickle mowed it, more grass would spring up the moment the blade passed. Faster and faster he cut the grass; faster and faster it grew back. Marveling at the strangeness of it all, Little Wong soon had so much grass bundled up that his carrying pole nearly broke under the weight of it.

For days after this, Little Wong went back to the curious field. It was always the same; the grass grew back as fast as he cut it.

When the farmer saw that the boy was returning early each day with a full load of grass, he asked, "How are you able to cut so much grass and return so quickly?"

When Little Wong explained about the wonderful field, his **greedy** master said only, "Fine! Then you can bring a double load each day, and my horses will be fatter for it."

So the boy had to work twice as hard.

 Stop here for the Strategy Break.

Strategy Break

If you were to create a cause-and-effect chain for this tale so far, it might look like this:

CAUSES

EFFECTS

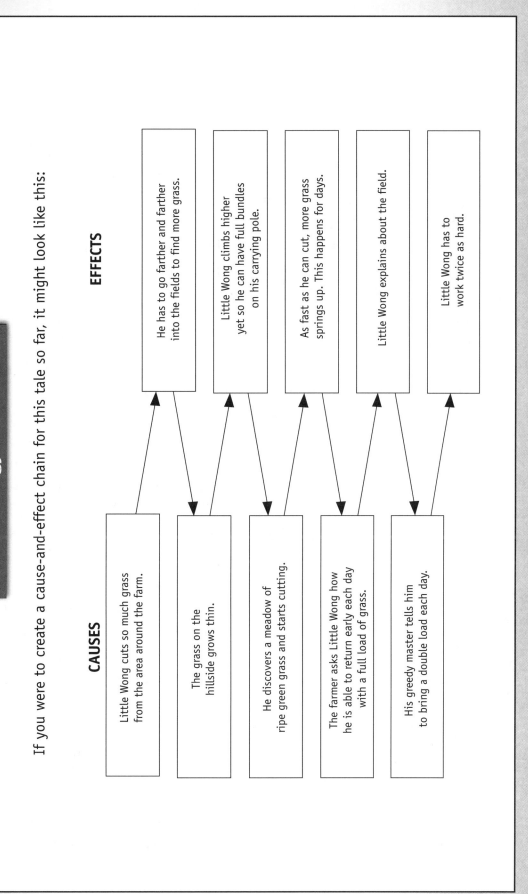

CAUSES	EFFECTS
Little Wong cuts so much grass from the area around the farm.	He has to go farther and farther into the fields to find more grass.
The grass on the hillside grows thin.	Little Wong climbs higher yet so he can have full bundles on his carrying pole.
He discovers a meadow of ripe green grass and starts cutting.	As fast as he can cut, more grass springs up. This happens for days.
The farmer asks Little Wong how he is able to return early each day with a full load of grass.	Little Wong explains about the field.
His greedy master tells him to bring a double load each day.	Little Wong has to work twice as hard.

Go on reading to see what happens.

At last his mother asked what had happened that he now made two trips into the hills each day.

When her son told her about the meadow with the ever-growing grass, she said, "My son, take me along with you tomorrow morning."

At sunrise, the two went into the hills. There his mother watched in amazement as Little Wong swiftly cut two bundles of grass, yet the meadow seemed untouched by his sickle. "There is something magical about this place," she said.

At that moment, Little Wong's sickle struck an object half-hidden in the grass. "Perhaps this is the source of the magic!" he exclaimed.

Quickly they dug, thinking to find some magical treasure. But all they found was a shallow earthenware bowl. "Surely there is nothing magical about this," said Little Wong in disappointment.

"Since we have gone to the trouble of digging it up," his mother said, "I will take it home and use it for feeding the master's ducks."

The next day, while her son was cutting grass, the woman put a handful of grain into the bowl to feed the ducks. Then she went to do some sewing.

But the master soon came to scold her, crying, "**Foolish** woman, you must pay more attention to your job. Look at how the ducks have scattered feed all over the yard! Why did you give them so much?"

When Little Wong's mother tried to explain that she had only put a handful of duck feed in the bowl, the man angrily shook his finger. "Do not lie to me," he said. "I know what I see."

Puzzled, the woman picked up the earthenware bowl, washed it out, and set it inside her house. She thought no more about it until she dropped a bit of thread into the bowl while she made herself some tea.

To her astonishment, when she tried to take up the thread, it kept coming until she had a pile of thread upon the floor. Only when she lifted the bowl to look more closely at it did the thread stop coming.

At that moment, Little Wong entered the room very upset.

"Mother, the grass in the meadow no longer grows back when I cut it. Since I must bring back twice as much for our master, the meadow will soon be grassless. Because there is so little grass anywhere else, the master will surely beat me. Perhaps he will turn us both out." The boy began to weep.

But his mother put her arm around his shoulder. "Do not cry, my son! The magic that was in the meadow is here now."

Quickly, she told him about the duck feed and the thread that had come from the little bowl.

"Could this be a treasure bowl?" asked Little Wong. He reached into the little cloth pocket at the front of his belt and took out a single copper coin. He tossed it into the bowl. Instantly, the bowl filled with coins.

"It is a miracle!" cried the woman. "We won't be poor any longer."

From that moment, they no longer worked for the farmer, though they remained in their little hut, not far from the man's gatepost. They lived carefully, spending their money **wisely**.

Each time they had used up their supply of copper coins, they placed one in the bowl and it would fill itself with coppers.

Little Wong still went into the hills every day, but now he cut and gathered firewood. When the money he made from his work was added to the coins from the magic bowl, Little Wong and his mother lived quite comfortably.

But their neighbors grew **jealous**. Rumors spread that there was something mysterious about the two who lived so well on a woodcutter's earnings.

No one was more curious than the greedy farmer who had once been their master. One day, he spied through the window as Little Wong's mother tossed a copper coin into the bowl. He could barely believe his eyes when he saw the bowl fill itself with coins. The woman took out the coins and put them in a cloth bag.

He stormed into the house and snatched the bowl, crying, "This belongs to me! It was my ducks' feeding bowl."

Little Wong returned at this point and argued that the bowl belonged to him and his mother because they had dug it up in the meadow.

"The meadow also belongs to me!" said the farmer. When mother and son tried to rescue the bowl, the man called to the neighbors to back his claim. Because the others were jealous of Little Wong and his mother, they let the farmer have his way. Little Wong's mother began to weep, but her son said, "We have more than enough put aside for our needs. And I will continue to gather and sell firewood."

Meanwhile, the farmer raced home with the ill-gotten treasure bowl. So eager was he to increase his wealth that he took a heavy silver ingot and dropped it into the bowl.

But the fragile bowl shattered. Though the man tried to repair it, it would never yield up so much as an extra bit of thread or a single copper coin, no matter what was put in it. And from the moment the bowl broke, the farmer's luck turned bad. His fields and orchards turned dry; his ducks and horses wasted away.

But Little Wong and his mother continued to prosper, and lived out their days contentedly. ●

Strategy Follow-up

Work with a group of classmates to create a cause-and-effect chain for the second part of this tale. You may want to use a long sheet of butcher paper and turn it lengthwise. Begin by dividing the story into several sections. Then take turns finding and recording the causes and effects in each section.

✓Personal Checklist

Read each question and put a check (✓) in the correct box.

1. How well were you able to use the information in Building Background to identify the characters' personalities in "The Magic Bowl"?
    - ☐ 3 (extremely well)
    - ☐ 2 (fairly well)
    - ☐ 1 (not well)

2. In the Vocabulary Builder, how well were you able to think of characters who are greedy, jealous, and wise?
    - ☐ 3 (extremely well)
    - ☐ 2 (fairly well)
    - ☐ 1 (not well)

3. In the beginning of this tale, how well do you understand why the Little Wong's master makes him work twice as hard?
    - ☐ 3 (extremely well)
    - ☐ 2 (fairly well)
    - ☐ 1 (not well)

4. How well do you understand why the bowl will not work for the farmer?
    - ☐ 3 (extremely well)
    - ☐ 2 (fairly well)
    - ☐ 1 (not well)

5. In the Strategy Follow-up, how well were you able to help your group create a cause-and-effect chain?
    - ☐ 3 (extremely well)
    - ☐ 2 (fairly well)
    - ☐ 1 (not well)

Vocabulary Check

Look back at the work you did in the Vocabulary Builder. Then answer each question by circling the correct letter.

1. Which vocabulary word best describes how Little Wong and his mother act in this tale?
    - a. greedy
    - ⓑ wisely
    - c. jealous

2. How did the neighbors feel about Little Wong and his mother's comfortable life?
    - a. They were happy about it.
    - ⓑ They were jealous of it.
    - c. They were afraid of it.

3. Which word best describes how the master acts?
    - ⓐ greedy
    - b. wisely
    - c. jealous

4. What is an example of greed in this tale?
    - a. Little Wong explains the wonderful field to his master.
    - b. When Little Wong tosses a coin into the bowl, it fills with coins.
    - ⓒ The farmer takes the bowl home and drops a silver ingot into it.

5. Which characters are usually the happiest at the end of traditional tales?
    - a. greedy characters
    - b. jealous characters
    - ⓒ wise characters

Add the numbers that you just checked to get your Personal Checklist score. Fill in your score here. Then turn to page 205 and transfer your score onto Graph 1.

Check your answers with your teacher. Give yourself 1 point for each correct answer, and fill in your Vocabulary score here. Then turn to page 205 and transfer your score onto Graph 1.

Strategy Check

Review the cause-and-effect chain that you helped create in the Strategy Follow-up. Then answer these questions:

1. What is the cause of the master scolding Little Wong's mother?
   - **a.** He thinks she gave the ducks too much food.
   - b. He thinks she didn't give the ducks enough food.
   - c. He's angry with her for making a mess with the thread.

2. What is the effect when Little Wong's mother puts a bit of thread into the bowl?
   - **a.** The thread keeps coming until she lifts the bowl.
   - b. The thread disappears completely.
   - c. The bowl shatters, and her luck turns bad.

3. What does the farmer do right after he learns about the magic bowl?
   - a. He breaks it.
   - **b.** He steals it.
   - c. He cleans it.

4. What is one effect of the farmer's luck turning bad?
   - **a.** His fields and orchards turn dry.
   - b. His grass grows as fast as he can cut it.
   - c. His neighbors all become jealous of him.

5. After Little Wong and his mother lose the bowl, what causes them to live out their days contentedly?
   - a. They get the bowl back and begin to use it again.
   - b. They go back to work for the greedy farmer.
   - **c.** They have more than enough put aside for their needs.

Comprehension Check

Review the tale if necessary. Then answer these questions:

1. What was amazing about the grass that Little Wong cut high on the hillside?
   - a. It grew thin.
   - **b.** It grew quickly.
   - c. It was easy to cut.

2. What do Little Wong and his mother think after they dig up the bowl?
   - **a.** There is nothing magical about it.
   - b. There is something magical about it.
   - c. It must belong to the farmer.

3. What gives you a clue about the farmer's personality?
   - a. Little Wong is afraid that his master will beat him.
   - b. The farmer steals the bowl from Little Wong and his mother.
   - **c.** Both of the above answers are correct.

4. Why do you think the magic bowl works for Little Wong and his mother?
   - a. They have very bad luck.
   - b. They are very greedy.
   - **c.** They use it wisely.

5. Why do you think the bowl is not magical for the farmer?
   - a. He already has many treasures.
   - **b.** He got the bowl by stealing it.
   - c. It only works for its first owner.

Check your answers with your teacher. Give yourself 1 point for each correct answer, and fill in your Strategy score here. Then turn to page 205 and transfer your score onto Graph 1.

Personal
Vocabulary
Strategy
Comprehension
TOTAL SCORE
✓ T

Check your answers with your teacher. Give yourself 1 point for each correct answer, and fill in your Comprehension score here. Then turn to page 205 and transfer your score onto Graph 1.

Personal
Vocabulary
Strategy
Comprehension
TOTAL SCORE
✓ T

Extending

Choose one or both of these activities:

WRITE A STORY ABOUT A MAGICAL OBJECT

First think of something that you use in your life that you wish were a magical object. Then imagine that it *is* a magical object. Write a short story to describe the object and what it does.

LEARN ABOUT CHINA

Use the resources listed on this page or ones you find yourself to learn more about China and its people. You might work in a group and have each person choose a topic to research, such as people, government, language, food, religion, natural resources, art, and music. Share your information with the class in a panel discussion about China.

Resources

Books

Armstrong, Jennifer. *Chin Yu Min and the Ginger Cat.* Random House, 1996.

Chin, Charlie. *China's Bravest Girl: The Legend of Hau Mu Lan.* Children's Book Press, 1997.

Cotterell, Arthur. *Ancient Chica.* Eyewitness Books. DK Publishing, 2000.

Rankin, Louise. *Daughter of the Mountains.* Puffin Newbery Library. Puffin, 1993.

San Souci, Robert D. *Fa Mulan: The Story of a Woman Warrior.* Hyperion Books for Children, 1998.

———. *Little Gold Star: A Spanish American Cinderella Story.* Harpercollins Juuvenile Books, 2000.

———. *Six Foolish Fishermen.* Hyperion Books for Children, 2000.

Wu, Priscilla. *The Abacus Contest: Stories from Taiwan and China.* World Stories. Fulcrum Publishers, 1996.

Web Site

http://www.merechina.com/facts
This Web site provides information on China and Chinese culture. There are recipes, a photo gallery, and links to other interesting sites.

Building Background

Why are folktales and other traditional tales told over and over? Well, it's usually because they reflect people at their best—and worst. No matter what the setting of the tale, it's fun to read about different characters and the situations they get themselves into. Many times, the characters in traditional tales are animals that act like people. Their personalities often reflect things about us or people we know. Often the tales teach us lessons about life. Sometimes they use magic to do it, as you discovered in "The Magic Bowl."

Think back to some of the traditional tales that you have read or heard. What lessons might they be trying to teach? Fill in the chart below with some of your ideas. If you need help getting started, an example is provided.

Traditional tale	Common folktale elements	Lesson it is trying to teach (if any)
The Tortoise and the Hare	• animals that act like people • flat characters (tortoise is patient; hare is impatient)	Slow and steady wins the race. Or, if you patiently keep at something, you'll finish it in good time.

Vocabulary Builder

complaints

ford

gazelle

patiently

peace

punish

tone

yam

1. Before you read "Talk," read the following descriptions. Then choose the vocabulary word in the margin that fits each description. Write that word on the line.

a graceful animal that resembles a deer	gazelle
a vegetable that looks like an orange potato; also called a sweet potato	yam
a shallow place in a river	ford
when you take your time, you are acting in this way	patiently
a time when there is no war	peace
when you do something wrong, someone may do this to you	punish
a list of things that are wrong	complaints
the way in which you say something	tone

2. Save your work. You will use it again in the Vocabulary Check.

Strategy Builder

Using Folktale Elements to Make Predictions

- As you know, folktales have certain common elements. In "The Magic Bowl" you learned that one of those elements was "flat," or one-sided, **characters**.

- In "Talk" you will learn about other common elements. For example, folktales often have a **repetitive pattern**. In some tales, the same thing happens to several characters. In other tales, one character repeats the same action.

- Another common element is **irony**. Often a tale will follow a predictable, repetitive pattern right up until the end. Then without warning it takes an unexpected turn, leaving readers surprised and amused.

- Look for the above elements as you begin reading "Talk." Use the elements—especially the repetitive pattern—to help you predict what will happen next. When you get to the end of the tale, see if your predictions match what happens.

Talk

an Ashanti Tale by Harold Courlander and George Herzog

Once, not far from the city of Accra on the Gulf of Guinea, a country man went out to his garden to dig up some **yams** to take to market. While he was digging, one of the yams said to him, "Well, at last you're here. You never weeded me, but now you come around with your digging stick. Go away and leave me alone!"

The farmer turned around and looked at his cow in amazement. The cow was chewing her cud and looking at him.

"Did you say something?" he said.

The cow kept on chewing and said nothing, but the man's dog spoke up. "It wasn't the cow who spoke to you," the dog said. "It was the yam. The yam says leave him alone."

The man became angry, because his dog had never talked before, and he didn't like his **tone** besides. So he took his knife and cut a branch from a palm tree to whip his dog. Just then the palm tree said, "Put that branch down!"

The man was getting very upset about the way things were going, and he started to throw the palm branch away, but the palm branch said, "Man, put me down softly!"

He put the branch down gently on a stone, and the stone said, "Hey, take that thing off me!"

This was enough, and the frightened farmer started to run for his village. On the way he met a fisherman going the other way with a fish trap on his head.

"What's the hurry?" the fisherman asked.

"My yam said, 'Leave me alone!' Then the dog said, 'Listen to what the yam says!' When I went to whip the dog with a palm branch the tree said, 'Put that branch down!' Then the palm branch said, 'Do it softly!' Then the stone said, 'Take that thing off me!'"

"Is that all?" the man with the fish trap said. "Is that so frightening?"

"Well," the man's fish trap said, "did he take it off the stone?"

"Wah!" the fisherman shouted. He threw the fish trap on the ground and began to run with the farmer, and on the trail they met a weaver with a bundle of cloth on his head.

 Stop here for Strategy Break #1.

Strategy Break #1

Use the information in the story to help you answer these questions:

1. What do you predict will happen next?

Students' responses will vary but should be supported with

clues from the text.

2. Why do you think so?

3. What clues from the story helped you make your prediction(s)?

Go on reading to see what happens.

"Where are you going in such a rush?" he asked them.

"My yam said, 'Leave me alone!'" the farmer said. "The dog said, 'Listen to what the yam says!' The tree said, 'Put that branch down!' The branch said, 'Do it softly!' And the stone said, 'Take that thing off me!'"

"And then," the fisherman continued, "the fish trap said, 'Did he take it off?'"

"That's nothing to get excited about," the weaver said. "No reason at all."

"Oh, yes it is," his bundle of cloth said. "If it happened to you, you'd run too!"

"Wah!" the weaver shouted. He threw his bundle on the trail and started running with the other men.

They came panting to the **ford** in the river and found a man bathing. "Are you chasing a **gazelle**?" he asked them.

The first man said breathlessly, "My yam talked at me, and it said, 'Leave me alone!' And my dog said, 'Listen to your yam!' And when I cut myself a branch the tree said, 'Put that branch down!' And the branch said, 'Do it softly!' And the stone said, 'Take that thing off me!'"

The fisherman panted, "And my trap said, 'Did he?'"

The weaver wheezed, "And my bundle of cloth said, 'You'd run too!'"

"Is that why you're running?" the man in the river asked.

"Well, wouldn't you run if you were in their position?" the river said.

The man jumped out of the water and began to run with the others. They ran down the main street of the village to the house of the chief. The chief's servant brought his stool out, and he came and sat on it to listen to their **complaints**. The men began to recite their troubles.

 Stop here for Strategy Break #2.

Strategy Break #2

Use the information in the story to help you answer these questions:

1. Do your earlier predictions match what happened? _____ Why or why not?

Students' responses will vary but should be supported with

clues from the text.

_____

_____

_____

2. What do you predict will happen next?

_____

_____

_____

_____

_____

3. Why do you think so?

_____

_____

_____

_____

_____

4. What clues from the story helped you make your prediction(s)?

_____

_____

_____

_____

_____

Go on reading to see what happens.

"I went out to my garden to dig yams," the farmer said, waving his arms. "Then everything began to talk! My yam said, 'Leave me alone!' My dog said, 'Pay attention to your yam!' The tree said, 'Put that branch down!' The branch said, 'Do it softly!' and the stone said, 'Take it off me!'"

"And my fish trap said, 'Well, did he take it off?'" the fisherman said.

"And my cloth said, 'You'd run too!'" the weaver said.

"And the river said the same," the bather said hoarsely, his eyes bulging.

The chief listened to them **patiently**, but he couldn't refrain from scowling. "Now this is really a wild story," he said at last. "You'd better all go back to your work before I **punish** you for disturbing the **peace**."

So the men went away, and the chief shook his head and mumbled to himself, "Nonsense like that upsets the community."

"Fantastic, isn't it?" his stool said. "Imagine, a talking yam!" ●

Strategy Follow-up

Go back and look at the predictions that you wrote in this lesson. Do they match what actually happened in the tale? What about the ending—did your prediction match what happened? Why or why not?

_____

_____

_____

_____

_____

_____

_____

_____

_____

✓Personal Checklist

Read each question and put a check (✓) in the correct box.

1. How well were you able to add information to the chart in Building Background?
   - ☐ 3 (extremely well)
   - ☐ 2 (fairly well)
   - ☐ 1 (not well)

2. How many words in the Vocabulary Builder were you able to match with their descriptions?
   - ☐ 3 (6–8 words)
   - ☐ 2 (3–5 words)
   - ☐ 1 (0–2 words)

3. As you read "Talk," how well were you able to identify the folktale elements described in this lesson?
   - ☐ 3 (extremely well)
   - ☐ 2 (fairly well)
   - ☐ 1 (not well)

4. How well were you able to use the folktale elements to predict what would happen next in this tale?
   - ☐ 3 (extremely well)
   - ☐ 2 (fairly well)
   - ☐ 1 (not well)

5. How well do you understand why everyone is frightened of the talking objects?
   - ☐ 3 (extremely well)
   - ☐ 2 (fairly well)
   - ☐ 1 (not well)

Vocabulary Check

Look back at the work you did in the Vocabulary Builder. Then answer each question by circling the correct letter.

1. In this tale, what is the graceful animal that resembles a deer?
   - (a.) gazelle
   - b. yam
   - c. ford

2. Which vocabulary word means "waiting while not complaining"?
   - a. complaints
   - b. punish
   - (c.) patiently

3. Which word is the antonym (opposite) of *war*?
   - a. tone
   - b. punished
   - (c.) peace

4. In the beginning of this tale, the man's dog talks and the man gets angry. What is one reason that the man gets angry?
   - a. He is tired of the dog's complaints.
   - (b.) He doesn't like the dog's tone.
   - c. The dog doesn't answer patiently.

5. What does the farmer want to use to punish the dog?
   - a. a yam
   - b. a knife
   - (c.) a palm branch

Add the numbers that you just checked to get your Personal Checklist score. Fill in your score here. Then turn to page 205 and transfer your score onto Graph 1.

Check your answers with your teacher. Give yourself 1 point for each correct answer, and fill in your Vocabulary score here. Then turn to page 205 and transfer your score onto Graph 1.

Strategy Check

Look back at what you wrote at each Strategy Break. Then answer these questions:

1. At Strategy Break #1, you probably predicted that the weaver would tell the men not to be afraid, and an object of his would talk. What would have helped you make that prediction?

    a. the weaver's one-sided personality

    (b.) the repetitive pattern of the tale

    b. the irony of the tale

2. At Strategy Break #2, in what order did you predict the men would recite their troubles?

    (a.) farmer, fisherman, weaver, bather

    b. bather, weaver, fisherman, farmer

    c. farmer, weaver, fisherman, bather

3. If you predicted that the chief would tell the men not to get excited, which clue would have best supported your prediction?

    a. Every other person has had the opposite reaction.

    (b.) Every other person has had the same reaction.

    c. Since the chief is wise, he'll have the same reaction.

4. If you predicted the chief's stool would talk, which clue would have supported your prediction?

    a. The chief tells everyone to go back to work before he punishes them.

    b. The chief says, "Nonsense like that upsets the community."

    (c.) If the stool talked too, it would be repeating the pattern of the story.

5. What is ironic about the ending of this tale?

    a. The men are surprised by a talking stool.

    (b.) The stool is surprised by a talking yam.

    c. The chief is surprised by a talking yam.

Comprehension Check

Review the tale if necessary. Then answer these questions:

1. What does each man do when he hears his object speak?

    a. Each man tells his object to be quiet.

    (b.) Each man starts running with the other men.

    c. Each man starts running in a different direction.

2. At first, each man doesn't believe the others' story. What causes all the men to change their minds?

    a. The yam talks to each of the men.

    b. The farmer tells the men to believe him.

    (c.) Something of their own speaks to them.

3. Why does the chief tell the men they are disturbing the peace?

    (a.) He thinks they are disturbing others with their nonsense.

    b. He thinks they are telling their troubles too loudly.

    c. All of the talking men and objects are making too much noise.

4. What do you predict the chief will probably think after the stool talks?

    a. He still won't believe the men.

    (b.) He finally will believe the men.

    c. Neither answer is correct.

5. What message or lesson do you think this tale is trying to teach?

    a. When you tell the truth, people always believe you.

    (b.) Things aren't always what they seem.

    c. Talking objects really do exist.

Check your answers with your teacher. Give yourself 1 point for each correct answer, and fill in your Strategy score here. Then turn to page 205 and transfer your score onto Graph 1.

Personal
Vocabulary
Strategy
Comprehension
TOTAL SCORE
✓ T

Check your answers with your teacher. Give yourself 1 point for each correct answer, and fill in your Comprehension score here. Then turn to page 205 and transfer your score onto Graph 1.

Personal
Vocabulary
Strategy
Comprehension
TOTAL SCORE
✓ T

SILVER FRAME

This is an easy and cost-effective way of making a fancy frame without any special tools. All you need is some corrugated cardboard and silver baking foil.

YOU WILL NEED
Metal rule
Pencil
Craft knife
Heavy corrugated cardboard
Card
Paper glue
Silver baking foil
Scissors
Picture hanger
Masking tape

1 Scale up the template to the size required. Using a craft knife and metal rule, cut out all the frame pieces from corrugated cardboard. Again using a craft knife and metal rule, cut out the spacers from card. Then glue together the two smaller borders of the frame.

2 Glue the three spacers onto the underneath of the front frame. Stick the spacers onto the sides and bottom so that a gap is left at the top to insert a photograph.

3 Cover the border of the corrugated cardboard with foil. Trim it to size using scissors and glue down. Cover the back piece with foil.

4 Using the point from a pair of scissors, pierce the back piece of the frame at the top, beneath the front border. Insert a picture hanger from the back. Cover the front of the hanger with masking tape.

5 Finally spread glue onto the spacers and stick the front piece of the frame to the back.

PAPER QUILLS

The old-fashioned paper craft known as quilling is used to make this distinctive card. You can design a picture in the same way, and hang it on the wall.

YOU WILL NEED
Assorted coloured papers
Scissors
Strong clear glue
Contrasting coloured card

1 Cut long narrow strips of various shades of coloured paper. First curl one end of each strip with the blunt edge of a pair of scissors, then, starting at this end, roll the strip into a tight coil.

2 Release the coil slightly and glue the end. Hold this in position until the glue is dry. Pinch the outside of the coils between your fingers to form different shapes such as a pear, scroll or eye.

3 Fold a rectangular piece of card in a contrasting colour in half. Arrange the shaped quills on the card and stick down, spreading the glue on the bottom edge of each quill.

KITCHEN TOOL HOLDER

Turn an empty can into a decorative holder for kitchen tools. Try to find paper that emphasizes some detail in the kitchen, or even paint your own design on plain paper.

YOU WILL NEED
Empty can
White matt emulsion paint
Large paintbrush
Ruler
Pencil
Wrapping paper
Scissors
Strong clear glue
Clear polyurethane varnish

1 Prime the can with white matt emulsion paint. Measure the height and circumference of the can and draw two rectangles on the back of the wrapping paper slightly larger than these measurements, one for the inside of the can and one for the outside. Cut out the pieces. Spread glue on the piece for the inside.

2 Insert this piece inside the can carefully and press it against the walls. Make cuts in the paper projecting at the top of the can so that the paper can be glued down neatly to the outside of the can.

3 Glue the second piece of paper to the outside of the can, making sure the top edge is flush with the rim, and that there is a small overlap at the base. Cut the projecting paper so it can be glued to the bottom.

4 Cut out a circle in the paper, using the can as a guide, and glue this to the base.

5 Cut out a slightly smaller circle in the paper, glue it and lower it into the base of the can. Press into place. Allow to dry. Then apply two coats of clear polyurethane varnish. Allow to dry overnight.

RECYCLED BOX

This 'green' idea should appeal to everyone. Recycle clean old cardboard boxes which perhaps once contained tea bags and cover them with wrapping paper. They make attractive storage boxes for little bits and pieces such as necklaces or bracelets.

YOU WILL NEED
Cardboard box
Metal rule
Patterned and plain wrapping paper
Scissors
Paper glue
Coloured tissue paper

1 Measure all the sides of the box and cut patterned wrapping paper to the approximate size. Wrap the outside of the box with the paper, trim to size with scissors and stick it down with paper glue.

2 Line the inside of the box with plain wrapping paper for neatness.

3 Scrunch up some tissue paper that complements the colours of the wrapping paper and use to line the box.

TISSUE BOX COVERS

This is a novel way to disguise tissue boxes and hide the brand names. Choose a wrapping paper that blends neatly into your colour scheme.

YOU WILL NEED

Tissue box
Metal rule
Thin white card
Pencil
Craft knife
Clear glue
Wrapping paper
Scissors

fold

cut

1 Scale up the template to the size required to fit the tissue box, adding 12 mm (½ in) to all the measurements of the original tissue box. Transfer the pattern onto thin white card. Using a craft knife, cut out the pattern. Using a metal rule and craft knife lightly score all the edges that need to be folded. Be careful not to cut right through the card.

2 Fold the top edges and the tabs, and stick the corners together with glue.

3 Using the same template cut out the wrapping paper. Leave an overlap for the hole in the middle. Fold the paper under and cut darts in the paper. Glue underneath.

4 Next stick the wrapping paper onto the white card with clear glue. Slip the cover over the tissue box and pull the tissues through the opening.

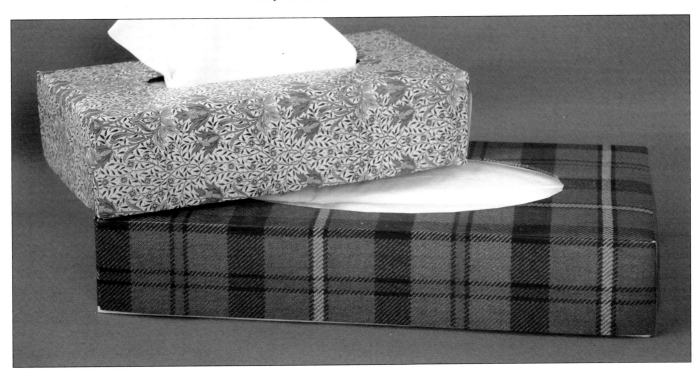

GIFT-WRAPPED

Add to the excitement of a special gift by packing it in this effective box. You can make the box any size, scaling the template up or down to fit the contents. Choose card and ribbon in colours to match your gift, if you like. The 'gems' can be bought from most craft suppliers.

YOU WILL NEED
Ruler
Pencil
Square of stiff card
Craft knife
Paper glue
Ribbon
Stapler
Jewel decorations

1 Scale up the template to the size required and transfer the measurements onto the card. Cut out the box using a craft knife and ruler. Score along the inside fold of the tabs. Fold the card inwards to make a box. Glue down the tabs onto the inside of the box.

2 Staple one piece of ribbon under the front flap of the box and fold the other piece under the staple onto the front flap of the lid in such a way that the staple does not show when the ribbon is tied.

3 Arrange the 'gems' on the lid in a pretty pattern and glue down. Tie the ribbon in a bow to finish and to hold the box shut.

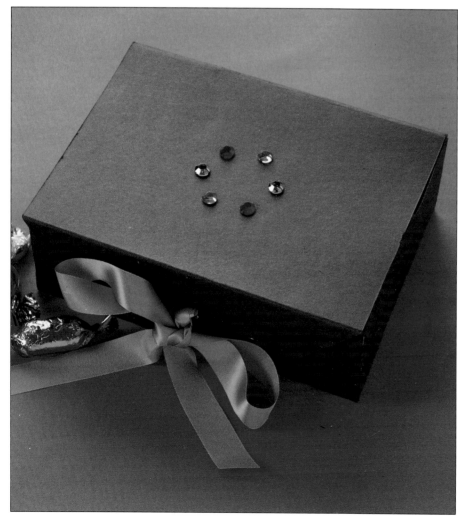

POP-UP CARD

This jolly cat pops out of a flowery garden and languidly surveys the scene. Use this simple design to make a variety of pop-up cards for different occasions.

YOU WILL NEED
Tracing paper
Pencil
Assortment of coloured cartridge papers
Scissors
Black paint
Small paintbrush
Ruler
Paper glue

1 Scale up the cat and flower templates. Draw in base tabs. Trace them onto coloured papers and cut out.

2 Paint the details of the cut-outs in black.

3 Cut a piece of paper 25 cm × 15 cm (10 in × 6 in). Fold it in half to form the base of the card. Measure a point 2.5 cm (1 in) from the top of the paper on the folded edge. Measure another point 4 cm (1½ in) from the folded edge along the top of the card. Draw a diagonal line between these two points. Make a fold inwards along this line, and open out the paper.

4 Fold the cat cut-out in half, and then open it out. Glue the base tabs, and stick the cat along the diagonal lines on the inside of the card.

5 Stick the flowers in position on the inside left of the card.

CHRISTMAS CARD

Black card makes a dramatic background for the angel on this stylish handmade Christmas greeting. Try making a series of different designs on a similar theme.

YOU WILL NEED
Stiff card
Scissors
Image from old card or wrapping paper
Paper glue
Silver glitter pen
Gold self-adhesive stars

1 Cut the card to the size you require and fold it in half. Score along the inside of the fold to make a sharp, neat edge. Cut out an image and glue onto the centre of the card.

2 Draw some elegant lines with a silver glitter pen around the edge of the card, and allow to dry.

3 Arrange a cluster of gold stars around the central image and a line of them spaced evenly on top of the silver lines to create a border.

DECORATING PAPER

It is fun to design your own wrapping paper. This rustic paper with its oak leaf motif could be used to wrap a woolly sweater in earthy colours, or perhaps some gardening tools. You could even print a friend's name with rubber stamps in the form of letters, or perhaps your own special message.

YOU WILL NEED
Pencil
Erasers
Craft knife
Assorted poster paints, or ink pads
Small paintbrush
Assorted wrapping papers

1 Draw a simple design onto an eraser and cut around it with a craft knife, taking great care to avoid your fingers.

2 Apply a coat of paint to the image on your rubber stamp, and press the stamp down firmly onto the wrapping paper. Take care not to make the paint too runny, as it would spread and blur the image. Alternatively, press the stamp onto an ink pad.

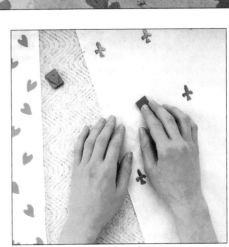

3 A more delicate effect is achieved by printing on white tissue paper, which would be partic-ularly suitable for wrapping wedding or christening gifts.

GIFT TAGS

Why buy expensive gift tags when you can make your own from scraps of paper? Match or contrast the tags with the wrapping paper, or make plain ones and decorate them with sequins, scraps of felt, coloured foil or glitter.

YOU WILL NEED
Ruler
Scraps of coloured paper
Scissors
Pencil
Paper glue
Hole punch
Thin string

1 Cut a 10 cm × 5 cm (4 in × 2 in) piece of coloured paper. Fold it in half.

2 Draw hearts and wavy lines onto contrasting pieces of coloured paper and cut them out.

3 Stick them in place with paper glue.

4 Punch a hole on the inside top left-hand corner of the gift tag. Thread a length of thin string through the hole.

STATIONERY SET

Co-ordinated stationery looks very attractive — you might like to make a complete set for all your correspondence, including invitation cards. You could choose a simple motif such as a star or heart, or perhaps your initials or a monogram. You could also make this stationery wallet to keep everything together.

YOU WILL NEED
Pencil
Scraps of paper in contrasting colours
Sheets of writing paper and envelopes
Scissors
Paper glue
Piece of thin card in complementary colour

1 Draw your design onto paper that contrasts with or complements the colour of your writing paper. Cut out each element of the design.

2 Place the cutouts on the stationery and stick in position. You might prefer the top left-hand corner, or perhaps the top centre of each sheet of paper. The back or front of each envelope may be decorated similarly.

3 Cut out a stationery wallet in thin card to hold the paper. The wallet may be decorated in the same way as the stationery.

PLACE CARDS

Place cards can set the mood for a meal. Perhaps you want to convey a sophisticated atmosphere with very plain cards, or a jazzy, fun air with bright, vivid colours and clever cut-outs. You can also follow the theme of the occasion such as a birthday or anniversary celebration.

YOU WILL NEED
Paper in a variety of colours
Scraps of paper in contrasting colours
Pencil
Scissors
Paper glue
Black felt-tip pen

1 Cut a small rectangle of cartridge paper. Draw your chosen design onto contrasting paper and cut it out.

2 Fold a small piece of coloured paper in half to form the place card. Position each element of the design, and stick it in place.

3 Write the name of a guest on each place card.

CHRISTMAS CRACKER

Decorate your Christmas tree with lots of fancy crackers. Fill them with tiny gifts and pull them during the festive season.

YOU WILL NEED
Cardboard tube
Silver doily
Scissors
Crêpe paper
Strong clear glue
Ribbon
Foil ribbon

1 Place the cardboard tube on top of the silver doily and trim the doily to size using scissors.

2 Place the cardboard tube on a length of crêpe paper which will cover the whole tube. Trim the ends, leaving at least 10 cm (4 in) at both ends. Glue the crêpe paper where the seam is formed. Next place the silver doily on top of the tube and glue down.

3 When this is secure, fringe the ends of the crêpe paper. This is done by cutting into the ends with scissors at regular intervals all around the circumference.

4 Next cut two lengths of ribbon about 30 cm (12 in) long and tie a bow at both ends of the cracker.

5 Pull long strips of the foil ribbon through closed scissors to make it twist and curl into ringlets. Tie onto both ends of the cracker.

FLOWER GARLAND

Festoon a ceiling and walls with
festive flower garlands made of
coloured tissue paper. Use bright
colours for the flowers, and green for
the leaves.

YOU WILL NEED

Coloured tissue paper
Thin card
Black felt-tip pen
Scissors
Paper glue
Coloured string

3 Fold the shapes
in half so that
you can cut a hole
neatly in the centre,
using the scissors.

4 For each
flower, glue the
centre of a brightly
coloured shape and
place directly on
top of another
shape of the same
coloured tissue
paper. Press down
firmly.

1 Fold sheets of
tissue paper so
that a number of
shapes can be cut
simultaneously.
Scale up the flower
shape on the
template onto card
and draw around it
with a black pen
onto the folded
sheets of tissue.

2 Cut out the
flower shape
with scissors,
keeping the layers
together. Repeat
this until you have
enough shapes of
different colours.

5 The leaves are
formed in the
same way as the
flowers, by gluing
in the centre. To
join the flowers and
leaves, glue the tips
of three petals on
one side of a flower
shape and place a
green shape on top.
Continue sticking
the shapes
alternately at the
tips and centre.
Alternate leaves and
flowers until the
garland is built up.

6 Finally, thread a
piece of
coloured string
through the central
holes to hang the
garland.

LAMPSHADE

Dress up that jaded shade by covering it with wrapping paper or wallpaper. The design or colours of the shade can be chosen to co-ordinate with the furnishing scheme of your room.

YOU WILL NEED

Lampshade
Brown parcel paper
Wrapping paper or wallpaper
Pencil
Craft knife
Coin
Scissors
Clear glue
Masking tape
Clear polyurethane varnish
Large paintbrush

1 Lay the lampshade on its side on the brown parcel paper and slowly rotate it, drawing the shape as you go along to achieve the correct measurement. Use this shape as the template for the lampshade.

2 Cut out the brown parcel paper shape slightly outside the drawn line using a craft knife. Draw a scalloped edge using a coin as a template and cut out scallops.

3 Place the template onto the wrong side of the wrapping paper and secure with masking tape. Then draw around the template and cut out this shape.

4 Spread glue onto the lampshade and stick down the paper slowly, smoothing out any bumps or air pockets as you go round.

5 Make cuts in the protruding paper at the top so that it can be glued down neatly to the inside of the frame. Apply two coats of clear polyurethane varnish so that the lampshade may be wiped clean.

GIFT BOXES

Presents always seem more intriguing if packed in a special box — here are two that have been decorated with holly leaves for Christmas and flowers for spring. Other suitable motifs include Christmas trees, angels and reindeer.

1 Using a pencil, draw your designs onto coloured paper.

YOU WILL NEED
Assortment of coloured paper or old catalogues
Pencil
Scissors
Gift boxes
Paper glue

2 Cut them out carefully using scissors.

3 Arrange the cut-outs on the gift box and stick them in position with paper glue.

4 As an alternative, cover a plain gold gift box with photographs of flowers cut out of a seed catalogue.

MODEL CLOCK

This highly original timepiece would delight any collector of bizarre objects! The figure is typical of the models daringly featured in Victorian mail-order catalogues.

YOU WILL NEED
Drill
Piece of plywood
Paper images from old magazines
Scissors
Diluted PVA glue
Pencil
Dark oak-coloured varnish
Small paintbrush
Soft cloth
Clear matt varnish
Clock mechanism
Clock hands
Battery

1 Drill a hole, large enough for a clock mechanism, in a primed piece of plywood. Cut out suitable paper images and clock face and arrange on the piece of plywood.

2 Make sure that the centre of the clock face is directly above the drilled hole. Stick the design in position using diluted PVA glue. Rub the paper with your hands until it is smooth. Using a pencil, pierce a hole in the centre of the clock face.

3 Allow 1 hour for the glue to dry, then apply dark oak-coloured varnish with a small paintbrush. Before it dries, rub it off in circular movements with a soft cloth, working from the centre outwards. Leave to dry.

4 Apply a coat of clear matt varnish. When this is dry, fit the clock mechanism and connect the hands to the front. Insert the battery.

WASTE PAPER BASKET

Decoupage decoration quickly covers surfaces in beautiful and unusual designs. It is particularly effective on shiny materials, such as this metal waste paper basket.

YOU WILL NEED
Flat brush
Diluted PVA glue
Metal waste paper basket
Pale blue and yellow tissue paper
Scissors
Flowery wrapping paper
Clear polyurethane varnish

1 Brush PVA glue liberally all over the waste paper basket.

2 Tear long strips of tissue paper and paste them round the middle area of the basket.

3 Cut out an assortment of strips and pretty motifs from wrapping paper.

4 Decide on the design of the basket and dip the pieces of wrapping paper in PVA glue. Stick them onto the basket according to your chosen design, brushing them flat as you work. Add more strips of tissue paper until the design is complete. Leave to dry. Finish with a final coat of glue and leave to dry. Cover with a coat of clear polyurethane varnish and leave to dry.

HAT BOX

This traditional hat box can be used to store a variety of objects other than hats. It is also an attractive piece to display in your home. A simple form of decoupage using wrapping paper is shown here. You can of course cut out pictures from magazines, old postcards and greeting cards, building up layers of images.

YOU WILL NEED
Hat box
White matt emulsion paint
Large paintbrush
Fine sandpaper
Piece of natural sponge
Poster paint
Rag
Wrapping paper
Scissors
Diluted PVA glue
Coloured varnish

1 Paint the hat box with matt white emulsion paint. Rub down using fine sandpaper. Using a piece of natural sponge, add a wash of watery paint to age the box, removing some of the paint with a rag as you go.

2 Choose a paper with an attractive design and cut out the images that most appeal to you. Arrange the paper on the box ready to glue on.

3 Glue your images onto the box using diluted PVA glue and leave to dry.

4 Varnish the box with a coloured varnish, again removing a lot of it with a rag to give the box warmth and to add to its antiqued look.

SHOE BOX

The pictures of shoes decorating this box have been dipped in cold tea to antique them. This technique is very effective, and a variety of different images could be used. For example, pictures of hats could adorn a circular hat box, or jewels a trinket box. Good sources of illustrations are old clothing catalogues, greetings cards, and any Victorian or Edwardian technical manuals.

YOU WILL NEED
Brown wrapping paper
Cardboard shoe box
Scissors
Paper glue
Old shoe catalogues
Cold tea

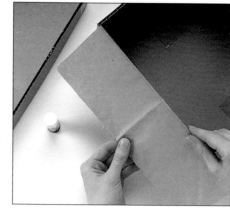

1 Cut out pieces of brown wrapping paper to fit a cardboard shoe box. Use to cover the box and lid completely and glue in place.

2 Roughly cut out the chosen images from the catalogues. Fill a small bowl with cold tea, and submerge each image for a few seconds so that the tea penetrates the paper. Pin each image up to dry. If the images hang vertically, this should prevent them from wrinkling as they dry. If they do become a little creased, press them quickly on the reverse using a cool iron.

3 Cut around the pictures carefully with small scissors and arrange them on the box and lid.

4 When you are satisfied with your design, stick each picture in position.

HAND MIRROR

Decorate a dull hand mirror with ornate decoupage motifs to add a beautiful touch to the dressing table. You could even make a matching set with a decorated hairbrush and other toilet items.

YOU WILL NEED
Plastic hand mirror
Fine sandpaper
Plain paper
Masking tape
Scissors
Poster paint in a complementary
*   colour*
Small paintbrush
Wrapping paper
Diluted PVA glue

1 Lightly sand the plain surfaces of the mirror using fine sandpaper.

2 Cut out a plain paper shield to fit over the mirror glass and stick in place with masking tape.

3 Paint the plastic surfaces with poster paint, allowing each coat to dry thoroughly.

4 Cut out motifs from wrapping paper and arrange over the handle and back of the mirror. Dip each piece into diluted PVA, place on the mirror and brush more glue on top.

5 Using small strips of wrapping paper, decorate the rim and front edge in the same way. Leave to dry overnight. Remove the paper and tape from the front edge.

CAKE TIN

This metal cake tin has been given a new lease of life with some white paint and jazzy tartlet motifs — you could, of course, depict any type of confectionery you wanted!

YOU WILL NEED
Metal cake tin
White poster paint
Paintbrush
Pencil
Coloured cartridge paper
Scissors
Paper glue
Clear gloss varnish

1 Wash the cake tin to remove any grease and then prime the outside with a coat of white paint. Leave to dry, then apply a second coat to give a good dense base colour.

2 Draw your designs onto cartridge paper and cut them out.

3 Arrange the cutouts on the sides and lid of the tin. Stick them in position with glue.

4 Seal the tin with two coats of varnish. Allow to dry thoroughly before you use the tin.

PRIVATE
LETTER BOX

This ornate box can be used to store those secret letters, or to keep documents safe. Use brightly coloured wrapping paper to decorate it, saving oddments for extra details.

YOU WILL NEED
Thin cardboard
Scissors
Craft knife
Metal rule
Strong clear glue
Masking tape
Wrapping paper
Large paintbrush
Diluted PVA glue
Narrow ribbon
Button

1 Scale up the template to the size required and transfer to a piece of thin cardboard. Cut out the box shape. Score along the folds using a craft knife and metal rule. Fold in the tabs and glue firmly in place along the sides.

2 Strengthen the edges of the box with strips of masking tape.

3 Cut out motifs from wrapping paper and decide where to position them on the box. Stick down with diluted PVA glue, brushing an extra coat of glue over the pieces to varnish them. Allow to dry. Fix a loop of ribbon under the flap of the lid and a button on the front of the box to fasten.

CUPID CUPBOARD

If you see a shabby old cupboard in an auction sale, why not bid for it? Decoupage is an easy way to turn such a piece of furniture into a charming addition to your home, and you do not need to have any special artistic skills.

YOU WILL NEED

Scissors
Decorative paper images
Small cupboard
Medium sandpaper
White spirit
White matt emulsion paint
Diluted wood glue
Small paintbrush
Acrylic varnish
Large paintbrush
Antique oak-coloured varnish
Soft cloth

1 Using scissors, cut out the decorative images required for the decoupage.

2 To prepare the cupboard, rub down with sandpaper, clean with white spirit and coat twice with white matt emulsion paint. Arrange the cut-out images on the cupboard and stick down with diluted wood glue. Make sure the glue is spread evenly over the images. Leave to dry for 1 hour.

3 Using a small paintbrush, apply a coat of acrylic varnish to the decoupage images only. This will protect them against the next stage of varnishing. Allow the acrylic varnish to dry for 30 minutes.

4 Using a large paintbrush, apply the antique oak-coloured varnish to small areas at a time. As soon as you have brushed on the varnish, wipe it off quickly with a soft cloth. Repeat this process until the whole cupboard has been varnished. This stains the white painted areas while the oak-coloured varnish stays intact in cracks and grooves.

MOSAIC TRAY

Create a useful and evocative souvenir of your travels with a collection of postcards. Select a variety of pictures that capture your memories, or those of a friend or relative, and use to transform an old tray into a piece of art.

YOU WILL NEED
Old tray
Sandpaper
White matt emulsion paint
PVA glue
Blue poster paint
Large paintbrush
Scissors
Assorted picture postcards

1 Clean and lightly sand the tray. Prime with one coat of white emulsion. Leave to dry. Mix two tablespoons of PVA glue with the blue poster paint and apply one coat to the tray. Leave to dry. Cut up picture postcards into triangles.

2 Decide on the arrangement of the images on the tray. Mix ¾ cup PVA to ¼ cup water. Dip each triangle into the glue and position on the tray, turning the tray as you work. Add small strips cut from postcards along the top edges of the tray. When the design is complete, varnish the tray with two coats of PVA glue.

IVY MIRROR

'Mirror, mirror on the wall — who is the fairest of them all?' By painting a trail of ivy on the frame, this mirror becomes a decorative feature for a country bedroom. Experiment using alternative designs made up of flowers or intricately-shaped leaves.

YOU WILL NEED
Wooden-framed mirror
Masking tape
White matt emulsion paint
Large paintbrush
Paper
Pencil
Carbon paper
Small paintbrush
Green and white acrylic paint
Soft cloths
Finishing wax

1 Prepare the mirror. Put strips of masking tape all round the edges of the mirror close to the frame to prevent paint from getting onto the mirror. Apply two coats of white matt emulsion paint.

2 Draw an ivy design onto paper to fit the mirror. Place a strip of carbon paper face down on the mirror frame and secure with masking tape. Lay the ivy design on top and secure in the same way. Draw around the design with a pencil so it is reproduced on the frame in carbon. Repeat this process until the whole design is copied onto the frame.

3 Using a small paintbrush, paint the meandering ivy with a mixture of green and white acrylic paint.

4 Use a darker mixture of green to paint an outline and other details. Using a soft cloth, polish the mirror frame with two coats of finishing wax. Allow each coat to dry and polish again.

5 When the wax is dry, remove the masking tape to reveal a clean mirror.

PAINTED BUCKET

This bucket is influenced by the canal boat painters and uses their traditional colours of green, red and yellow.

YOU WILL NEED
Metal bucket
Wire (steel) wool
Green, red, yellow and black enamel paint
Large paintbrush
Pencil
Tracing paper
White paper
Chalk
Masking tape
Small paintbrush

1 Rub down the bucket with wire wool. Paint it with two coats of green enamel paint using a large paintbrush. Scale up the template to fit your bucket, tracing the design onto paper. Rub chalk onto the back of the template and attach to the bucket side with masking tape. Draw the design on top with a pencil and the image will be duplicated in chalk.

2 Remove the template carefully so as not to disturb the chalk. Paint the areas of red and yellow using a small brush. Apply two coats and allow to dry for 6 hours between each coat.

3 When all the colours are dry, finish off by adding black outlines and details with a small paintbrush. Allow the paint to dry forming a tough coat. Varnish is not necessary for this piece.

TOY CHEST

This colourful chest can be used in a child's room for storing toys and puzzles. Try to think of as many different colours as you can for the kites and bows — experiment with mixing your own shades.

YOU WILL NEED

Toy chest
White matt emulsion paint
Large paintbrush
Sandpaper
White chalk
Stiff black card
Scissors
Pencil
Assorted acrylic paints
Small paintbrush
Masking tape
Clear satin polyurethane varnish

1 Prepare the chest. Paint it white, leave to dry and rub down with sandpaper. Apply a second coat of white paint and leave to dry. Scale up and draw the shape of the kite and bows with white chalk on black card and cut them out. Hold the templates against the chest and move them around until you have arranged them satisfactorily. Then draw around each template with a pencil. Draw in the detail and link up the bows and kites with a flowing pencil line.

2 Using a small paintbrush, paint the edges of the chest in blue acrylic paint, covering the borders with masking tape to give a neat line.

3 Start painting in the design. You may need to give it a couple of coats to achieve an even finish. Using a small paintbrush in a confident manner, link up the bows following your flowing pencil line with burnt umber acrylic paints. Add the finishing touches with a paler tone of each colour to add movement and dimension. Allow to dry. Apply polyurethane varnish, giving the chest at least two coats for maximum protection. Leave to dry overnight.

FOOT STOOL

The red tulips and blue decoration on this stool are reminiscent of early American folk art. This idea can be adapted to transform any piece of secondhand furniture.

YOU WILL NEED
Stool
Sandpaper
White matt emulsion paint
Metal rule
Plain paper
Pencil
Scissors
Coloured chalk
Masking tape
Soft cloth
Assorted gouache paints
Small paintbrush
Gloss polyurethane varnish

1 Rub down the stool with sandpaper and paint with matt white emulsion paint. Measure the surfaces to be decorated, then draw the planned design onto paper. Cut out to size. Completely cover the back of the paper with chalk. Hold it in place on the stool with masking tape. Draw over the design firmly with pencil, and remove the drawing paper. Follow the chalk design carefully and lightly with pencil, and wipe off the loose chalk with a soft cloth.

2 Paint on the design with gouache paints using a small paint-brush. Leave to dry. Then seal the stool with two coats of gloss polyurethane varnish.

SIDE TABLE

You might find an old piece of furniture that has a pleasing shape or line but is in terrible condition. Strip off any old paint and start again. This is a very simple linear design painted on just such a 'rescued' table. Masking tape is invaluable for helping to paint straight lines.

YOU WILL NEED
Table
White matt emulsion paint
Large paintbrush
Yellow ochre and raw umber acrylic
*   paints*
Ruler
Pencil
Masking tape
Small paintbrush
Antique pine-coloured varnish
Soft cloth
Matt varnish

1 Prepare the table. Apply two coats of white matt emulsion. For the base cream colour, mix yellow ochre acrylic paint and white matt emulsion paint. Apply two coats. Measure and mark out the linear design on the table with a pencil. Using the markings as a guide, lay down long parallel strips of masking tape to protect the areas not to be painted.

2 Using a small paintbrush, fill in the exposed areas. This design starts with a dark tone which gets gradually lighter. To achieve this, mix raw umber acrylic paint and white matt emulsion paint in the required proportions. Allow to dry for 30 minutes.

3 When the paint is completely dry, peel off all the masking tape carefully. A little re-touching may be needed at this point.

4 Next, brush on the antique pine-coloured varnish with a large paintbrush, working in small areas at a time, and rub it off immediately with a soft cloth. Repeat this until the whole table has been covered to give it a nice warm tone. Finally, give the table a coat of matt varnish with a large paintbrush, in a well-ventilated room.

WICKER BASKET

Here an ordinary wicker basket is given a new lease of life for a baby's room. When choosing a basket, look out for little details which you can emphasize to give it that personal touch.

YOU WILL NEED
Wicker basket
White matt emulsion paint
Large paintbrush
Blue and red acrylic paint
Small paintbrush

1 First paint the inside and outside of the wicker basket with white matt emulsion paint, using a large paintbrush.

2 When the white paint is dry, mix a little blue acrylic paint with some white matt emulsion paint to make a baby blue. Also mix a little red acrylic paint with some white matt emulsion to make a baby pink. Using a small paintbrush, pick out the detail on the wicker basket in contrasting colours.

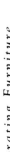

DESIGNER SHELVES

These pretty shelves are in the tradition of tole painting. You can make them to any size or renovate old or existing shelving. Choose colours to match the room; a combination of blue and white is both simple and effective. Practise the brush strokes on a piece of paper before you start, to gain enough confidence to achieve the design.

YOU WILL NEED
Shelves
White matt emulsion paint
Large paintbrush
Fine sandpaper
Pencil
Blue acrylic paint
Small paintbrush
Clear polyurethane varnish

1 Prime the shelves with white emulsion paint and rub down with fine sandpaper. Pencil on the design.

2 Mix the blue acrylic paint to a creamy consistency. Paint the design gently but precisely using single confident brush strokes.

3 Varnish the finished shelves with clear polyurethane varnish to protect the design and so that they may be wiped clean.

HOOK BOARD

Brighten up your hallway by painting a simple bow motif to join coat hooks on an old length of board, and attach it to the wall.

1 Sand the length of board until it is smooth. Then wipe the surface with white spirit and a soft cloth.

YOU WILL NEED
Length of board with coat hooks
Medium sandpaper
White spirit
Soft cloth
White matt emulsion paint
Large paintbrush
Assorted acrylic paints
Pencil
Small paintbrush
Metallic gold paint
Clear gloss varnish

2 Apply a coat of white matt emulsion paint with a large paintbrush. Leave for 30 minutes to dry.

3 Mix up a buttermilk colour with a little yellow ochre acrylic paint and some white matt emulsion paint. Apply two coats, avoiding the hooks.

4 Then draw a bow motif onto the board using a pencil. Fill in the design with red acrylic paint using a small paintbrush. Leave for 10 minutes to dry.

5 Using a small paintbrush, make little strokes to suggest highlights with a mixture of red acrylic and white matt emulsion paint, and shadows with a mixture of red and raw umber acrylic paint. Allow to dry.

6 Then using a small paintbrush, paint the metal hooks with metallic gold paint.

7 Finally, when all the paint is dry, apply a coat of clear gloss varnish, working in a well-ventilated room.

KITCHEN CHAIR

Here the technique of distressing is used. The yellow underneath the top coat of paint shows through on the finished chair as if the colour had worn away with time. On this piece, less traditional colours have been used. The colours you use on your chair can of course complement those in your kitchen.

YOU WILL NEED
Kitchen chair
White matt emulsion paint
Yellow and blue vinyl matt emulsion paint
Large paintbrush
Soft cloth
Beeswax
Medium sandpaper
Pencil
White paper
White chalk
Masking tape
Small paintbrush
Diluted blue acrylic paint

1 Prepare the chair. Prime it with two coats of white matt emulsion paint, then apply two coats of yellow vinyl matt emulsion paint using a large paintbrush. Allow to dry for 2 hours.

2 Using a cloth, apply a liberal layer of beeswax on the areas where the chair would normally become worn, such as the edges and the seat. Leave to dry for 2 hours.

3 Then apply one coat of blue vinyl matt emulsion paint with a large paintbrush. Leave for 1 hour or until the chair is completely dry.

4 Next, using a piece of medium sandpaper, rub down the entire chair, concentrating particularly on the areas where the beeswax was applied. This will expose patches of the yellow under-coat. Remove all dust with a soft dry cloth before the next step.

5 Using the template, scale up the flower pattern separately on two pieces of paper as necessary to fit on the back of the chair. Cover the reverse of the paper with white chalk and attach each to one bar of the chair with masking tape. Pencil over the design so that the chalk is transferred onto the chair.

6 Using a small paintbrush, fill in the areas of the design with diluted blue acrylic paint. The paint sits lightly on the wax and has a faint textured effect when dry.

7 To finish off the piece and to protect it, apply two layers of beeswax, allowing 1 hour to dry between coats.

Decorating Furniture

57

BEDSIDE CUPBOARD

A fleur-de-lys is always an elegant motif and looks most impressive gilded, as on this bedside cupboard.

YOU WILL NEED
Bedside cupboard
White matt emulsion paint
Large paintbrush
Paper
Pencil
Green acrylic paint
Sponge
Gold pigment
Acrylic varnish
Small paintbrush
Clear gloss varnish

1 Prepare the cupboard. Apply two coats of white matt emulsion paint. Scale up and cut out the fleur-de-lys motif template.

Place the template on the top of the cupboard and draw around it using a pencil. Repeat this process on the door.

2 Mix a base colour that is a mid-tone with a mixture of green acrylic and white matt emulsion paint. Cover the whole piece of furniture using a large paintbrush. Paint carefully around the fleur-de-lys motif so that it remains white. Leave this to dry for 1 hour.

3 Mix a darker shade of green, using more green acrylic and less white matt emulsion paint. Place a small quantity of paint on a dish so that it can be spread out thinly. To keep the fleur-de-lys motif white, cover it with the original template. Sponge the darker green up to the edge and onto the paper. Work quickly and lightly all over the cupboard to ensure that there is an even pattern and texture.

4 While the green is drying, mix the gold pigment and acrylic varnish to form a liquid gold. Then paint the fleur-de-lys using a small paintbrush. It may need two coats to ensure it is covered completely.

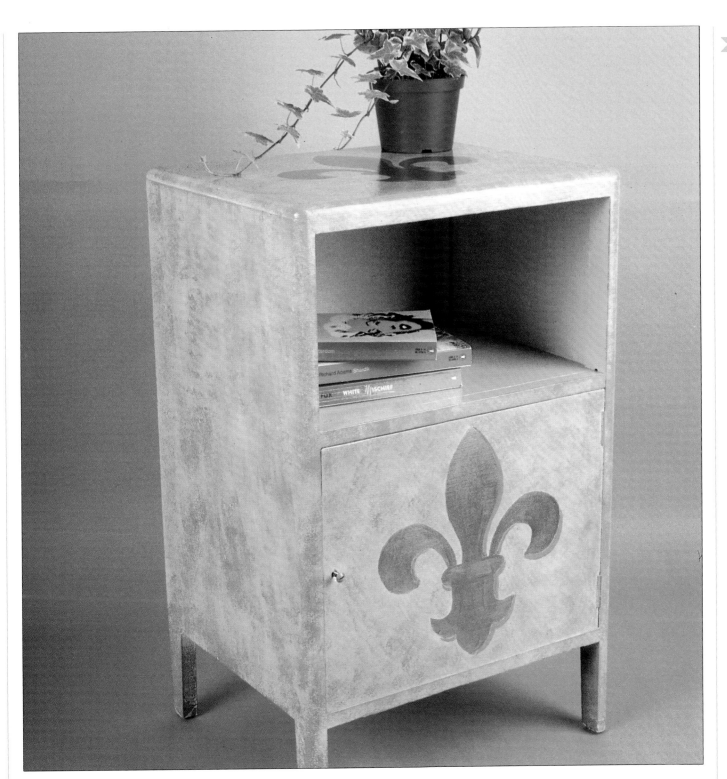

5 When the gold is dry, paint a shadow and further detail on the fleur-de-lys in a dark green acrylic colour with a small paintbrush. Allow 30 minutes for the paint to dry completely.

6 Then apply a coat of clear gloss varnish using a large paintbrush.

CUP AND SAUCER

The appeal of the bold design on this cup and saucer is its look of spontaneity. If you do not feel confident enough to copy the fluent brush strokes, practise on a piece of broken china. Unless you are absolutely certain that the paints you are using are food-safe, adapt the design by stopping the decoration at least 4 cm (1½ in) below the rim of the cup.

YOU WILL NEED
Non-toxic ceramic enamels
Small paintbrush
White spirit
White china cup and saucer

1 Dip the brush in green ceramic enamel and make bold squiggles on the cup. Leave to dry. Clean the brush before changing colours using white spirit. Between the green shapes paint purple squiggles. Leave to dry.

2 Decorate other white spaces with red ceramic paint. Paint red dots on the handle. Decorate the saucer in the same way.

FEEDING TIME

It is not easy to find attractive bowls for pets, so why not decorate a brightly coloured one with cold enamels? You might like to write your pet's name on the bowl too, to personalize it. Make absolutely certain that you use non-toxic enamels, and only paint the outside of the bowl, *not* the inside.

YOU WILL NEED
China bowl
600 ml (1 pt) warm water with 10 ml (2 tsp) vinegar
Chinagraph pencil
Cold ceramic enamel
Small paintbrush

2 Paint around the design with enamel colour.

1 Wash the bowl in the vinegar solution to remove any grease. Dry thoroughly. Draw your design directly onto the bowl with a chinagraph pencil.

3 Paint a row of fine spots around the outside edge of the bowl.

THAT'S TORN IT

This is a very easy way of giving an inexpensive china mug a distinctive design. You can also decorate a plate to match. Make absolutely sure the ceramic enamels are non-toxic.

YOU WILL NEED
Tape measure
China mug
Masking tape
Scissors
Non-toxic ceramic enamels
Small paintbrush

1 Measure the circumference of the mug and cut three strips of masking tape. Rip the masking tape in half lengthways and place it with the straight edges back to back round the mug in bands.

2 Press the masking tape down so that the paint can not seep under the edges. Apply ceramic enamel to the white areas. Leave to dry overnight.

3 Peel off the masking tape.

> ### WARNING
> Take care with the selection of paints. Not all ceramic paints and enamel paints are non-toxic or food-safe. Always study the manufacturer's instructions carefully and follow them exactly. If you have the slightest doubt, NEVER paint any surface that will come into contact with food or the lips or mouth. To adapt a design such as this you would stop the decoration at least 4 cm (1½ in) below the rim of the cup.

TERRACOTTA PLANTER

Brighten up a plant collection with a set of unusually decorated terracotta flowerpots. The clay absorbs some of the colour to create an attractive matt effect. Try experimenting with patterns and colours to create a whole range of designs.

YOU WILL NEED
Terracotta flowerpot
Pencil
Tape measure
Small paintbrush
Assorted ceramic enamels

1 Using a pencil, draw two parallel horizontal lines around the top and bottom of the rim of the flowerpot. Keep the lines as straight as possible.

2 Calculate the circumference of the rim with a tape measure and divide it into an uneven number of equal sections, marking each one with a small pencil mark. Join the marks with two parallel zigzag lines.

3 Using a small paintbrush, paint the zigzags in one colour and the surrounding area of the rim in a contrasting shade. Mark in vertical zigzags in pencil on the side of the flowerpot and paint in. Paint dots inbetween. Leave to dry.

FANCY TILES

Why not brighten up your bathroom with the minimum of fuss by decorating the tiles? If you use cold enamels that set without heating, you can paint tiles that are already in place — just remember to follow the manufacturer's instructions, and let the tiles dry thoroughly before you take a bath or shower!

YOU WILL NEED
Ceramic tiles
600 ml (1 pt) warm water with 10 ml (2 tsp) vinegar
Chinagraph pencil
Cold ceramic enamels in a variety of colours
Paintbrushes in various sizes
Tile adhesive and grout (optional)

1 Wash the tiles down with the vinegar solution to remove any grease. Dry thoroughly. Draw your design directly onto the tiles in chinagraph pencil. Any mistakes can be easily removed with a piece of paper or your fingers.

2 Start to fill in the largest area of your design with enamel, using a fairly thick brush. Work quite loosely, as you can add fine details when the first coat of enamel is dry.

3 Add definition to your design by painting on top of the first colour with a darker-toned enamel.

4 If you want a bold effect, outline your design with black enamel. If you are painting loose tiles, stick them in position with tile adhesive. When the adhesive is thoroughly dry add the grouting. Do not allow the tiles to come into contact with water for at least 48 hours.

CANAL BOAT MUG

This colourful mug would make a perfect gift for any canal boat enthusiast. The stylized form of decoration is a traditional feature not only of the boats, but also of buckets and other utensils.

YOU WILL NEED
Small paintbrush
Ceramic enamels
Enamel mug
White spirit

1 Dip the brush in ceramic paint and paint circular shapes onto the mug as a background for the roses. Leave to dry.

Clean the brush before changing colours using white spirit. Paint circles in other colours to form a design.

2 Paint petals on the roses and turn some of the shapes into leaves. Emphasize the detail with black or white ceramic enamels.

3 Outline the design with red dots and paint a wavy red line on the handle.

CHRISTMAS CANDLE HOLDERS

Why not create decorative candle holders especially for the festive season? Green holly leaves and red berries are quite easy to paint directly onto the china, using a sprig of fresh holly as a pattern.

YOU WILL NEED
Plain white candle holder
Red and green ceramic enamels
Small paint brush
White spirit (paint thinner)

1 Paint outlines of the holly leaves in green ceramic enamel all round the candle holder, then fill in each leaf in the same colour. Leave to dry.

2 Clean the brush before changing colours using white spirit. Paint red berries between the leaves.

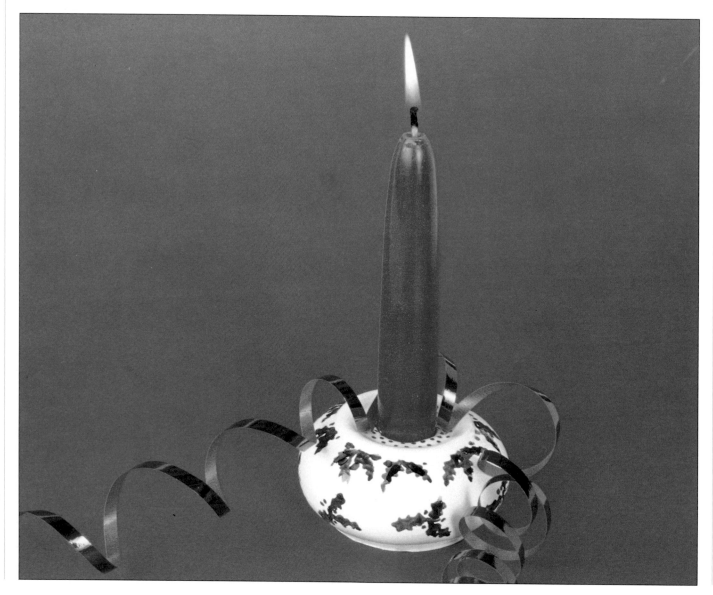

PLANT POT
IN RELIEF

Many pieces of china are available with patterns that are raised or 'in relief'. The detail can be further emphasized by colouring the design in ceramic paint, perhaps in the shades suggested by the patterns on the china or even to match a particular interior decor scheme. Cold ceramic enamels are easy to apply but it is best to avoid painting china used for food.

YOU WILL NEED
China pot with relief design
Cold ceramic enamels in different
  colours
Small paintbrush
Clear polyurethane varnish

1 Wash the china pot in warm soapy water to remove any grease or grime. Allow to dry thoroughly.

Choose a colour scheme and apply the first shade of paint carefully using a small paintbrush.

2 Paint in the areas chosen for the second colour, wiping off any paint that might go over the edge of a particular detail.

3 Continue to paint in the design until the china pot is decorated all over.

Allow the paint to dry thoroughly. For extra protection apply a coat of clear varnish.

DESIGN IN THE NEGATIVE

Draw on a white plate with a black chinagraph pencil and then colour the remaining areas. The chinagraph pencil marks are then rubbed away, leaving white lines in their place. Make sure the ceramic enamels are of the non-toxic variety.

YOU WILL NEED
Black chinagraph pencil
White china plate
Ceramic enamels
Small paintbrush
Paper towel or tissue paper

1 Using the chinagraph pencil, draw your design onto the plate.

2 Paint in the larger areas of colour. If you wish to mix colours, make sure you mix enough. Ceramic enamels look better slightly dappled, as it is very difficult to achieve a flat even surface over a large area.

3 When the large areas have been painted, fill in the details. Do not overload the brush with paint but build up the colour gradually. Leave the paint to dry. Rub away the chinagraph pencil marks using a paper towel or tissue paper.

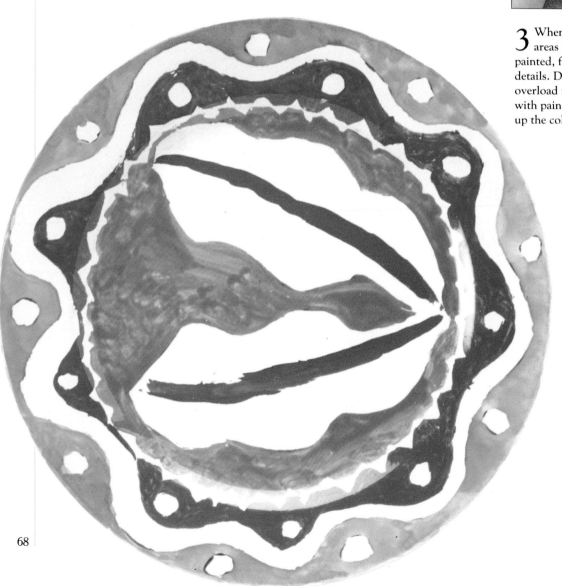

EGGCUPS

These eggcups will help to get your day off to a good start! They are bright and jazzy, and take their inspiration from European folk art designs. As when painting all crockery, make absolutely sure that you are using non-toxic cold ceramic enamels, and do *not* paint any surface that comes directly into contact with food. Bon appetit!

YOU WILL NEED
600 ml (1 pt) warm water with 10 ml
*   *(2 tsp) vinegar*
Chinagraph pencil
Plain white eggcups
Cold ceramic enamels in a variety of
*   colours*
Paintbrushes in various sizes

1 Wash each eggcup in the vinegar solution to remove any grease. Dry thoroughly. Draw your design directly onto the china using a chinagraph pencil.

2 Start to fill in the first colour of enamel. Work from the lightest shades to the darkest, so that you can paint on top of initial coats of enamel if you like.

3 Continue to paint in the design.

4 For a bolder effect, first block in the design with bright colours, and then outline with black enamel.

PLANT POT

A fern or other non-flowering house plant looks very effective in this plain white pot with a bold stencilled design.

YOU WILL NEED
15 cm (6 in) white china plant pot
4 cm (1½ in) wide masking tape
Pencil
Craft knife
Ceramic enamels in 2 basic colours
Small plate for paints
2 small pieces of sponge
Plastic glove

1 Cover the rim of the pot with masking tape, overlapping the outer edge by 12 mm (½ in). Cover the side of the pot with masking tape, leaving a 4 cm (1½ in) space between each strip of tape. Draw a flower design on each strip of tape and pencil in the parts to be cut out.

2 Holding the pot firmly with one hand, take the craft knife with the other and carefully cut out the shapes drawn onto the masking tape. Peel off the cut-out tape as you go along. Continue until the design is complete all round the pot.

3 Pour a little paint onto a plate. Using a small piece of sponge, dab the first colour onto alternating cut-out spaces. Repeat with the second colour. Wear a plastic glove on the hand you use to apply the paint to protect yourself from splashes. Sponge under the rim and around the base of the pot. Leave to dry thoroughly. When dry, peel off all the masking tape.

STENCILLED TRINKET BOX

This charming trinket box can be used to keep many things such as coins, keys or spare buttons. The traditional method of stencilling enables you to repeat a design quickly and easily.

YOU WILL NEED
Round box
White matt emulsion paint
Small paintbrush
Pencil
Plain paper
Tape measure
Clear acetate
Black felt-tip pen
Craft knife
Masking tape
Blue acrylic paint
Stipple brush
Clear polyurethane varnish

2 Lift the stencil carefully and tape it down onto the lid. Stipple it with undiluted blue acrylic paint, using a dry stipple brush. Leave to dry.

3 Repeat this process for the side design, remembering to tape down the stencil, moving it around the box as necessary.

1 Prime the box with a coat of white matt emulsion paint. Draw around the lid onto a sheet of plain paper to get the correct size for the design. Measure the circumference and depth of the box and transfer these measurements onto the paper. Scale up the design within the measurements. Place the box lid on the acetate, draw around it with a felt-tip pen and then cut out the shape. Stick down the acetate onto the lid design with masking tape. Cut out the stencil with a craft knife. Repeat this process to make the stencil for the side design.

4 Paint the rim of the lid with blue acrylic paint. Leave to dry and then coat with clear polyurethane varnish to protect the box.

STENCILLED NOTELETS

Choose a pattern that will look good repeated on the head of the notelets. If you have not used stencils previously, it is best to practise on newspaper before working on expensive writing paper.

YOU WILL NEED
Sheets of coloured writing paper
Strip of stiff card
Pencil
Scissors
Assorted poster paints
Small plate
Small round stencil brush or small sponge
Soft cloth

1 Fold the sheets of writing paper in half. Take the strip of card and concertina into 15 mm (⅝ in) folds.

2 Keep the card folded and draw out a pattern. Cut out using scissors. Open the pattern out flat and lay it across the top of the folded writing paper.

3 Mix a little poster paint on a small plate. Dab the stencil brush or sponge into the paint, wiping off any surplus on a soft cloth. It is very important not to overload the brush or sponge with paint if you want to avoid smudges.

Place the cut-out card onto the head of the folded sheet of writing paper, holding the card firmly in position with one hand. Dab paint through the opening of the cut-outs. Lift up the card gently and leave the paper to dry.

ROSE CARD

This romantic birthday card is very effective, particularly on the black background colour which adds depth to the stencilled single rose.

YOU WILL NEED

Square of stiff card
Ruler
Pencil
Plain paper
Masking tape
Clear acetate twice the size of the folded card
Craft knife
Natural sponge
Assorted acrylic paints
Small paintbrush

1 Fold the square of stiff card in half, scoring along the inside line. Measure the front of the card to ensure your design fits the available space. Draw a rose design onto plain paper, taping it down onto a clean flat board. Cover the design with half of the acetate and tape down. Cut out only the shape of the rose. Remove the stencil carefully. Move the acetate up so that the bottom half covers the design. Repeat the cutting process, only this time cut out only the shape of the leaves.

2 Place the stencil of the leaves onto the card, securing with the masking tape and making sure the stencil is central. Moisten the natural sponge, squeezing out any excess water. Use green and white acrylic paint for the leaves, making sure the paint is not too wet. Fade the sponging from the edge towards the middle of the leaves. Leave to dry and remove carefully.

3 Place the stencil of the rose carefully onto the centre of the card, moving it around until it fits snugly in the middle of the bed of leaves. Repeat the process with pink and white acrylic paint, again fading the stippling with the natural sponge in towards the middle. Leave to dry and remove the acetate carefully.

4 Add a finishing touch with a twirl of paint using a paintbrush, and your card is completed.

COSMIC STATIONERY

The intricate design of shooting stars and fireworks demands neat fingers and plenty of patience! Use the stencil to make a harlequin set of writing paper in a variety of colours.

YOU WILL NEED
Strip of stiff card
Masking tape
Pencil
Craft knife
Sheets of coloured writing paper
Poster paint in assorted colours
Round stencil brush or small sponge
Soft cloth

1 Cover a strip of stiff card completely with strips of masking tape. Using a pencil draw a design of shooting stars and fireworks on it. Working on a hard-surfaced board and using a craft knife cut out all the shapes carefully to form the stencil template.

2 Place the stencil over a sheet of writing paper, and secure in position with a little masking tape. Have your paints ready on a plate. Dab the brush or sponge into each colour, wiping off any surplus on a soft cloth. It is very important not to overload the brush or sponge with paint if you want to avoid smudges. Dab the paints through the stencil until the design is completed. Lift up the stencil gently and leave the paper to dry.

STENCILLED TRAY

The traditional technique of stencilling is an extremely effective form of decoration. This tray is pretty enough to be displayed in your kitchen when not in use. Why not try using colours to match a favourite set of china?

YOU WILL NEED
Wooden tray
White matt emulsion paint
Large paintbrush
Sandpaper
Masking tape
Diluted blue acrylic paint
Stipple brush
Sheet of plain paper
Pencil
Clear acetate
Craft knife
Clear satin polyurethane varnish

1 Prepare the tray. Prime with white matt emulsion paint, rub down with sandpaper and give it another coat for a nice smooth finish. When the paint is dry, put masking tape all along the inside edges of the tray. Brush diluted blue acrylic paint thinly onto the edges of the tray and stipple off while the paint is still wet; work swiftly and only do a section at a time so that the paint does not have a chance to dry.

2 Draw your design onto plain paper, stick the paper down onto a smooth board and then place a sheet of acetate on top, making sure you stick it down on top of the design with masking tape. Place on a hard surface and start to cut out the shapes of your stencil very carefully, using a craft knife and holding down the acetate with your free hand where necessary.

3 When you have finished cutting out the design, transfer the stencil onto the tray, remembering to remove the masking tape very carefully. Tape down the stencil in the centre of the tray. It is also a good idea to tape down some paper around the edges of the acetate so that splashes of blue do not go on to the surrounding area. Stipple on the paint with a dry stipple brush using fairly dry acrylic paint; get rid of any excess paint before beginning by stippling on a scrap of paper. Leave to dry, remove the stencil and give the tray two coats of clear satin polyurethane varnish.

PHOTO FRAME

Jazz up a favourite photograph with a simple stencilled frame. Choose colours that enhance those in the photograph and mount it on the wall for all to see. If a stencil is made for one frame, it can be used again to make a series.

YOU WILL NEED
Thick coloured card
Metal rule
Craft knife
Thin card
Clear acetate
Permanent black ink pen
Masking tape
Stencil brush
Acrylic paint
Clear glue
Picture hanger

1 First draw up the pieces of your frame on thick coloured card. Then carefully cut these out using a metal rule and craft knife. In the same way, cut three spacers out of thin card.

2 Take a piece of clear acetate of the same width as the front frame piece and draw on the design with a permanent black ink pen. Then cut out the design with a sharp craft knife.

3 Place the acetate on the front frame piece, securing it with masking tape. Using a stencil brush with a little acrylic paint, stipple on the paint. Allow the paint to dry before removing the acetate.

4 Glue the three spacers onto the sides and the bottom to the back of the stencilled frame piece. Then stick the spacers to the back piece of coloured card frame.

5 When the frame is complete, attach a light picture hanger to the back, strengthen with masking tape, and hang on the wall.

STAR SCARF

Stencilling a plain scarf is a wonderful way to show off your artistic talent and look original.

YOU WILL NEED
Thin card
Clear acetate
Permanent black ink pen
Craft knife
Scarf
Masking tape
Fabric paints
Stencil brush
Iron
Tissue paper

1 Make a star template in thin card to fit the scarf. Draw round the template onto clear acetate using a permanent black ink pen. Cut out the star image from the clear acetate, following the black lines using a craft knife.

2 Secure the acetate stencil on a corner of the scarf with masking tape. Put a little fabric paint onto the stencil brush and stipple the paint straight onto the fabric. Start at the tip of each star point and lightly work towards the middle. Concentrate more on the points and edges to get a 3-dimensional look.

3 Repeat on all four corners and the centre of the scarf and allow to dry. Iron the star images with a medium hot iron. Place a piece of tissue paper between the iron and the fabric to protect the paint. The heat of the iron fixes the fabric paint so that it can be washed.

SEAHORSE SHIRT

Transform a white cotton turtle-neck with a stencilled design of an exotic seahorse painted in three bright colours.

YOU WILL NEED
Thin card
Craft knife
Black felt-tip pen
Thick card cut to turtle-neck size
White cotton turtle-neck
Masking tape
3 round stencil brushes
Fabric paints in 3 colours
Small plate
Fine flat brush

1 Cut a piece of thin card to fit the area of the front of the turtle-neck you would like to decorate. Scale up the design to the required size. Insert the thick card inside the shirt to stretch the fabric, and prevent the paint from leaking onto the back.

2 Place the design on a hard-surfaced board and cut out all the black shapes carefully. This is your stencil.

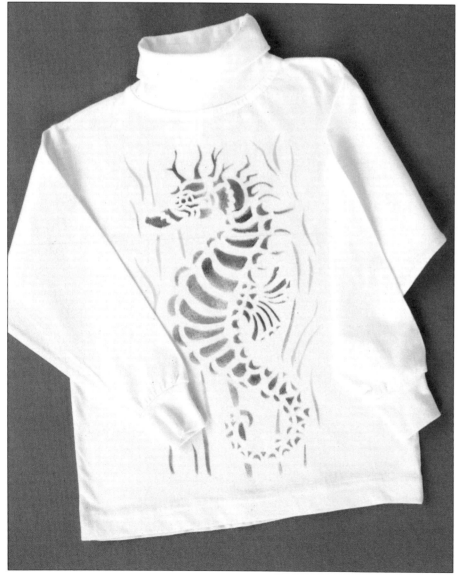

3 Secure the stencil on the front of the turtle-neck using masking tape. Hold the stencil brush vertically and dab the paint through the cut-out holes of the stencil. Change colours and brushes as you go along. When you have finished colouring the design lift up the stencil carefully and put it aside to dry. If there are any smudges, touch up carefully with a fine flat brush. Leave the turtle-neck to dry thoroughly. Remove the piece of thick card. Fix according to the instructions on the paints.

FLOWER POT STENCIL

Enhance your plant with an individual flower pot. Decorate a terracotta plant pot to give it individuality; try varying the sizes for a whole collection.

YOU WILL NEED
Terracotta flower pot
Clear acetate
Permanent black ink pen
Craft knife
Masking tape
Acrylic paint
Small stencil brush

1 Wash the flower pot thoroughly with soapy water so that all grease and dirt marks are removed. Leave to dry thoroughly. Scale up the flower design from the template. Then draw it onto clear acetate with a permanent black ink pen. Cut around the black pen lines on the acetate carefully using a sharp craft knife.

2 Secure the acetate stencil onto the terracotta flower pot with masking tape. Then apply the acrylic paint directly onto the terracotta pot through the acetate, using a stencil brush. Use small amounts of paint; if too much is applied, it may leak under the acetate. Do not remove the acetate until the paint is dry.

3 Move the acetate stencil around the pot repeating the process until you are satisfied with the total design.

Clear acetate has the advantage of your being able to see through it for perfect placement when spacing your design.

CAT CUSHION

Most 'bean bag' cushions are very popular with pets, but this one with its additional filling of catmint (irresistible to cats) with tansy and cotton lavender (which fleas and other fur 'visitors' hate) should make for a very happy cat.

YOU WILL NEED
Lengths of cotton and calico (muslin)
*   fabrics*
Scissors
Needle and thread
½ cupful of dried tansy
½ cupful of dried catmint (nepeta)
½ cupful of dried cotton lavender
*   (santolina)*
1 heaped teaspoon of orrisroot powder
Small polystyrene (styrofoam) 'pearls'
*   for filling*

1 Cut out two pieces each of the calico (muslin) and your chosen cotton outer cover fabric, measuring 50 cm × 41 cm (19½ in × 16 in). Stitch the two short sides and one long side of the calico together, and part of the remaining long side, leaving a 7.5 cm (3 in) opening. Turn through. Repeat with the cover fabric, remembering to start with the material inside out. Leave a bigger opening so that the filled calico inner can be inserted.

2 Mix the tansy, catmint, cotton lavender and orrisroot powder together in a bowl. Make up a calico sachet about 10 cm (4 in) square, fill with the special cat pot-pourri and sew together. Fill the calico inner with the polystyrene 'pearls', pop in the sachet and sew together.

3 Slide the calico-covered cushion into the outer cover and slipstitch the gap.

POT-POURRI

This simple and lightly spiced pot-pourri has a careful selection of material, chosen for its appearance in a basket as well as for its perfume.

YOU WILL NEED

3 cupfuls dried blue larkspur flowers,
    a few dried red roses for colour,
    1 cupful geranium leaves, 1 cupful
    of soapwort leaves and flowers
1 teaspoon grated lemon rind
½ teaspoon sandalwood powder for
    smell
½ cupful orrisroot powder (perfume
    fixative)
Mixing bowl
5 drops of geranium essential oil for
    smell
Plastic ice-cream container with tight-
    fitting lid
Sticky tape
Display bowl or basket
Lace ribbon

1 Remove the larkspur florets from the stems and break up the roses, reserving some whole for decoration.

2 Add the geranium leaves, soapwort leaves and flowers, lemon rind, sandalwood and orrisroot powders.

Place all the ingredients in a mixing bowl and stir gently as you slowly drip in the geranium essential oil.

3 Transfer the mixture to a plastic ice-cream container and seal the lid carefully with sticky tape. Store in a warm place for 6 weeks, stirring occasionally. When the pot-pourri is ready, empty into a display bowl, or fill a small basket. Decorate with a small bunch of larkspur and roses tied with a lace ribbon.

TABLE DECORATION

This soft, delicate arrangement is an ideal table decoration for a small or intimate dinner party and a chance to display that very special plate.

YOU WILL NEED
Florist's adhesive clay tape
Florist's scissors
Plastic pin holders
Small pretty plate
Florist's plasticine (putty)
2 plastic candle holders
Scrim ribbon
Silver and black reel wires
Florist's wire cutters
Reindeer moss
Dried larkspur
Fir cones
Dried roses
Candles

1 Cut a short length of florist's adhesive clay tape and use it to fix a florist's plastic pin holder off-centre on your chosen pretty plate.

3 Cut several 15 cm (6 in) lengths of scrim ribbon and form into single loops using silver reel wire.

2 Knead a piece of florist's plasticine (putty) into a 5 cm (2 in) diameter ball and fix onto the pin holder. Push two plastic candle holders into this.

4 Cut 5 cm (2 in) pieces of silver reel wire and bend into hairpin shapes. Cover the candle holders and clay with pieces of reindeer moss, securing it in place with the wire pins.

5 Wire the larkspur and fir cones using black reel wire.

6 Cut down rose stems to suitable lengths. Start to place the various elements, by pushing into the florist's plasticine (putty). Insert the ribbon loops to simulate bows and disguise the candle holders. Finally place the two candles in their holders. Take great care not to let lighted candles burn down near the decorations.

SCENTED NOTEPAPER

The tradition of 'scenting' notepaper goes back many centuries; often a drop of the sender's favourite scent was used but this stained the paper. It is much better to leave a lavender sachet with the paper for a month.

YOU WILL NEED
Muslin (cheesecloth)
Needle and thread
½ cupful lavender flowers
Handmade or fine acid-free notepaper
Pressed flowers
Tweezers
Rubber-based adhesive
Toothpick
Box or bag
Sticky tape
Cellophane

1 Make up a square sachet of muslin and fill with lavender.

2 Decorate the notepaper using pressed flowers. Arrange the flowers or petals using tweezers, sticking them in place with a dab of rubber-based adhesive applied with a toothpick.

3 Put the notepaper in a box – or a bag if you do not have a box big enough – with the sachet and seal the box.

Leave for a month. Take the notepaper out of the box or bag, and wrap it in cellophane to keep in the perfume.

PRESSED FLOWER CANDLE

Making these candles is challenging, but good fun. Turn a plain white candle into an elegant decorated gift that will give hours of pleasure.

YOU WILL NEED
Heatproof cylindrical container (taller and wider than the candle)
4-5 cm (1½-2 in) diameter white candle
Selection of pressed flowers, leaves or grasses

1 Fill the container with enough hot water to reach the shoulder of the candle when it is immersed. Holding the candle by the wick, immerse in the hot water for about 30 seconds. Remove the candle, and working quickly, press a few leaves and flowers onto the softened wax around the lower part of the candle.

2 Refill the container with very hot water and dip the candle again briefly to soften the wax surface and seal in the pressed flowers.

ROSEBUD POMANDER

This long-lasting pomander looks beautiful and its perfume can be renewed when necessary with a few drops of rose essential oil.

YOU WILL NEED

90 cm × 12 mm (36 in × ½ in) green
  satin ribbon
Length of florist's wire
9 cm (3½ in) diameter florist's foam
  (styrofoam) ball
Dried rosebuds of different sizes
*White woodworking glue or rubber-
  based glue*
Paste brush
Rose essential oil

1 Cut the ribbon into 3 equal lengths. Tie a bow in the centre of each piece of ribbon leaving two long ends. Tie the third piece into a double bow and leave the ends long to make a hanging loop. Twist a florist's wire around each bow leaving one long end and push the wires through the foam ball. Pull the bows down to the ball and tuck in the end of each wire to secure.

2 Grade the rosebuds from smallest to largest. Divide the ball into quarters by painting a line of glue and pressing in a row of medium-sized rosebuds along it.

3 Cover one quarter at a time with glue and press in rosebuds, the smallest at the top and bottom and getting larger as you reach the centre, until the ball is completely covered. A few drops of rose essential oil can now be dripped onto the pomander ball.

PRESSED FLOWER CARD

Winter months are the time to use the flowers that you pressed in the summer. It is fun arranging them into a picture, which makes such a lasting gift when covered with protective film, available from specialist suppliers. Folded cards are available from most artist's suppliers.

YOU WILL NEED
Rubber-based adhesive
Small dish
Selection of dried flowers including verbena, forget-me-not, spiraea and gypsophila (baby's breath) and foliage
Folded blank card with aperture
Tweezers
Toothpick
Heat-sealing protective covering film
Steam iron

1 Squeeze out a little adhesive onto a small dish. Start by positioning foliage in an irregular oval shape to fit within the cut-out aperture of the card. Fix the foliage in position using tweezers to pick up each leaf. Using a toothpick transfer the smallest spot of adhesive to the reverse side of the leaf and touch it down.

2 Position and touch down verbena and forget-me-not flowers in the same way.

3 Use florets of spiraea and gypsophilia (baby's breath) to complete your design.

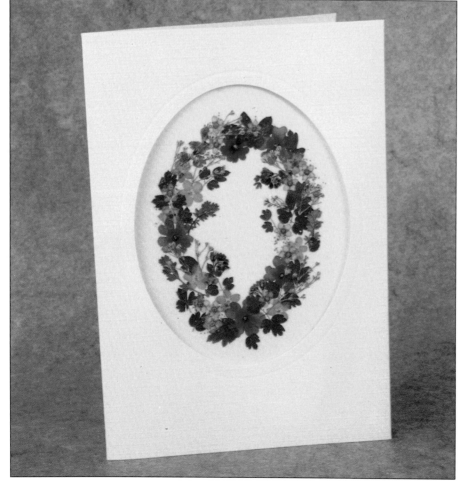

4 Protect the design with iron-on heat sealing laminate. Cut out a piece of the laminate slightly smaller than the page size. Open up the card and cover the design with the sheet of protective film, and iron down in accordance with the manufacturer's instructions. Re-fold the completed card.

FESTIVE WREATH

The materials and colours for this wreath have been chosen to suit any festival or occasion from an anniversary or birthday to Christmas. All the items are readily available from craft or florist's suppliers. A spring or summer wreath can be made using the flowers available.

YOU WILL NEED
Florist's scissors
Dried nigella orientalis seed-heads
Florist's foam (styrofoam) wreath base
Florist's wire cutters
Bunches of artificial fruit and leaves
Dried ambrociana
Florist's black and silver reel wires
Lace ribbons
Dried red roses

1 Cut short stems of nigella orientalis, and insert around the inner circumference of a foam wreath at an angle of about 15°.

2 Cut down the wires of the bunches of artificial fruit and leaves to about 4 cm (1½ in) in length, and insert around the top of the wreath at regular intervals.

3 Wire together small bunches of ambrociana with florist's black reel wire and insert all around the outside of the wreath to form a soft edge.

4 Cut eight 30 cm (12 in) lengths of ribbon to make bows with two loops and two ends. Bind with florist's silver reel wire, leaving two ends, and insert evenly around the wreath. Then cut five 12.5 cm (5 in) lengths. Fold in half, bind with florist's silver reel wire at the centre and insert around the outer edge of the wreath.

5 Position the roses evenly around the centre of the wreath and fill in with more nigella and ambrociana where required to give a balanced effect.

LAVENDER BAG

These lavender bags, smelling so fresh and clean, make very pretty gifts that look charming and are so practical in a linen cupboard.

YOU WILL NEED

35 cm × 6 mm (14 in × ¼ in) ribbon
28 cm × 5 cm (11 in × 2 in) piece of lace
Scissors
4 pieces of muslin (cheesecloth), each 12.5 cm × 10 cm (5 in × 4 in)
Needle and thread
Lavender pot-pourri
5 stems of lavender
Small elastic band

1 Cut a 12.5 cm (5 in) length of ribbon and lace. Place a length of lace and one of ribbon 7.5 cm (3 in) from the bottom edge of a piece of muslin (cheesecloth) and stitch into place. Gather the remaining length of lace and stitch to the top of the muslin.

2 Turn through and stitch the sides. Fold to the centre seam, stitch the bottom edge and turn through.

3 Fill with the lavender pot-pourri and tuck the five stems of lavender into the top of the bag, protruding from the neck, and secure with an elastic band.

4 Take the remaining ribbon and tie in a bow around the neck, to cover the elastic band.

FLOWER POSY

The posy is a very old form of flower arrangement with its origins dating from the medieval nosegay. Using dried and silk flowers means it can be treasured as a keepsake for years to come.

YOU WILL NEED

Florist's foam (styrofoam) posy holder
*   and ready-formed lace frill*
Dried gypsophila (baby's breath)
Florist's scissors
Florist's silver reel wire
Florist's wire cutters
Stems of silk peony flowers, buds and
*   leaves*
Sticky tape
2.5 cm (1 in) wide length of cream silk
*   ribbon*

1 Fix the frill around the foam head of the holder by pulling it down until it is firmly in place.

2 Cut short heads of gypsophila and wire together with silver reel wire.

3 Remove the leaves from the peony stems and insert a row around the edge of the foam block.

4 Cut the stem of a peony bud and insert into the centre of the foam block, and position open flowers around the edge.

5 Add more leaves and peonies. Fill in by inserting bunches of wired gypsophila to create an even but soft effect.

6 Tape the ribbon to the end of the handle and bind upwards towards the under-side of the posy. Secure with sticky tape. Make several 'figures of eight' from the remaining ribbon and bind at the centre to form a multiple bow. Wire to the base of the posy to cover the back. Stick down.

HERBAL BATH SACHETS

These scented sachets hang under the hot water when the bath tub is being filled. They create a refreshing fragrance as well as being naturally soothing and softening for the skin.

YOU WILL NEED
1 cupful oatmeal
½ cupful powdered milk
¼ cupful wheat bran
Handful of dried lavender or
*   rosemary flowers*
Handful of soapwort leaves and
*   flowers*
Plastic bowl
Teaspoon
Nappy (diaper) liners or thin
*   cheesecloth*
6mm (¼ in) wide ribbon or string
Pinking shears

1 Mix all the ingredients together in a plastic bowl.

2 Place two teaspoons of the mixture in the centre of a nappy (diaper) liner. Gather up the liner around the mixture and tie with a ribbon or string, leaving ends long enough for the sachet to hang beneath the running water.

3 Cut off the corners of the nappy liners using pinking shears and arrange so that you achieve a pretty frill.

SCENTED
SHELLS

As sea shells are generally associated with water, the ideal place to display a collection is in the bathroom. Add a further pleasing dimension to their colour and form by making them fragrant.

YOU WILL NEED
Collection of sea shells
Dish-washing liquid
Bleach
Towel
1 vanilla pod (bean)
Small cuttlefish bone
Lemon, bay and rosemary essential oils
Plastic ice-cream container with tight-fitting lid
Glass dish or bowl

1 Scrub and wash the shells carefully in soapy water to which a little bleach has been added, and set aside to dry thoroughly on a towel.

2 Moisten a cuttlefish bone with 25 drops of lemon, 15 drops of bay and 5 drops of rosemary essential oils. Place a bruised vanilla pod and the cuttlefish bone into a plastic ice-cream container. Add the shells, seal down the lid and leave for 4 weeks. Remove half the shells and arrange in a glass dish or bowl for display. After a few weeks or whenever the shells lose their fragrance, replace with the other shells left in the container. Do this on a regular basis, and occasionally refresh the cuttlefish bone with a few drops of the essential oils.

ALMOND BUBBLE BATH

This bubble bath makes a delightful gift – it is excellent for the skin, adds a beautiful perfume and foams when a little is poured slowly under fast-running hot water, when you are starting to fill the bathtub. It also looks good displayed in the bathroom.

YOU WILL NEED
300 ml (½ pint) non-biological dishwashing liquid
Screw-top jar
15 drops peach essential oil
2 drops pink food colouring
2 tablespoons almond oil
Presentation bottle
Label

1 Pour the dishwashing liquid into the screw-top jar and add the peach essential oil and food colouring.

2 Add the almond oil, screw on the lid and shake vigorously for about a minute. Fill the presentation bottle immediately. Decorate the bottle as liked and label carefully with a list of the contents and instructions to shake the bottle for a few seconds before use.

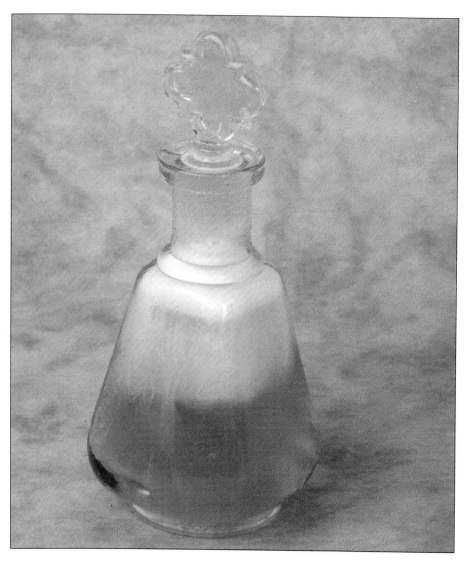

SUGGESTED LABEL:

ALMOND BUBBLE BATH

A mild soap base combines with peach essential oil to produce foaming frothy pink bubbles for a gentle soak in the bath tub.

SWEET VIOLET CREAM

This sweet-smelling rich beauty cream makes an interesting change to the usual commercially produced cosmetics.

YOU WILL NEED

1 teaspoon beeswax
3 tablespoons almond oil
Heatproof mixing bowl
Small saucepan
Newspaper
½ teaspoon cornflour (cornstarch)
2 tablespoons boiling water
Balloon or electric whisk
6 drops violet essential oil
Presentation jar
Label

1 Melt the beeswax in the almond oil in a bowl over a saucepan of hot water. When melted, remove the bowl and stand on some folded newspaper.

2 Add the cornflour (cornstarch), stir well and then add the water gradually, beating with the whisk until the mixture becomes creamy.

3 Add the violet essential oil, and continue to whisk until the cream is cool. Then pour into the presentation jar and leave to set. Label with a list of the contents.

SPICE AND LEMON COLOGNE

This cologne with its fresh, spicy aroma makes a super gift for any man. The miniature bottles are ideal for packing when travelling.

YOU WILL NEED
2 handfuls of lemon geranium leaves
Sharp knife
2 cinnamon sticks
Screw-top jar for mixing
3 teaspoons grated lemon rind
1½ cups vodka (or ethyl alcohol)
Coffee filter paper
Plastic or glass funnel
Small glass jug
Presentation miniature bottles
Labels

1 Wash the geranium leaves, pat dry and chop finely. Break up the cinnamon sticks and pack with the leaves into the jar. Add the grated lemon rind to the jar and fill with vodka. Secure the lid and store in a warm place for 4 weeks, shaking daily.

2 Filter the mixture through a coffee filter paper in a funnel into a jug. Repeat if the liquid is not very clear.

Wash and dry the storage jar and pour in the filtered cologne. Put the lid on the jar and keep in a dark place for 6 months.

3 Taking care not to disturb any sediment, decant the liquid carefully into the miniature bottles and label with the contents.

ROSE MOISTURIZER

This moisturizer, made from natural ingredients, is light, nourishing and soothing and will make a most welcome gift.

YOU WILL NEED

1 teaspoon beeswax
3 teaspoons lanolin
Small heatproof mixing bowl
Small non-aluminium saucepan
3 tablespoons almond oil
150 ml (¼ pint) rose-water
Pinch of borax
Cooking thermometer
Balloon whisk
Screw-top presentation jar
Label

1 Melt the beeswax and lanolin in a small mixing bowl resting in the saucepan of hot water over a low heat. Add the almond oil and beat together. Put the mixing bowl in a warm place.

2 Wash and dry the saucepan. Heat the rose-water and borax to about 50°C (122°F) and add slowly to the mixing bowl. Whisk the mixture together.

3 Stand the bowl in cold water and continue whisking until the cream is cold. The cream will still be soft and can be spooned into the presentation jar. Label with a list of contents.

AROMATIC BODY OIL

Almond oil can be bought inexpensively in large quantities from specialist shops. It is very light and soothing to the skin and is specially beneficial with this exotic blend of essential oils. Remember that essential oils are very strong, and should never be used undiluted directly on the skin. If some is splashed on by accident, wash it off immediately with soap and water. The body oil can be used after baths, or rubbed on elbows, knees and hands at any time.

 1 Pour the almond oil into the screw-top jar.

YOU WILL NEED
150 ml (¼ pint) almond oil
Screw-top jar for mixing
15 drops peach essential oil
10 drops melissa essential oil
Presentation bottles
Labels

2 Add the peach and melissa essential oils, drop by drop. Secure the lid and shake for 1 minute. Leave for 1 hour before pouring into the presentation bottles. Label with contents.

SUGGESTED LABEL:

AROMATIC BODY OIL

A refreshing and soothing body oil for use after bathing or on dry skin at any time, with the delicate scents of peach and melissa essential oils.

PEPPERMINT FOOT-BATH

This rejuvenating pick-me-up for tired and aching feet would be much appreciated by a busy hostess hard at work. The given quantity will be enough for four foot-baths. To use, fill a large bowl with moderately hot water, stir in the peppermint mixture and soak the feet for 10 minutes.

YOU WILL NEED
Several stems of fresh peppermint or
 60 g (2 oz) dried peppermint leaves
125 g (4 oz) juniper berries
Non-aluminium saucepan with lid
750 ml (1¼ pints) water
12 drops sandalwood essential oil
6 drops cypress essential oil
Coffee filter paper
Funnel
Storage jars or bottles
Labels

1 Place the peppermint and juniper in the saucepan, add the water and heat slowly to just below boiling point, stirring occasionally. Cover the saucepan and leave to cool.

2 Before the mixture is cold, add the sandalwood and cypress essential oils and stir well.

3 Strain off the liquid through a coffee filter paper in a funnel into the storage jars. Seal and label with instructions on how to use and a list of contents.

ROSEMARY HAIR RINSE

This rosemary rinse should be massaged into the scalp as a final rinse to make the hair beautifully soft and well-conditioned.

YOU WILL NEED
2 handfuls of fresh rosemary stems
2 jars with plastic screw-tops
600 ml (1 pint) white vinegar
600 ml (1 pint) water
Non-aluminium saucepan
Coffee filter paper
Funnel
Presentation bottles
Labels

1 Wash the rosemary stems carefully in cold water and shake dry. Break into manageable lengths and divide between the jars.

2 Put the vinegar and water in a saucepan and bring to the boil. Leave to stand for 2 minutes and pour over the rosemary in the jars. Stand on a warm window-sill for 2 weeks, shaking occasionally. Then strain the liquid through a coffee filter paper in a funnel into the presentation bottles. Label with a list of the contents and instructions on how to use.

SCENTED BATH SALTS

This is a very easy way to make beautifully scented, coloured bath salts. You can use any colouring and any variety of essential oil you like.

YOU WILL NEED
3 tablespoons vodka
Small yogurt pot
Pink food colouring
Peach essential oil
1 teaspoon almond oil
Plastic spoon
1 kg (2 lb) washing soda crystals
1 litre (1¾ pint) plastic ice-cream container with a well-fitting lid
Presentation jars
Ribbon
Labels

1 Pour the vodka into the clean yogurt pot, and add about 5 drops of pink food colouring, 15 drops of peach essential oil and the almond oil. Stir until the mixture is thoroughly blended.

2 Put the washing soda crystals into the ice-cream container, give the vodka mixture a final stir, and pour it over carefully. Keep turning the crystals over with a plastic spoon for a few minutes, and then seal with the lid.

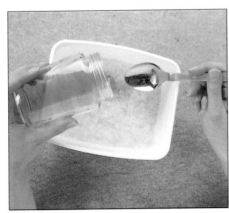

3 After 3 days, stir the bath salts again and pack into attractive jars. Add a ribbon bow and label with the contents.

MARINATED OLIVES

A jar of these marinated olives makes an original hostess gift. As they will cause a minor explosion on the palate, warn people when offering them at a drinks party with other nibbles!

YOU WILL NEED
Jar of pitted black olives in brine
Jar of pitted green olives in brine
Sieve
1 fresh hot chilli
3 cloves of garlic
Chopping board and knife
Storage jar
5 ml (1 tsp) dried oregano
Olive oil
Presentation jar
Label

1 Empty the jars of olives into a sieve and rinse thoroughly under a running cold tap. Set aside to drain. Chop the chilli and garlic very finely and put into the storage jar with the oregano. Add a little oil and shake well.

2 Add the drained olives and enough oil to cover. Shake gently for a minute every day for a week, then transfer to the presentation jar, topping up with more olive oil if necessary. Label the jar, listing all the ingredients.

ALMOND TREATS

While these 'fruits' are traditionally eaten at Christmas, they also make a super gift at any time of the year. Try to use white marzipan (almond paste) which will enable you to mix more realistic colours.

YOU WILL NEED
White marzipan (almond paste)
Sharp knife
Board
Rolling pin
Gel food colourings
Icing (confectioners') sugar
Toothpicks
Petits fours paper cases
Lidded container
Greaseproof (wax) paper

1 Divide the marzipan (almond paste) into pieces for the basic colouring. Roll out one piece thinly. Dot the food colouring very lightly on the surface. Then knead the marzipan (almond paste) until it is evenly coloured. Repeat this process for each colour.

2 Mould the marzipan (almond paste) into appropriate fruit shapes to suit the different colours. Use a little extra colouring in some areas.

3 Use icing (confectioners') sugar to achieve a soft or peach-like effect, and food colourings on the tip of a toothpick to define areas, add 'blemishes' and colour stems. Place the fruit in petits fours cases to protect them and enhance their appearance. Store in a lidded container, lined with grease-proof paper, until they are packed into a presentation box.

HERB BUTTER

Decorative containers filled with herb-flavoured butters make thoughtful gifts for busy cooks. Rosemary butter is good with green peas and roast lamb, mint with new potatoes, and fennel with fish.

YOU WILL NEED

Fresh herbs of your choice
Paper towels
Chopping board
Sharp knife or herb chopper
Best quality unsalted butter
Salt
Saucers or small mixing bowls
Spatula

2 Cut up the unsalted butter into medium-sized pieces and allow to soften at room temperature.

Sprinkle a little salt over the herbs — this will help to crush the herbs and release their flavour.

1 Rinse small bunches of herbs carefully in cold water and pat dry with paper towels. Chop each herb very finely on a chopping board, keeping each herb separate.

3 Mix the herbs with the softened butter using a spatula. When thoroughly mixed together pack into decorative containers and chill in the refrigerator until required.

GINGERBREAD TREES

Try baking a light gingerbread mixture in decorative Christmas tree shapes, and edge with icing (confectioners') sugar 'snow'. Finish them off with pretty seasonal ribbon bows.

YOU WILL NEED

100 g (4 oz/1 stick) butter, slightly softened
100 g (4 oz/⅔ cup) soft brown sugar
100 g (4 oz/½ cup) golden (corn) syrup
2 eggs
Sieve
450 g (1 lb/4 cups) white self-raising flour
15 ml (1 tbsp) ground ginger
Rolling pin and board
Christmas-tree shape cutter
Baking sheet
Ribbon
Shallow dish
Icing (confectioners') sugar

1 Beat the butter, sugar and golden (corn) syrup into a cream and then beat in the eggs. Sift in the flour and ground ginger and mix into a dough.

2 Roll the dough out thinly and stamp out Christmas tree shapes. Arrange on an oiled baking sheet. Bake for 20 minutes at 180°C (350°F/gas 4).

3 When cool, tie a ribbon bow on each tree shape and then dip the sides carefully in a shallow dish containing about 6 mm (¼ in) depth of icing (confectioners') sugar to decorate the upper edges of the branches with 'snow'.

ROSE AND JASMINE TEAS

Both rose and jasmine teas are lightly but beautifully flavoured, are drunk without milk, and are delicious either hot or cold. Dried rose and jasmine petals are available from specialist suppliers. Green 'gunpowder' teas are made with large leaves which, like the petals, will sink, so they are suitable for using when making tea directly in a cup or glass. Only use half a teaspoon for each cup.

YOU WILL NEED
Rose petals
Net bag
Lemon zest-peeler or sharp knife
Lemon
Plate
Dried jasmine petals
Gunpowder tea
Airtight storage containers

1 To dry your own rose petals, choose a variety that is sweet rather than bitter-tasting. Half-fill a little net bag with rose petals and hang in a warm dark place until dry.

2 Using a lemon zest-peeler or a sharp knife, remove only the zest (no pith) from a lemon, shred finely and leave to dry on a plate in the bottom of a cooling oven for 30 minutes.

3 Combine equal parts by weight first of dried rose petals and gunpowder tea, and then of jasmine petals and the tea, adding a quarter part of dried lemon zest to the jasmine mixture. Store the teas in separate airtight containers.

HERB-INFUSED OILS

Now lighter, healthier dressings for salads are popular, these delicately flavoured oils make very welcome gifts. It is best to use only one variety of herb in each bottle of oil, but oregano and basil do go well together. Olive or sunflower oil is recommended, or use walnut or grapeseed for a gourmet treat.

YOU WILL NEED
Stems of fresh rosemary, thyme,
*   oregano or basil*
Paper towel
Attractive presentation bottles
Plastic or glass funnel
Scissors
Fine quality salad oils of your choice
Self-adhesive labels

1 Choose only the freshest stems of herbs, wash in cold water and pat dry on a paper towel.

2 Using a funnel, fill the bottles with the chosen oils. Using scissors, trim the herbs to about two-thirds the height of the chosen bottles, and discard any dis-coloured leaves, but leave any flowers – dead or alive. Insert the herbs into the bottles.

3 Seal the bottles and label with the ingredients. Leave for two months before use.

CHOCOLATE FUDGE

This is a beautiful rich fudge, made in the traditional way. It will make a delectable gift for anyone with a sweet tooth.

YOU WILL NEED
450 g (1 lb/2¼ cups) granulated
   sugar (preferably cane)
150 ml (¼ pint/⅔ cup) milk
50 g (2 oz/¼ cup) cocoa powder
50 g (2 oz/2 squares) dark chocolate
Saucepan
6 drops vanilla essence (extract)
150 ml (¼ pint/⅔ cup) double (heavy)
   cream
100 g (4 oz/½ cup) unsalted butter
Shallow non-stick baking sheet
Metal spatula
Sharp knife
Gift boxes

1 Heat the sugar, milk, cocoa and chocolate in a pan, stirring until the mixture has dissolved. Add the vanilla essence, cream and the butter, then re-heat stirring occasionally until the butter melts. Remove from the heat and beat with a wooden spoon until the fudge mixture starts to granulate.

2 The mixture will now be thick. Transfer to an oiled non-stick shallow baking sheet and spread out evenly using a metal spatula. Leave to set for 12 hours in a cool place.

3 Invert the fudge onto a chopping board and cut into even squares, frequently dipping the knife blade in water. Pack into your chosen gift boxes.

TANGY VINEGARS

Flavoured red wine or cider vinegars are invaluable in preparing many dishes, sauces and dressings. They keep well for several months after maturing, but should be stored away from bright light. Here are recipes for tarragon vinegar and red chilli with ginger vinegar. Alternatives are numerous: try making a salad dressing with grapeseed oil and ginger and garlic vinegar, or tarragon vinegar and yogurt with cold chicken; or black pepper, coriander and cardamom vinegar in a meat stew; and red chilli and cumin vinegar on fried fish.

YOU WILL NEED
Fresh tarragon stems
Screw-topped bottle of cider vinegar
Whole dried red chillies
Fresh ginger root
Screw-topped bottle of red wine
*   vinegar*
Ribbon for decorating
Self-adhesive labels
Felt-tip pen

1 Trim three freshly picked tarragon stems to fit under the surface of the cider vinegar, and put into the bottle.

2 Place two whole red chillies and two small pieces of ginger root in a bottle of red wine vinegar.

3 Screw the lids onto the bottles, decorate with ribbon and add labels listing the ingredients. Store in a dark cool place for at least a month.

BOUQUET GARNI

The traditional bouquet garni is made from three sprigs of parsley, two of thyme and a bay leaf tied together with string, and often enclosed in muslin (cheesecloth) so that it can easily be removed. Other herbs may be added, such as fennel for fish dishes, three sage leaves for pork dishes, four short sprigs of rosemary for lamb dishes, two sprigs of fresh coriander (cilantro) and an extra bay leaf for beef dishes.

YOU WILL NEED
Sprigs of fresh or dried parsley and
 thyme
Bay leaf
Sharp pointed scissors
Muslin (cheesecloth)
White string

1 Mix together three parts chopped parsley, two parts chopped thyme and one part broken bay leaves.

2 Cut out circles of muslin (cheesecloth) 9 cm (3½ in) in diameter. Put two heaped teaspoons of the herbs into the centre of each circle.

3 Gather the muslin around the herbs and tie in little bundles with white string. Store in an airtight container.

CHERRIES IN BRANDY

Only use the best quality canned cherries as cheaper varieties might split open in the brandy. A decorative jar filled with perfect fruit makes a most acceptable hostess gift.

YOU WILL NEED

1 can best quality pitted red cherries
    in syrup
Can opener
Small saucepan
1 cinnamon stick
3 tablespoons granulated cane sugar
Wooden spoon
Strainer
2 screw-top jars (sterilized)
¼ bottle of cooking brandy
3 drops vanilla essence (extract)
Small jug
Fancy lidded glass jar (sterilized)
Ribbon
Label

1 Drain the syrup from the cherries into a saucepan, add the cinnamon stick and sugar and stir continuously while bringing to the boil. Allow to cool and strain off into one of the screw-top jars and store in the refrigerator.

2 Reject any damaged fruit and place the remainder in the other screw-top jar.

Add the brandy and vanilla essence. Screw on the lid and store in a cool place for 3-4 weeks.

3 Pour off the brandy into a jug, and stir in small quantities of the chilled syrup to taste. Place the cinnamon stick in the fancy glass jar and pack in the fruit in a decorative manner. Fill the container with the sweetened brandy, seal and finish with a ribbon bow. Add a label listing the ingredients.

FRILLY SOCKS

Transform a pair of white socks with frilled ribbon for a little girl to wear to a party.

YOU WILL NEED
2.5 m × 15 mm (2¾ yd × ⅝ in) narrow ribbon
Scissors
Needle and thread
Pins
Pair of plain socks

1 Cut the ribbon into six equal lengths. Sew a line of running stitches as near to one edge as possible of each piece of ribbon.

2 Pull the ribbon up the thread to gather the length of ribbon. Repeat with the other pieces of ribbon.

3 Starting at the back, pin the gathered edge of the ribbon to the top of the sock to hold it in place. When you have pinned the ribbon all the way round, make sure both ends overlap slightly.

4 Tack the ribbon in place and then secure it with a line of backstitch, stretching the sock as you work, so it will still fit over the child's ankle.

5 Sew on the other two lengths at 10 mm (⅜ in) intervals. Repeat with the other sock.

GIANT BOW

Make a giant bow to trim a gift-wrapped package. Choose colours that tone with the paper or make a good contrast.

YOU WILL NEED
2 m (2 yd) lengths of twisted paper rope in 2 different colours
2 m (2 yd) satin ribbon
Sticky tape

1 Untwist the lengths of coloured paper rope and spread them out.

2 Twist the paper rope strands together with the satin ribbon.

3 Wrap around the middle of a gift-wrapped package and tie the remaining loose untwisted ends into a bow. Use a small piece of sticky tape to fasten in place if necessary.

DRAUGHT EXCLUDER

Make your home cosy and keep draughts at bay in a colourful way. Cushions in matching fabric would give a co-ordinated look.

YOU WILL NEED
Ruler
25 cm × 122 cm (¼ yd × 48 in)
*   furnishing fabric*
Scissors
Pins
Needle and thread
Wadding (batting) or stuffing
1.6 m (1¾ yd) wide ribbon

1 Measure the width of the door; upstairs doors are usually narrower than those downstairs. Allow an extra 18 cm (7 in) width for seam allowances and cut out the fabric to the required size. Turn in and pin 9 cm (3½ in) at each end and machine sew two rows of a long (gathering) stitch, stopping just short of the seam allowance. Pull the threads through to the right side of the fabric.

2 Fold in half lengthways, right sides together. Pin and machine along the edge, taking care not to stitch over the long threads.

3 Turn through to the right side and pull up the gathering threads at one end. Knot to fasten off.

4 Stuff from the open end until the 'sausage' feels firm. Pull up the gathering threads from the open end. Tie securely and fasten off.

5 Cut the ribbon in half and cut a 'V' shape in the ends. Tie an extravagant bow at each end of the 'sausage'.

LACE HANDKERCHIEF

It is very simple to add delicate detail to a plain handkerchief with a trimming of lace. Scraps of unusual or antique lace are worth collecting and saving for such a project.

YOU WILL NEED

21 cm (8½ in) square of Swiss lawn
(fine cotton)
Steam iron
Tailor's chalk
Scissors
130 cm (51 in) fine cotton lace
Needle and thread

1 Fold the square of lawn into a triangle and press. Fold again to make a smaller triangle.

Unfold once. Chalk the position of the lace inside one corner, chalking on both sides.

2 Cut off the corner of lawn along the chalked lines.

3 Pin a strip of lace along the raw edge allowing a 6 mm (¼ in) overlap on the lawn. Pin the lawn corner to the lace again allowing a 6 mm (¼ in) overlap. Secure with oversewing. Turn in the lawn overlap making a fine rolled hem along both sides, catching the edge of the lace at the same time.

4 Sew four pieces of lace, each 28 cm (11 in) long, along each side of the handkerchief, leaving a 6 mm (¼ in) overlap. At each corner leave enough lace to overlap into a square. Trim the lace along the diagonal at each corner leaving 3 mm (⅛ in) overlapping. Hem the lawn overlap into a fine rolled edge along all four sides of the handkerchief. Neatly sew up the diagonal lace corners and sew the lace onto the hemmed edges.

STRAWBERRY BERET

Berets are available in a wide range of colours and are not expensive. Appliquéd felt strawberries make an original decoration for this classic yet elegant hat.

YOU WILL NEED
Red and green felt
Scissors
Needle and thread
Miniature beads
Beret
Rubber-based glue

1 Cut out some red strawberry shapes and green stems from the felt.

2 Sew some beads onto each strawberry.

3 Stick the motifs on the beret using rubber-based glue. Allow to dry.

BERIBBONED
SPECTACLE CASE

Make this pretty padded case to protect a pair of glasses. Choose brightly coloured fabric and ribbons so that the case will always be easy to find!

YOU WILL NEED

4 pieces of fabric, each measuring 14 cm × 21 cm (5½ in × 8½ in)

2 pieces of foam interlining, each measuring 14 cm × 21 cm (5½ in × 8½ in)

Pins

Needle and thread

Metal rule

Scissors

1.6 m (64 in) length of wide ribbon

1.6 m (64 in) length of narrow ribbon

1 Place a rectangle of fabric on top of each piece of foam interlining so that they fit flush. Pin and tack (baste) in place.

2 Place the rectangles of fabric together. Pin and tack (baste). Sew around three sides with a 15 mm (⅝ in) seam allowance, leaving one short end open. Trim the seams. To make the ribbon front mark the front edge on the right side of one of the remaining rectangles of fabric 5 cm (2 in) from the top. Lay the first piece of ribbon from the corner to the mark. Secure with pins. Continue to lay the ribbon diagonally across the fabric, alternating the wide and narrow ribbons and leaving a gap of 5 mm (¼ in) between each ribbon. When you have reached the bottom of the material, do not forget to finish the top triangle. Tack (baste) into place.

3 Next, start weaving the ribbon in the opposite direction, again alternating between the narrow and wide ribbons. Secure with pins. When complete, tack (baste) into place and trim the ends.

4 Sew the ribbon side to the right side of the fabric rectangle. Sew around three sides, using a 20 mm (¾ in) allowance and leaving the bottom end open. Trim and turn through.

5 Use a closed pair of scissors to push the lining gently and carefully into place. Turn the raw ends under by 3 cm (1¼ in). Pin and stitch in place.

MAKE-UP BAG

This eye-catching make-up bag is made in quilted satin, with a contrasting zip and a co-ordinated lining.

YOU WILL NEED
25 cm × 115 cm (¼ yd × 45 in) satin
25 cm × 115 cm (¼ yd × 45 in)
    cotton lining
Flat wadding (batting) or flannelette
Scissors
Pins
Needle and thread
20 cm (8 in) zip
Tiny piece of ribbon

1 Cut out two pieces of satin and lining, each 20 cm × 15 cm (8 in × 6 in), and two pieces of wadding (batting) 20 cm × 14 cm (8 in × 5½ in). Pin and tack together the satin, wadding (batting) and lining, leaving a gap where the wadding (batting) does not reach to the top. This will make it easier to put in the zip.

2 Quilt by hand or machine. Fold in the top edges of the bag and tack in place.

3 Lay the zip right side up and place the two folded sides of the bag over it. Pin, tack and sew in place. If you use a machine, attach the zipper foot. Open the zip, then turn the bag through right sides together. Pin, tack and sew around the sides and base edge. Trim then overstitch to neaten. Trim the corners diagonally and turn through to the right side. Tie a tiny piece of ribbon to the zip pull for decoration.

PADDED COAT HANGER

Padded coat hangers are a must for the well-dressed person, preventing clothes from having hanging marks on the shoulders. These are both decorative and easy to sew. You could also add some pot-pourri in the hanger for a scented gift.

YOU WILL NEED
140 cm × 10 cm (55 in × 4 in) *wadding (batting) or a double thickness strip the same size as the coat hanger*
Wooden coat hanger
Needle and thread
Iron
60 cm × 15 cm (24 in × 6 in) *strip of fabric*
Pins
Ribbon

1 Wind the length of wadding (batting) around the coat hanger, making sure it is even. Sew the ends in place.

2 Press in a seam allowance of about 6 mm (¼ in) on all four sides of the strip of fabric.

3 Mark the centre with a pin. Fold the fabric around the hanger with the open edge at the top. Using a double thread, start at one end and sew a running stitch from one end up to the centre. Repeat, starting at the other end.

4 Gather up each end so that it curves around the hanger. Sew to fasten securely. Wrap the hook in green ribbon and sew in the end.

PEG BAG

Hanging out your washing on the line is easier if the clothes pegs are kept in a special bag. A rotary cutter and self-heal mat help to ensure the quick and accurate cutting of fabric for patchwork.

YOU WILL NEED
Saw
Wooden coat hanger
Tape measure
Rotary cutter or scissors
30 cm × 115 cm (⅓ yd × 45 in) patterned fabric
25 cm × 115 cm (¼ yd × 45 in) contrasting plain fabric
50 cm × 115 cm (½ yd × 45 in) lining
Needle and thread
Steam iron
Pair of compasses
Pencil
Ruler
Tracing paper
Pins
Bias binding

1 Using a saw, cut off the ends of the coat hanger so that it measures 33 cm (13 in). Cut out five strips measuring 70 cm × 5 cm (28 in × 2 in) of the patterned fabric and four identical strips of the plain fabric. Cut out a 70 cm × 35 cm (28 in × 13½ in) piece of lining.

2 Sew the strips in pairs with a 6 mm (¼ in) seam allowance until all nine are joined. Press the seams open. Trim the ends straight.

3 Draw a 15 cm (6 in) diameter circle on tracing paper and cut out. Place the lining right side down and the joined strips right side up on top. Place the template 7.5 cm (3 in) from the top and equidistant from the sides. Pin the two layers of fabric around the circle to stop them from moving, then draw around the template in pencil. Cut out the circle.

4 Measure the circumference of the circle and cut a piece of bias binding slightly larger. Join with a diagonal seam.

5 Pin, tack and sew the bias binding in place.

6 Fold the fabric in half right sides together, keeping the circular opening at the top. Place the coat hanger at the top and mark the curve of the hanger using a pencil. Cut just outside this line leaving about 6 mm (¼ in) seam allowance. Pin the three sides and sew, leaving a gap for the hook at the top. Trim the corners diagonally. Zigzag stitch around to neaten the seams. Turn through and insert the coat hanger.

PATCHWORK CUSHION

This striking design is surprisingly quick to make, using just one template. Experiment with placing the strips of triangles in different combinations.

YOU WILL NEED
Template plastic
Pencil
Ruler
Pieces of black and white fabrics, each about 36 cm × 18 cm (14 in × 7 in)
White pencil
Scissors
Pins
Patchwork square rule
25 cm × 115 cm (¼ yd × 45 in) turquoise fabric
25 cm × 115 cm (¼ yd × 45 in) blue fabric
Needle and thread
Iron
164 cm (64 in) strip of striped fabric
38 cm (15 in) cushion pad

1 Using the template as a guide and including 6 mm (¼ in) seam allowance, draw 20 triangles on the black fabric and 20 on the white, having first drawn two parallel lines along the grain of each fabric in which to fit the triangles.

2 Cut out and pin the triangles in pairs of one black and one white, keeping the straight grain along the top and bottom. Continue to pin pairs until you have four strips of five pairs. Each alternate strip should start with a white triangle and finish with a black one.

3 Pin the strips together, offsetting the black points to the centre of the black triangle in the next row.

4 Using a patchwork square rule draw a 20 cm (8 in) square plus 6 mm (¼ in) seam allowance on the wrong side, centred so that the points of the triangles balance. These lines will be your stitching lines. Trim to 6 mm (¼ in) seam allowance.

5. Measure opposite sides of the square and cut two strips of turquoise fabric 9 cm (3½ in) wide to fit. Pin with right sides together, sew and press flat. Measure remaining sides and cut two strips of blue fabric 9 cm (3½ in) wide to fit. Pin with right sides together, sew and press flat.

6 Continue in the same manner, cutting black and white striped fabric 3 cm (1¼ in) wide to fit. Pin, sew and press. To make the back of the cover, cut a piece of blue fabric to fit the width plus 6 mm (¼ in) seam allowance. Cut a piece of turquoise fabric of the same width but longer for the overlap. Turn in a hem at one end of each piece. Place the two pieces, right sides together, over the patchwork square. Pin, sew and snip off the corners diagonally, so that the corners will be sharp. Invert and press. Insert the cushion pad.

FELT NEEDLECASE

Make this attractive needlecase from brightly coloured scraps of felt to keep your sewing and embroidery needles safe.

YOU WILL NEED
Stiff white card
Ruler
Scissors
Small pieces of fuchsia, pink, orange, green and yellow felt
Black felt-tip pen
Coin
Stranded cotton in yellow, orange and green
Crewel needle
Tacking (basting) thread in a contrasting colour
Sewing needle

1 Cut out a 9 cm × 14 cm (3½ in × 5½ in) rectangle from white card to make a template. Lay the template on the fuchsia felt, draw round it with the black felt-tip pen and cut out. Repeat with the pink and orange felt.

2 Using a coin as a template, cut out a circle of both the green and yellow felt. Also cut out a small strip and a square of the fuchsia felt.

Arrange the shapes on half of the pink felt rectangle and attach them using blanket stitch and three strands of cotton with the crewel needle.

3 Tack (baste) the pink and fuchsia felt rectangles together. Work a row of blanket stitch round the edge using three strands of yellow thread. With the fuchsia side facing, stitch the orange felt down the centre, then fold in half to make a book shape. You may need to trim the orange felt slightly round the edges with sharp scissors.

HEART-SHAPED BOX

A porcelain box with an embroidered design set in the lid makes a lovely gift for a special friend. Fill the box with pot-pourri or some favourite bath pearls.

YOU WILL NEED

Tracing paper
Sharp HB pencil
Small piece of pink cotton or linen fabric
Stranded cotton in yellow, pink, light green and jade green
Crewel needle
Tapestry needle
Steam iron
Scissors
Heart-shaped porcelain craft box in pink

1 Scale up the template to the desired size and transfer it to the right side of the fabric using a sharp HB pencil. Make sure you transfer each part of the design, including the heart-shaped cutting line.

2 Following the colours shown on the template, embroider the design in whipped backstitch, chain stitch and French knots, using two strands of thread in the crewel needle. When working the whipping stage of the backstitch, use six strands of thread in the tapestry needle.

3 Press the embroidery lightly on the wrong side with a cool iron. Cut out along the heart-shaped cutting line with a pair of sharp scissors. Mount the embroidery in the box lid following the manufacturer's instructions.

SILVER PENDANT

A silver-plated pendant is the perfect way to display a tiny piece of beautifully stitched embroidery with a small-scale design.

YOU WILL NEED
Oval silver-plated craft pendant and
*   chain*
Small piece of 18-count ainring in
*   white*
Sharp HB pencil
Stranded cotton in yellow, orange,
*   light green and dark green*
Crewel needle
Scissors

1 Remove the card shape from the pendant and lay it on the fabric. Draw round the card with a pencil.

2 Each coloured square on the chart represents one cross stitch worked over one woven block in the fabric. Following the chart, embroider the design in cross stitch using two strands of thread. Embroider the linear details in half cross stitch worked over one fabric block using two strands of dark green thread.

3 Cut out the embroidery slightly inside the pencil line. Mount in the pendant following the manufacturer's instructions.

CHRISTMAS TREE DECORATIONS

Hand-embroidered Christmas decorations in shaped golden frames will make your tree trimming a talking point year after year.

YOU WILL NEED

Small pieces of 11-count pearl aida in white

Stranded cotton in red, dark red, light green, mid green, dark green and brown

Tapestry needle

Metallic-effect gold yarn

Small gold beads

Shaped gold-coloured craft Christmas frames with shaped red felt self-adhesive backing

Sharp HB pencil

Scissors

Narrow red ribbon for hanging

1 Each coloured square on the chart represents one cross stitch worked over one woven block in the fabric. Work the designs in cross stitch using three strands of thread (or one strand of gold yarn).

2 Outline the striped package in backstitch using two strands of brown thread. Add straight stitches and beads to the tree design.

3 Centre the frames over the embroidered motifs and draw round the outsides with a sharp HB pencil.

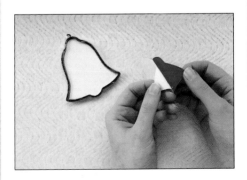

4 Cut out the embroideries slightly inside the pencil lines. Mount in the frames following the manufacturer's instructions. To finish, add the red felt backing and red ribbon for hanging.

TRINKET ROLL

A pretty and practical way to store your treasures when on holiday, this roll has two fat 'sausages' for rings and earrings, and a pocket for necklaces and bracelets.

YOU WILL NEED
Scissors
Ruler
30 cm × 115 cm (⅓ yd × 45 in) velvet
30 cm × 115 cm (⅓ yd × 45 in) lining
Pins
Iron
Needle and thread
18 cm (7 in) zip
2.5 m × 15 mm (2¾ yd × ⅝ in) bias binding
Small piece of velcro

top lining

Base lining

zip

1 Cut out one piece of velvet 33 cm × 23 cm (13 in × 9 in) and round off the four corners. Cut out two pieces of lining 25 cm × 23 cm (10 in × 9 in), and three pieces 23 cm × 11.5 cm (9 in × 4½ in) of velvet. One of these is a pocket and the others are tubes for rings and earrings.

2 Press in two edges of the lining, centre and place the zip between. Pin and sew in place. Curve the corners to fit the velvet top.

3 Cut a length of bias binding to fit the velvet pocket and press in half. Fold over the pocket, pin and sew on. Place the pocket on the lining, wrong side up and sew along the bottom. Bring the pocket up and pin the end before tacking (basting) in place.

4 Roll the last two velvet pieces into sausage shapes, pin and slip stitch.

5 Sew velcro to the end of the one for rings and sew the corresponding piece onto the lining.

6 Pin the lining onto the wrong side of the velvet, making sure the two sausage shapes are in place. Measure enough bias binding to fit around the edge and leave a length for the ties. Fold the ties in half lengthways and sew. Pin the ties to the centre of one end of the roll.

Place the binding, right sides together, on the velvet and pin, then tack (baste) and sew in place. Fold over to the inside and slip stitch. Check that you have caught the edges of the pocket and the 'sausage' for earrings on both sides, but on only one side for the 'sausage' for rings.

QUILTED CUSHION COVER

Scraps of furnishing fabric are excellent for making this comfortable quilted cushion cover. The quilting helps it to keep its shape well. The measurements can easily be altered to fit any size of cushion pad; try making an assortment to pile on a comfortable sofa.

YOU WILL NEED
Furnishing fabric in two patterns
Metal rule
Scissors
Needle and thread
Steam iron
45 cm (18 in) square of foam interlining
45 cm (18 in) square of backing fabric
1 m (1 yd) ribbon
41 cm (16 in) cushion pad

1 Cut out four squares measuring 15 cm (6 in) and one measuring 23 cm (9 in) of one pattern of furnishing fabric, making sure that the pattern is following the same direction. Cut out two pieces measuring 15 cm (6 in) long and 23 cm (9 in) wide and two pieces measuring 23 cm (9 in) long and 15 cm (6 in) wide of the other pattern of furnishing fabric, again making sure that the pattern is following the same direction. Sew the pieces of fabric together using a 20 mm (¾ in) seam allowance. Press open the seams. Sew the panels together using the same seam allowance and press open.

2 Lay the cushion front on the interlining, pin together and tack (baste). Machine sew very carefully along each seam line to create a padded appearance.

4 Make small bows from the ribbon and stitch into place. Push the cushion pad through the opening, making sure the pad is pushed into the corners. Once in position, slipstitch the opening.

3 With right sides together, pin and tack (baste) the backing fabric to the front. Sew together using a 20 mm (¾ in) seam allowance but leave an opening of about 20 cm (8 in) to enable the cover to be turned through. Trim the corners and seams. Turn through.

INDEX